PORTFOLIO 7

METROPOLITAN SEMINARS IN ART

Portfolio 7 · *Composition*

by John Canaday

CHIEF OF THE DIVISION OF EDUCATION

THE PHILADELPHIA MUSEUM OF ART

THE METROPOLITAN MUSEUM OF ART

COMPOSITION
Arrangement as Expression

IN THE two preceding portfolios we examined composition as a flat pattern and composition as structure, whether in two dimensions or three. These classifications, to a large extent arbitrary, were adopted in order to isolate for explanation some of the devices most frequently used in putting pictures together.

These portfolios, however, were not our introduction to composition. In the first paintings discussed, beginning with Whistler's *Arrangement in Gray and Black*, we saw composition as expression. Composition may be pattern or it may be structure, but in either case it is also always expression. It is in fact primarily expression, since the organization of a picture so largely determines its effect. The graceful, swinging arabesques that tie together the various figures in Botticelli's *La Primavera* (Plate 58, Portfolio 5) could never have served Leonardo da Vinci as a substitute for the geometrical framework of *The Last Supper* (Plate 61, Portfolio 6), and, in turn, this framework would be just as ruinous to Botticelli's lyrical allegory if we tried to force *La Primavera* into its general lines.

Frequently the subject of a painting is so special that standard compositional devices cannot be adapted to serve it. In this portfolio we are going to look at some pictures remarkable for the expressive ingenuity of their composition, as well as at some others that will help us to understand the special examples.

The first three color reproductions, Rembrandt's *The Shooting Company of Captain Frans Banning Cocq and Lieutenant Ruytenburgh*, called "The Night Watch" (Plate 73), Charles Willson Peale's *The Peale Family* (Plate 74), and Degas's *The Bellelli Family* (Plate 75) will be compared with one another, so it would be a good idea to put them side by side. Painted respectively by a seventeenth-century Dutchman, an eighteenth-century American, and a nineteenth-century Frenchman, they contrast strongly with one another. Yet they share a common problem in composition. All are group portraits, and the group portrait is as vexing a problem as a painter is ever required to solve.

In a group portrait each member must be awarded his proportionate share of interest and prominence. Obviously this condition limits the painter's freedom in arranging his pictorial material, since ordinarily he is free to assemble as many or as few figures as he wishes and to dispose them at will to build up whatever focal climax he wants. In a portrait where all the members share equal interest and importance his problem is to involve them in a composition that will be interesting in itself, rather than being merely a line-up of figures like, say, the usual graduating class photograph.

Rembrandt's problem in "The Night Watch," a large group portrait, was to catalogue the features of the individual members of an organization (which was essentially social in spite of the military suggestion of its name) and to create at the same time an inherently

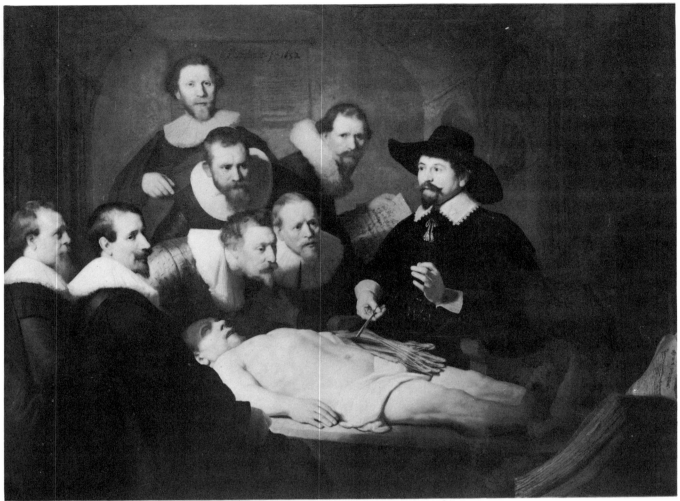

Figure 1

interesting picture. With some twenty figures to be included, Rembrandt chose the device of incorporating them into the expression of a dramatic moment when the company responds to the captain's order to march. Individual psychological delineation is not attempted, as being less appropriate here than in another kind of picture, say one of an actual call to battle in which every man responds to the emotional moment in his own way. In an earlier and smaller group portrait, *The Anatomy Lesson of Doctor Tulp* (*Figure 1*), Rembrandt has given the individuals their own psychological identities, but in "The Night Watch" it appeared more reasonable to subordinate these identities to the activity of the moment. In fact this was even indispensable to such a large and complicated picture. And so "The Night Watch," primarily a rendering of

light and movement organized in space, would be disrupted if our attention were called to a variety of psychological factors within it.

"The Night Watch" has long been a much misunderstood picture. For decades it was obscured by coats of yellowed varnish and layers of dirt that reduced its bright colors to murky gloom punctuated by figures, or suggestions of figures, revealed as if by torchlight. Thus it acquired its inaccurate popular title, "The Night Watch." But during the Second World War the canvas was dismounted (it is a huge picture, over thirteen feet high) and hidden for safekeeping. After the war it was cleaned before being put back on exhibition. Cleaning revealed details in the background that had been obscured, brought minor figures into proper relation with the others, and above all brightened the yellow

6

glow to reveal the members of the "night" watch occupying a spacious room into which early sunlight flows.

The figures in the picture are awarded varying degrees of prominence. The fact that some of them had all but disappeared was one of the things that gave rise to the legend that when Rembrandt completed the picture it was rejected by the company that had commissioned it, ruining his career and beginning his long decline into poverty and relative obscurity. This decline—in worldly success, not at all in Rembrandt's power as an artist—did in fact take place. But the reasons for it must be found elsewhere; there are no factual circumstances to support the legend that "The Night Watch" was a disastrous landmark in the painter's career. The introduction of incidental figures, especially the girl so conspicuous in the pool of light to the left (*Figure 2*), was by the same legend arbitrary on Rembrandt's part. He was supposed to have used these figures as convenient elements in the creation of his dramatic composition, in spite of the fact that they had no justifiable relationship to the shooting company whose members had paid to have their likenesses recorded. But these figures are now believed to have some emblematic significance.

However, if cleaning and historical reconsiderations have brought us back to a more proper understanding of the picture, it has suffered one irremediable disfigurement. The canvas was at some time cut down on all four sides, crowding the figures at left and right in a way that is obvious at a glance and making a less apparent but more serious shift in the relation of the two central figures to the rest. As the picture now exists, these figures are too obviously centered. Originally they were off-center; this placement emphasized the feeling of movement and excitement created by the diagonal movement of the composition, a device already familiar from previous discussions, especially on Géricault's *Raft of the Medusa* (Plate 71, Portfolio 6).

Figure 2

As a solution to a problem "The Night Watch" was a brilliant consolidation of a given number of figures into a group portrait and, under the conditions of this particular assignment, seems to have been satisfactory to the clients who commissioned it. In our two other examples, the Peale and the Degas family groups, the drama and monumentality of "The Night Watch" would of course have been altogether inappropriate. Family subjects demand intimacy rather than dramatic excitement and the expression of psychological interplay between individuals whose lives are closely bound together. Yet the two family groups contrast with one another just as much as the pair of them contrast with the Rembrandt. In both pictures of the family groups the painters relay contrasting psychological values in their subjects through composition.

The Peale Family

Peale began work on his group portrait about 1773. Nine of the people in the picture are members of his family by birth or by marriage. The tenth is a matriarchal family nurse who stands in the background, hands folded, with all the majesty of a great natural monument. For good measure Peale includes three familial portrait busts on the shelf to the right and as an afterthought adds the portrait head of a member who joined the family after the picture was half finished, the dog Argus.

Argus, as a pup, was left to the Peales by a grateful old Revolutionary soldier who pulled him out from under his blouse in return for a free meal. The Revolution had come and gone since Peale began the picture. For many years he kept it unfinished in his studio as a kind of demonstration piece. In finishing it he added the portrait of Argus, by then venerable, and the following inscription at the center right: *C. W. Peale painted these Portraits of his family in 1773. wishing to finish every work he had undertaken—compleated this picture in 1809!*

A little arithmetic shows that the picture was completed thirty-six years after it was begun. This explains why Peale, who was sixty-eight years old at the time, appears in it as a young man of thirty-two. He stands to the left side, holding a palette and bending over to inspect a drawing on which his brother, St. George Peale, is working (*Figure 3*).

The Peale Family is a delightful painting. John Adams, who saw it in 1776 in the painter's studio, wrote in a letter, "There was a pleasant, a happy cheerfulness in their countenances, and a familiarity in their air towards each other." And the intention of the picture is no more complicated than that. It presents an ideal façade of family life, informal, affectionate, harmonious, and secure. The canvas on the easel in the background, the picture-within-a-picture upon which Charles Willson Peale has been at work, originally bore the phrase *Concordia Animae* as a clue to the meaning of the whole painting. But Peale later eliminated these words, "the design being," he wrote to his son, "sufficient to tell the subject," as indeed it is. A glance at *The Peale Family* is enough to show that the ten people in it are happily united as a group. They are pleasantly disposed and share the limelight without competing for it (although Argus, it must be confessed, remains what he was when he was introduced into the composition, a postscript).

Compositionally, the subjects are divided into two groups, six figures clustered at the left and three at the right side, or, if you include the nurse, four. She stands in a nicely selected relationship to the family itself, expressive of her position in the household, closely allied with the other figures yet slightly removed, painted as she is in more subdued tones and standing as she does in the only attitude not physically bound to the rest by contact of a hand or a shoulder.

If all the figures had been massed together they would have looked crowded and monotonous. Hence, the division into two groups. But this is a family, a harmoniously united family, so it is necessary that we also be conscious of the two groups as a unit. And we are: the two halves are united by a slight overlapping and by a scattering of fruit across the table, a trivial detail, yet an important one in binding the two halves together (*Figure 4*). They are even more strongly held together by the fact that St. George (extreme left), sketching his mother as she holds a grandchild (extreme right), glances toward her as he draws. This play of interest across the breadth of the picture is a psychologically effective tie nullifying any feeling of disunity that might

8

Figure 3

Figure 4

have been produced by the physical division into two groups.

Within this firmly knit composition each figure is pleasantly varied. We are conscious of each one as an individual, but we cannot look long at one without being led to another. The composition is not brilliant or complicated; it need be neither to express the painter's conception, which is direct and simple.

Peale's style has a suggestion of dryness in it, like a pinch of salt in a dish that might otherwise have been too bland. There are occasional awkwardnesses in drawing. For instance, the hands of the sister standing at the left, one resting on the shoulder of Charles Willson, the other on the shoulder of his wife, are a touch oversize. These hands are not quite as fortunately incorporated as the rest. They remind us that the picture is a group of separate studies synthesized into a whole. Also, the arm of the grandmother cannot bear close examination. Instead of terminating as it should it continues as a tubelike form and disappears into the shadows a moment too late to conceal from us that it is too long and handless. But these imperfections have their own appeal; they account for the suggestion of engaging provincialism that distinguishes the work of this early American painter from that of the facile English portraitists who were his models.

Pictures of this general type, which go by the name of "conversation piece," are frequent in eighteenth- and early nineteenth-century painting. These pictures, based on the assumption that life is a matter of agreeable surfaces, are usually built around a theme with incidental reference to some pleasurable activity associated with the subjects, like the exercise in drawing that occupies St. George and Charles Willson here.

The picture is a happy interpretation of family life but not a very searching one, even for a pre-Freudian age. Families are more complicated than this. Family relationships produce frictions and irritations as minor evils, agonizing psychological conflicts as major ones. The brothers, sisters, and in-laws gathered around the Peale table were human beings and certainly not immune to these difficulties. Just as certainly, in other aspects of their family life they rose to joys more intense than the casual affection so uniformly expressed in the group. Peale does not hint that these human beings have more than an agreeably tepid experience of life, and they are not strongly differentiated from one another psychologically. The particular psychological circumstance does not interest this painter.

The Bellelli Family

But the particular circumstances of individual relationships in all their psychological subtleties fascinated another painter, a young Frenchman who painted a family group in about 1860 when he was less than thirty years old. This, you may remember, is younger than Peale was when he began his family portrait. But at that age the Frenchman, Edgar Degas, was already an urbane cosmopolite. He was a doubter, a speculator upon human nature, and basically a pessimist. He spent the better part of a year in Italy, in spite of his father's repeated insistence that he return to Paris, for Degas had begun work there on a large painting of his aunt, Baroness Bellelli, his two young cousins, and the baron. In this family there was a less happy state of affairs than the one Peale would have us believe existed in his family. Degas reveals it through a composition as original as any in the history of painting and, as Peale said of his own, "sufficient to tell the subject." "Sufficient" is an understatement. Superlatives are dangerous, but there is less danger than usual in describing *The Bellelli Family* as the finest psychological group portrait ever painted. The temperament of each of the four members is individualized for us, and, beyond that, their interrelationship is revealed. Before you read the following paragraphs you may want to ask yourself on the evidence of the picture what these people were like. In that case ask yourself what the relationship of the father to the rest of the family might be, what the emotional tie of each of the little girls is to each of the parents, and what the difference is, temperamentally, between these two children. The chances are that you will learn as much from the picture itself as you will know when you have read the following summary, with the exception of specific historical facts.

From references in family letters we infer that the baron was a man of uneven temperament, given to moods, and, at least during the time Degas visited the family, conscious of frustrations and discouragements in his personal life and in his career. His only son had died (the family is still in mourning in the portrait), and the baron was marking time as a political exile from his native Naples. His disturbed life made him a half stranger in his own household, a condition made no easier by an increasing rift between his wife and himself. Social conventions of respectability a hundred years ago placed limitations on a woman in the baroness's situation. A reserved, intelligent, and patient woman—if we can accept the judgment of her young nephew—she seems to have shouldered even more of the responsibility for the home and the children than did the average wife of the mid-nineteenth century. Of the two little girls, the elder, Giovanna (*Figure 5*), was placid and closely attached to her mother, whereas the younger, Giuliana (*Figure 6*), was more energetic and restless. She was temperamentally sympathetic to her father but, by force of circumstance, more securely bound within the life of her mother and sister.

The most casual observer must notice that in Degas's portrait the father is separated from the rest of the family by a series of vertical lines that, violating all accepted compositional rules, separate a generous third of the picture from the rest of it. In addition, he sits unconventionally with his back toward us,

Figure 5

the only one of the family who looks at us, although the others are aware of our presence. She looks at us unquestioningly, content to stay within her mother's support and protection.

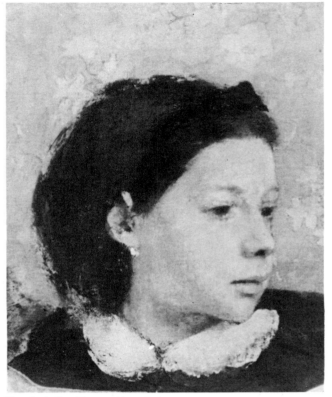

Figure 6

and he is painted less decisively than the other figures (*Figure 7*). He is the only one of the family who is not completely revealed to us as a person; we are left with the feeling that we do not know him as we know the mother and daughters. He has a life beyond this room; perhaps he leads a life more important to him than the life we are seeing here; he is an outsider.

But this vagueness, incompleteness, and isolation are reversed in the figure of the wife. She stands with decision, dignity, and forbearance, dominating the room by her quietness. Of all the figures hers is the simplest and strongest in silhouette. That is why we return to her always, no matter how interesting the other figures may be in their greater detail and variety.

Her right hand rests on the shoulder of Giovanna, who was so like her and so close to her. This little girl is held within the larger silhouette of the mother's figure. Her way of standing echoes her mother's, as does her general silhouette—and she is as quiet. She is

But the other child, Giuliana, partially breaks away from the pair. She occupies the side of the picture separated from the father, but we feel strongly her connection with him. She is the only one whose glance could, and in a moment might, meet her father's. She sits restlessly, one leg tucked up under her, as if impatient with sitting for her artist cousin, unable to remain still, the volatile member of the group. Just as she is divided in her loyalty to her mother and her father, so she does not belong wholly to either in the composition of the painting.

It is apparent, then, that Degas set about expressing a specific set of circumstances with the help of appropriate compositional means. When we know the circumstances the picture takes on some peripheral interest, but it is a great picture because it is expressive whether we know those circumstances or not. It has a life of its own beyond the immediate reasons for its creation. If the identity of the painter and the family were unknown to us, any meaning *The Bellelli Family* might lose would be superficial.

The Bellellis are not important to us as individuals. It makes no difference how they looked. Their troubles were never of any importance except to themselves. The relationships so brilliantly revealed were neither unique nor on the grand scale. The picture's greatness lies in its ability to stir us to thought beyond the limited considerations of a single family's not unusual circumstances. And it does so because Degas has crystallized his material into forms of perfect order, rid of all confusions, incidentals, vagaries, and distractions. In the resultant clarity our sensibilities and understanding may expand.

Degas was one of the greatest of all pictorial composers, and *The Bellelli Family*, an early painting, is only one (though one of the best) of a succession of startlingly original compositions. Degas is pre-eminent in this unconventionality. Other great masters of pictorial composition time and again demonstrate their ability to use conventional devices more skillfully than their contemporaries. But Degas invents compositions without direct precedent, and each of these compositions is so special to its subject that none is directly useful to followers hunting a formula. The composition of *The Peale Family* might be adapted to any number of group portraits, but that of *The Bellelli Family* could not. In our first portfolio we discussed the extraordinary portrait called *Woman with Chrysanthemums* (Plate 5) where, to describe a special personality, Degas used devices running counter to tradition in a way that appalled conventional artists.

At the same time Degas was a master of what we call classical composition, although even here he was original in his use of traditional devices. Compare Poussin's *Funeral of*

Photo by Archives Photographiques, Paris

Figure 7

Phocion (Plate 76), a standard example of classical composition at its zenith, and Degas's *Rehearsal in the Foyer of the Opera* (Plate 77), an exceptional classical composition, although it is seldom thought of as one. Beneath their surface dissimilarities the pictures have much in common.

Poussin's masterpiece, painted in the seventeenth century, is an arrangement of architectural and landscape forms, completely imaginary, beautifully disposed in space, studded here and there with some small human effigies of no very great interest or individuality in themselves. On the other hand, Degas's *Rehearsal* is an arrangement of human beings, drawn from life and sharply individualized, in an identifiable interior of the Paris Opera. The Poussin looks backward through centuries to the half-legendary world of classical antiquity for its subject, a subject involving the great and the mighty. Degas chooses a subject at hand, involving nobody more important than a few second-string ballet performers, their rehearsal master, and the fiddler who supplies practice

13

music. These people are not even involved in a performance, with its attendant excitement and glamour; they are engaged in a routine rehearsal, and some of the dancers are apparently a little bored with the whole thing.

Ultimately the subject of any classical composition is order. We have already seen that all composition is order of one kind or another, but in classical composition order is associated with the idea of repose and may exist almost for itself. What we call a classical composition is conceived in limited space, bounded space, rather than vast imaginative reaches into infinity. In our first portfolio we made this contrast between Cézanne's *Mont Sainte-Victoire* (Plate 8) and Durand's *Imaginary Landscape* (Plate 7). We have seen another classical composition in Vermeer's *The Artist in His Studio* (Plate 37, Portfolio 4) where the space was limited to a small room defined on all sides. Within the room various objects were so disposed that removing any one of them would disturb the perfect order created by the painter.

The Funeral of Phocion

Poussin's *The Funeral of Phocion* is designed on the same principle. The satisfaction it gives us is based on the sense of order within a limited world. True, this landscape presents a space much larger than Vermeer's small room, without walls and floor and ceiling to define its limits. But the sky is conceived more as a backdrop terminating a stage-set than as a continuation of space in nature. And even though we have no walls at the picture's sides, we are not offered temptations to wander beyond the frame. We may, however, wander at will in the picture. Space exists all around the architectural and landscape forms. To enjoy the picture fully we must think of it in three dimensions, not as the flat surface of a canvas.

Actually, we do not wander; we are led. The contour of a hill, the angle of a wall, the placement of a tree, the direction in which a cart moves—all these elements direct us as we

explore this microcosm, this small, complete world. We are never allowed to escape from it, any more than we are allowed to escape from Vermeer's small room. Yet the objects are so harmoniously ordered that we do not feel imprisoned.

Such a picture is the result not of rules but of the artist's feeling for what is right. This feeling, of course, is developed through study, contemplation, and practice. If the means used to achieve its order were too obvious the picture would be less satisfying. Some of these means, however, are definable and can be pointed out without marring our spontaneous enjoyment.

For instance, there is the device of "repetition of the picture plane." The picture plane is simply the plane defined by the frame or the surface of a canvas. It can be compared to the curtain of a stage. When the curtain is raised the "plane" where the curtain hung still exists psychologically. On a stage this plane would be repeated by, let us say, a piece of furniture facing the audience directly rather than at an angle. Likewise it would be repeated by any actor who stood directly facing us. It would be repeated finally by the terminating backdrop or set wall.

In the Poussin the picture plane is repeated again and again as the objects recede toward the final "backdrop," the sky. It is repeated by the facing surfaces of walls, by various buildings, and is suggested by long, low hills or mounds disposed across the picture space parallel to the picture plane.

A second series of planes at an angle to the picture plane is suggested first by the side plane of the wall at the right (*Figure 8*). We enter the picture from the lower left corner and move across it, but are kept from moving out by the tall tree at the right and by this plane of the wall, which is turned to deflect the "current" of our movement back into the picture. It is not noticeable that this plane is, in fact, a distortion of true perspective. In true perspective we would not see the side

Photo by Archives Photographiques, Paris

Figure 8

surface of a wall whose front plane was parallel to the picture, but Poussin turns this (and other planes that repeat it) slightly inward to create a series of checks to our movement, like objects placed on a stage to keep our eyes from wandering off toward the wings.

A corresponding but weaker set of planes serves the same function in the other direction. The rigidity of all these forms is alleviated by the curvings of streams or paths or pathlike areas winding backward and forward and around and about. Although the small figures, represented as seated, standing, walking, riding, and carrying the sheeted corpse, also turn us in directions in which the artist wants us to move, they themselves are not invested with motion. Essentially they are as static as the natural and architectural forms around them.

Classicism in Disguise

We commented in the preceding portfolio that this static quality, especially of figures represented as if in motion, is the element in classical composition that, to many people's way of thinking, limits its effectiveness. Degas, with his customary ingenuity, finds a way to avoid this difficulty in *The Rehearsal in the Foyer of the Opera* (Plate 77). The figures in *The Rehearsal* are classically static and classically balanced, but at the same time they are convincingly engaged in an activity based on a premise of motion—dancing. How does Degas solve this contradiction?

He chooses an instant of repose in the midst of continuous action. The ballet master, in the white suit at the right side of the picture, has just held up his hand and tapped the floor with his stick. Responding to this command, the dancer (extreme left) whom he has been rehearsing stops stock still (*Figure 9*), holding the attitude of the moment as she listens for the comment or correction he is about to make (*Figure 10*). The violinist has lowered his bow, taking the opportunity for a moment's relaxation. Most of the other dancers, attracted by

15

Figure 9

Figure 10

the tapping of the stick, pause to glance and listen, but others in casual attitudes chat with one another or stand waiting their turn for rehearsal. Thus the picture is full of life; it is, in a way, full of activity. But it is quite natural that every figure in it is perfectly still, and Degas is free to use each one as an object for disposition within a static, classical composition as if they were the walls, buildings, shrubs, and trees used by Poussin.

Degas has also turned his space at an eccentric angle. To increase the effect of informality in a paradoxically formal arrangement he abandons the picture-plane idea. But his pictorial space is still very precisely defined. The chair in the foreground, which appears to be so casually placed, repeats the angle of the walls, thus becoming a major factor in defining in the foreground the volume of space that the walls define in the background. The chair also serves as a barrier to keep us from entering the void in the center of the picture. It deflects us either to the ballet master and the group around him or to the dancer at the left.

To build a composition with a void at its center is another eccentricity, but Degas is not using it only for its novelty. In physically isolating the dancer from the ballet master he is unifying them psychologically. The tension of interest that vibrates between them would be weakened by any interruption of the space. This is the same device, more sharply employed, that Peale used when he bound his family portrait together by the glance St. George casts toward the figures he is sketching.

By all the rules Degas's *Rehearsal* is overbalanced on the right side, where a heavy mass of figures occupies one end of a kind of compositional seesaw whose other end must be held down by the lone figure of the dancer. But the two sides are in what is called "psychic balance." The dancer's isolation attracts our attention in a composition where the other figures, massed, compete with one another. The curious attitude of her legs and feet, opposed to the more ordinary gestures and attitudes of the several members of the group on the other side, also sets her apart. And finally, the "seesaw" is at the angle in space defined by the chair and the walls, so that the dancer's end of it is thrown nearer to us. Thus she is not only in a more conspicuous location but by reasons of perspective must be drawn larger than the figures she faces. For all these reasons she holds her own against superior forces.

The Degas is everywhere as neatly and beautifully balanced as the Poussin. Both painters set for themselves the problem of perfect balance of static objects within defined space. Of the two, the Poussin is more majestic in its implications, but the Degas is warmer. Poussin rejects the commonplace, and Degas accepts it, but both seek meaning through order. Neither one is much concerned with his apparent subject. The Poussin's sheeted corpse happens to be that of an Athenian general wrongly convicted of treason, who must therefore be buried outside the walls of the city. But the picture would not be much changed if the object on the stretcher were, say, the drum of a column being carried to a building site. The Degas has a much closer connection with its subject matter, but the longer we know the picture the more our satisfaction comes from the disposition of the objects rather than from our interest in who or what they are.

Degas admired both Poussin and Vermeer, and the gentle flow of light in *The Rehearsal* is suggestive of the latter's art. Similar, too, is the device of implying a wall by showing objects illuminated by light coming from a window not seen but clearly sensed.

In arresting a moment of action Degas has a classical precedent in Greek sculpture of the fourth century B.C. *The Discus Thrower*, which we know in several versions copied from a lost original by the sculptor Myron, represents an athlete engaged in violent action (*Figure 11*). But the sculptor seizes the instant when the arm has reached the apex of the upward motion of its arc, the instant before it starts the downward motion that begins the act of throw-

Figure 11

19

ing. This is also the instant when the body has reached the extremity of its twist in one direction and is ready to reverse this motion.

But every great picture is new, no matter what its connection with the past. Other painters have imitated Vermeer, have imitated the sculptor of *The Discus Thrower*, have imitated Poussin. Degas imitated nobody. If we made a long catalogue of the sources of the art of Degas and an equally long one of the sources of the art of some mediocre painter, these sources might be the same, yet Degas would still be an original painter, and the other would remain an imitator, an eclectic.

Composition as Narrative

Of the seventy-odd paintings discussed thus far in our series very few have been story-telling pictures. When they were, as in the case of Gérôme's *The Duel After the Masquerade* (Plate 21, Portfolio 2), we have found them lacking in interpretive power. This is understandable since by its very nature the story-telling picture is likely to be a compromise between pictorial art and verbal art, or narration. You may argue that Rubens's *Prometheus Bound* (Plate 18, Portfolio 2), which pictures a classical legend, and Delacroix's *Abduction of Rebecca* (Plate 72, Portfolio 6), which takes its subject from *Ivanhoe*, and the various Crucifixions we have seen, which tell that great story, are narrative paintings. This is true on the face of it, but it is also true, and much more important, that these paintings are first of all pictures of ideas. We do not have to translate them back into their original form of narrative in order to give them meaning. The medium of images is not playing second-best to the medium of words. But when he wants to tell a story, the painter's most vivid narrative device is composition.

Saint Anthony Tempted by the Devil in the Form of a Woman (Plate 78), painted by the Sienese artist Sassetta a little more than five hundred years ago, is as economical and ex-

pressive a bit of storytelling as can be found in any medium. Instead of showing us the incident as a kind of glorified snapshot of an actual happening, Sassetta reveals its dramatic and psychological atmosphere through the abstract means of color, line, and arrangement. It might be objected that the temptation of Saint Anthony could hardly suggest a snapshot since the incident is a fantastical one, but an unimaginative painter could have treated it as literally as if it were the factual record of a commonplace event. Even such a painter might be able to tell the story clearly enough, but we all know that a story told effectively by one person may fall flat when told by another. In this little picture it is not so much what Sassetta says as the way he says it.

What he says is that when the saint, who lives in the wilderness dedicated to a life of ascetic contemplation, returns to his cell one evening he discovers waiting near the door a woman, delightfully beautiful, who tempts him to the pleasures of the flesh. And the way he says it is this:

The saint, walking toward the door of his shelter, has just discovered the woman. In a wonderfully expressive attitude he hesitates, half turning toward her, his hand raised in a gesture of surprise that in the next moment can turn into a gesture of assent or one of rejection. He stands directly in the center of the picture, with the cell and the woman on either side of him like equal weights in a scale of which he is the pivot. The balance is emphasized by the fact that both objects offered him for choice are pink, the only bright color in the picture except the streak of light along the horizon. These pinks, however, clash with one another, the vermilion-pink of the shelter with the carmine-pink of the woman's robe. The woman is an exquisite little creature; the innocence of her pretty face and blonde hair is denied by slits in her bodice and skirt; even her jeweled batwings are pretty, although they are hidden from the saint and revealed only to us. In contrast to the graceful and orna-

Figure 12

mented forms of the woman the lines of the shelter are extremely severe.

The apparitional quality of the scene is created by the background. It is a never-never land of desert, its path sprinkled with stones to humiliate the flesh of the saint's bare feet, its odd rock-hills dotted with a few exotic trees that look like designs for jewelry (*Figure 12*), and its horizon so curved that it suggests the end of the world, the jumping-off place. Against this desolate isolation the temptress is all the more tempting.

This is not a complicated picture, and the story itself has been reduced to minimum terms. This minimum is reflected in the spareness of the objects represented. There are no parenthetical references, no hint that the subject may have further implications beyond its immediate terms. And that, of course, is where it fails in greatness, if it can be said to "fail" when it does not achieve something it never set out to achieve. The painting is utterly delightful and skillful, a joy; it tells its little story perfectly, directly, in succinct pictorial terms.

Figure 13

Philosophical Narrative

To see how much a painter may say beyond the mere narrative of an incident drawn from a literary source, we will look at *The Fall of Icarus* (Plate 79) by the sixteenth-century Flemish painter, Pieter Bruegel the Elder. According to the Greek legend, the boy Icarus fell to his death in the sea when he flew too close to the sun on a pair of wings invented by his father, Daedalus. The wings were made of feathers and wax; the heat of the sun melted the wax of the boy's wings and they fell apart. Daedalus, at a more cautious height between the sea and the sun, did not fall. The legend is given various meanings, most of them having to do with the vanity of pride or ambition.

Bruegel, however, finds its meaning in another direction. The composition of *The Fall of Icarus* carries this meaning by a kind of reverse emphasis. Whereas other compositions build every element toward a climax in the figure of the protagonist of the theme, at first Icarus does not seem to be in the picture at all. The most conspicuous figure is a plow-

man, his head bent toward the soil, who is not even a part of the legend (*Figure 13*). Beyond him, looking up with mild curiosity toward an odd speck in the sky, a shepherd tends flock. Stretching around these figures is a land- and seascape of intricate beauty. Ships move across the water, and in the cove below the plowman a particularly elaborate one is setting sail. When we have discovered this ship we have very nearly discovered Icarus at last. Our subject, or at least the small legs of our subject, is nearby, just disappearing into the water with a very small splash, lost in the picture's detailed patterns.

Bruegel's comment, then, has to do with the insignificance of personal tragedy in the great scheme of things. The death of this boy and the anguish of his father mean nothing at all in terms of a larger pattern. This could be a pessimistic conclusion, and the modern poet W. H. Auden makes it one in "Musée des Beaux Arts" inspired by this painting and others of the Flemish school where everyday events are combined with subjects like the Nativity and the martyrdoms of saints:

About suffering they were never wrong,
The Old Masters: how well they understood
Its human position; how it takes place
While someone else is eating or opening a
    window or just walking dully along;
How, when the aged are reverently, pas-
    sionately waiting
For the miraculous birth, there always
    must be
Children who did not specially want it to
    happen, skating
On a pond at the edge of the wood:
They never forgot
That even the dreadful martyrdom must run
    its course
Anyhow in a corner, some untidy spot
Where the dogs go on with their doggy life
    and the torturer's horse
Scratches its innocent behind on a tree.

In Brueghel's *Icarus*, for instance: how
    everything turns away
Quite leisurely from the disaster; the plough-
    man may
Have heard the splash, the forsaken cry,
But for him it was not an important failure;
    the sun shone
As it had to on the white legs disappearing
    into the green
Water; and the expensive delicate ship that
    must have seen
Something amazing, a boy falling out of
    the sky,
Had somewhere to get to and sailed calmly
    on.

We have here, then, a theme from literature, transformed in painting, with a con-
sequent literary restatement. By this interpretation Bruegel used the Icarus legend to
comment on human indifference to the suffering of others, the loneliness of the individual.
But this idea is not in harmony with the look
of Bruegel's picture. The pattern is of such
depth and serenity, such calm beauty, such
grandeur, that we may be consoled by the

Figure 14

23

Figure 15

knowledge that our individual troubles are absorbed within a greater order.

In its serenity and elegance *The Fall of Icarus* is an exception in Bruegel's work. Typically, he combines the fantastic and the grotesque with the earthiness of peasant life, unlikely as the combination may sound. In *Flemish Proverbs* (Plate 80) he has a ready-made vehicle, since proverbs grow directly out of the life of the people but are expressed in terms of fantasy. The man who is half-enclosed within a crystal globe (*Figure 14*) illustrates "I must stoop if I wish to go through the world" (*Ick moet my crommen, sae ick door de werelt commen*) and the man strewing roses before swine (*Desen stroyt roosen voor de vercken*) is no stranger to us if we substitute pearls for the blossoms (*Figure 14*).

Flemish Proverbs is conceived as a kind of drollery, although in the light of Bruegel's subsequent achievements critics like to believe that in painting it the artist intended a com-

pendium of human folly. Compositionally it is not remarkable, although the job of tying together some eighty *tableaux vivants* simultaneously enacted upon a large stage is admirably accomplished. *Flemish Proverbs* is a fascinating picture, but in a later one devoted

Figure 16

to a single proverb, *The Parable of the Blind* (Plate 81), we see Bruegel as a mature man and a mature artist doing a great deal more with the same kind of material.

The blind men are proceeding in single file across a bit of descending ground that ends in a ditch. The leader has tumbled in. The last man in line has no suspicion of what is happening. He will continue to follow, in complete docility, until he meets the catastrophe that the other men, in graduated stages, begin to suspect. The other figures are studies in the progressive emotions of uneasy suspicion that develops into terrified certainty and culminates in frantic and helpless confusion as the men are finally caught up in the disaster they failed to anticipate when they placed their trust in another no better equipped to avoid it than themselves.

If this were only a picture of blind men falling into a ditch it would be cruel. But it is a parable of human inertia, a comment on the weakness of men who follow blindly because it is too much trouble to find a way for themselves, who would rather shift responsibility for a course of action to someone else, just anyone, than make the effort to determine one for themselves. The blind men of the picture may be pitiable, but the "blind" men of the parable are not.

For expressive reasons the picture abandons all usual ideas of balance and catapults downward into one corner. Each man's face reflects his state of mind; in this respect the faces are a superb series of inventions. But if they were blanked out, the story would still be vividly told, since it is in the design of the figures that Bruegel has concentrated the expressive force. The last man in line is drawn in simple masses (*Figure 15*). His cloak hangs in straight lines. In each successive figure this simplicity is more and more replaced by complexity and agitation (*Figure 16*) until finally the first

Figure 17

25

figure is a tumbled silhouette, a tumbled broken mass (*Figure 17*). This is not because men tumbling or falling would happen to present such forms. They might, in fact, present quite simple ones. If you will recall newspaper photographs of people falling or jumping or lying on the pavement after an accident you may remember that it is a rare photograph in which the victim presents a shape expressive in itself. Abstractly, that is, without the attendant evidence of blood or wreckage, the form of a man who has died a violent death is not likely to be much different from that of a man lying in a drunken stupor or even one taking a peaceful nap. Nor is the form of the figure of a man in physical torment or some violent action of a tragic nature likely to be very different, objectively regarded, from that of a man dancing or engaged in sport.

The point we are making is that Bruegel's blind men are not realistic. They may be realistic in detail, but taken as a whole they are abstract patterns of line and form, expressively designed. If they seem realistic, it is because of Bruegel's power as a creative draughtsman.

The rest of the picture is a peaceful landscape that, like the one in *The Fall of Icarus*, is in emotional contrast with the tragedy being enacted. The landscape in *The Fall of Icarus* was made elaborate and fanciful to suggest the unimportance of the single detail of the legs of the boy. In *The Parable of the Blind* the landscape is as simple as the procession of men is complicated. Its lines are as straight and spare as those of the hapless men are knotted. By contrast the quiet landscape emphasizes the dramatic inventions of the foreground figures.

Three Pictures for Study

It is hardly possible to exhaust the subject of pictorial composition since it is limited only by the number of pictures, good or bad, that exist for discussion. And in concluding the third of the portfolios devoted to composition we are not abandoning it. Our next portfolios will explain the techniques of painting— fresco, tempera, oil, water color, and the rest. But we are still talking about pictures, which means that we will continue to look at them as expressions of ideas, of emotions, and of their times.

In the meantime, here are three great paintings that may be studied independently in the light of what has been said in the seven portfolios of this series to date: Andrea Mantegna's fifteenth-century *The Adoration of the Shepherds* (Plate 82), El Greco's sixteenth-century *View of Toledo* (Plate 83), and Georges Seurat's *Sunday Afternoon on the Island of La Grande Jatte* (Plate 84), painted late in the nineteenth century. None of these pictures follows any compositional formula very closely, but all of them are organized with high degrees of definition. In the first one, the reader might ask himself how Mantegna has organized the multitude of precisely executed detail into a composition where each one has its proper place and emphasis; in the second, how El Greco's uses of line, light, and color invest this landscape with an air of rapturous mysticism. The third picture is a meticulously studied placement of static forms to which Poussin's *Funeral of Phocion* might provide a key. Some further comments are included in Notes on the Painters.

Notes on the Painters

Rembrandt Harmensz. van Ryn, 1606-1669, Dutch

73. THE SHOOTING COMPANY OF CAPTAIN FRANS BANNING COCQ
AND LIEUTENANT RUYTENBURGH ("THE NIGHT WATCH"),
1642

Oil on canvas. Height 13'4⅜". The Rijksmuseum, Amsterdam

Rembrandt was born in Leiden but in his middle twenties he moved to Amsterdam, where he spent the rest of his life. He is probably the most widely known of all painters (except in Italy), even though individual works like Leonardo's *Mona Lisa* and *The Last Supper* and Michelangelo's Sistine Ceiling may be better known.

Until 1642, when at the age of thirty-six he was commissioned to paint "The Night Watch," his life followed the pattern of the exceptionally talented and successful young man. His work during this period reflects a joyousness in life—not a gaiety but a profound joy. He was happily married and had one son. He was creatively vigorous, financially prosperous. But to a man of Rembrandt's nature prosperity was less important than the solution of problems in painting and the expression of his own philosophical ideas. Personal tragedy—the loss of his first three children and then his wife—contributed to a new, introspective moodiness in his work. He was no longer painting in accord with popular taste, but he was unwilling to modify his painting to regain his popularity. In the end, in miserable quarters, he sank into professional obscurity, at any rate, obscurity in comparison with the prominence he enjoyed during his early years. He lived by teaching and by occasional commissions, painting now for himself. Today we are accustomed to the idea that an artist creates for himself, but in Rembrandt's century it was still exceptional for an artist to regard his work first of all as a personal experience and only secondarily as one that the public might or might not be ready to share.

In these years Rembrandt pondered the relation of the human soul to the circumstance of human existence, its relation to God, the reconciliation of the world we experience physically, in all its accidents and imperfections, with the conviction that life is justified by some cosmic good. His images of the world are seldom beautiful in themselves; his models are usually homely and battered, subject to all the chance, misfortune, and indignity of daily life. But by revealing them in pools of light glowing within vibrant dark areas, he invests them with a spiritual majesty corresponding to his belief in the ultimate nobility of the human being, no matter what the ignobleness of daily experience.

The wide appeal of Rembrandt's painting suggests that its philosophical content must be sensed to some degree by anyone who sees his work, even those who have never pondered his question and would be puzzled by it as a verbal statement. And in the end, since it is an affirmation of good, Rembrandt's art remains joyous.

Charles Willson Peale, 1741-1827, American

74. THE PEALE FAMILY, 1773-1809

Oil on canvas. Height 56½". The New-York Historical Society

Peale is one of the most engaging personalities in American art. He was indefatigably curious about the world. His enthusiasm for science was as great as his enjoyment of painting; he was a silversmith and clockmaker, a

lively politician, a soldier in the Revolution, and a significant force in education, having been influential in founding the oldest art school in this country, the Pennsylvania Academy of the Fine Arts. In addition, he had his own museum of anthropological and zoological specimens, including the bones of a mastodon he himself discovered near Newburgh, New York. These specimens were combined with some of his own sculpture and painting on the second floor of Independence Hall, and some of the paintings are still there. Peale appears to have been a sort of Early-American Leonardo.

As if he had more creative energy than a single lifetime could accommodate, he made painters of his brothers and his children, naming the latter after great painters of the past. He saw his work continued in portraits by his son Rembrandt and in remarkable still lifes by his son Raphael.

Hilaire Germain Edgar Degas, 1834-1917, French

75. THE BELLELLI FAMILY, ABOUT 1862

   Oil on canvas. Height 6′6⅝″. The Louvre Museum, Paris

77. REHEARSAL IN THE FOYER OF THE OPERA, 1872

   Oil on canvas. Height 13″. The Louvre Museum, Paris

Degas was discussed in our first portfolio in connection with his *Woman with Chrysanthemums* (Plate 5), which may now be compared with an earlier painting by him, *The Bellelli Family* of this portfolio. *Woman with Chrysanthemums* is painted more freely—it is generally true that painters develop a more flexible style in their later periods—but both pictures are superb examples of the dominating factors in Degas's art: an acute perception of character, draughtsmanship of the very first order, and composition of expressive originality. The more rigid composition of *The Bellelli Family* is, superficially at least, more conventional than that of *Woman with Chrysanthemums*, but the picture could hardly be more unlike the conventional happy family group portrait it resembles at first glance. A more detailed study of this early masterpiece, with illustrations of preliminary drawings for it and a more detailed account of the Bellelli family itself, is given by Jean S. Boggs in *The Art Bulletin* for June 1955.

Both *The Bellelli Family* and *Woman with Chrysanthemums* are oil paintings. In his latest work Degas abandoned oil for pastel, bringing to this technique a strength and decision unique in its history. In respect to this technique Degas is further considered in Portfolio 10.

Nicolas Poussin, 1593/94-1665, French

76. THE FUNERAL OF PHOCION, 1648

   Oil on canvas. Height 46¾″. The Louvre Museum, Paris

For French artists, Poussin holds a position of special significance. Painters of every school have found in him a model or a mentor. At first this may not seem reasonable since his art is so carefully disciplined that it would seem to have nothing to offer a painter who is interested in emotional expression. And it would also seem true that its high idealism and its subject matter drawn from the world of classical antiquity would have nothing to offer the painter interested in the everyday world. Yet we have just seen that Degas, who was one of these painters, draws upon Poussin's tradition without imitating his subject matter or his style of drawing and painting. The explanation lies in the fact that a foundation of logic and order is a constant in French art, and French artists have always found Poussin to be its apotheosis.

There are further comments on Poussin in Portfolio 6, in connection with *The Rape of the Sabine Women*.

Sassetta (Stefano di Giovanni), 1392-1450, Italian

78. SAINT ANTHONY TEMPTED BY THE DEVIL IN THE FORM OF A WOMAN

Tempera on wood. Height 14½". Yale University Art Gallery, New Haven

Sassetta was a painter of the school of Siena. Sienese refinement, delicacy, and sophistication were commented on in Portfolio 3 in the discussion of the great Sant'Ansano altarpiece *The Annunciation* by Simone Martini (Plates 31 and 32). Simone, working a century before Sassetta, was his true master. Sassetta continues in spirit Simone's medievalism. Although he takes advantage of some renaissance discoveries in perspective, anatomy, and especially modeling, he uses them merely as adjuncts to the creation of graceful compositions, brilliantly continuing the Sienese tradition of pictorial narrative and poetic sensitivity.

Other painters have depicted the temptation of Saint Anthony in terms of horrifying and violent struggle. But one does not look for power and intensity in Sassetta's work. He is an utterly charming painter, and it is one of the beauties of his art that he never forces a subject beyond the natural limits of his ability to conceive it. He offers us perfection within small boundaries.

Pieter Bruegel the Elder, active by 1551—died 1569, Flemish

79. THE FALL OF ICARUS, ABOUT 1558

Oil transferred from wood to canvas. Height 29". The Royal Museum of Fine Arts, Brussels

80. FLEMISH PROVERBS, 1559

Oil on wood. Height 46⅛". Kaiser-Friedrich Museum, Berlin

81. THE PARABLE OF THE BLIND (a copy, probably by Jan Brueghel, of the one dated 1568 in the National Museum, Naples)

Oil on wood. Height 46⅜". The Louvre Museum, Paris

Bruegel combines a love for the fantastic, grotesque, and humorous with a faith in the ebullient force of human life. His grotesqueries recall the gargoyles and diableries of the Middle Ages, but his love of the world and his investigation of it are those of a renaissance man. But whether he is painting scenes from hell or rollicking peasant festivals his comment is humanistic. His medieval inheritance of fantastic allegory is most apparent in his early work; later, when he discovers the Flemish peasant, his style broadens in a series of pictures that celebrate human vitality. These streams merge in pictures like *The Fall of Icarus* and *The Parable of the Blind.*

Following a trip to Italy in 1552 and 1553 when he visited Rome and quite probably Naples, Bruegel returned to Antwerp where he was a member of the painters's guild. He produced a wealth of marvelous drawings, many of which are now in the celebrated collections of Europe. Many were also engraved and published by his business associate, Hieronymous Cock, thus finding a wider audience for his unusual work. During the last six years of his life he apparently devoted the greater part of his attention to painting. Some of his most famous pictures date from this period.

Bruegel's two sons assisted him and frequently imitated him. Both were sound technicians but neither approached the force and originality in the father's work.

Andrea Mantegna, 1431-1506, Italian

82. THE ADORATION OF THE SHEPHERDS

Tempera transferred from wood to canvas. Height 15¾". The Metropolitan Museum of Art, anonymous gift, 1932

Mantegna is the most important master of the North Italian school, which centered around Padua, and one of the most important ones of the fifteenth century in all Italy. He shared the passion of the Renaissance for the revival of classical antiquity, but he differs from his contemporaries because instead of striving for classical repose he created a vision of antiquity that was almost ferociously masculine although exquisitely controlled. A series of frescoes in the church of the Eremitani in Padua, depicting scenes of the martyrdoms of Christian saints in ancient Rome, afforded him the perfect vehicle for the double expression of his particular kind of classicism and his taste for violence. The destruction of these paintings in the Second World War was one of the most tragic of all losses in Italian art.

Mantegna appears again in Portfolio 9, where *The Adoration of the Shepherds* is discussed in some detail and a portion of it is reproduced at full size. In the meantime the reader may be interested in analyzing the composition as a variation on the triangular scheme.

El Greco (Domenicos Theotocopoulos), 1541-1614, Spanish

83. VIEW OF TOLEDO

Oil on canvas. Height 47¾". The Metropolitan Museum of Art, H. O. Havemeyer Collection, 1929

El Greco was considered as an expressionist in Portfolio 3. *View of Toledo* differs from the paintings discussed there in being a landscape. In certain other respects, however, the comments made in that portfolio are applicable here. The picture is not exactly a "view" of the Spanish city because it does not correspond with its actual appearance. In reality Toledo is a dun-colored city rising upon hills so dry, so barren, and so forbidding as to be nearly desertlike. Nevertheless, it is a city permeated with the intense emotional mysticism of Spanish Catholicism. It is this spirit that El Greco has painted. The bridge still stands and most of the buildings are identifiable, but their disposition does not correspond with El Greco's composition.

Earlier in these discussions we said that every picture we learn to know increases our understanding of every other one. *View of Toledo* is related to pictures as different as Van Gogh's *Starry Night* (Plate 25, Portfolio 3) and Ruisdael's *Wheatfields* (Plate 66, Portfolio 6). Both pictures may help in making an analysis of the composition of *View of Toledo*.

Georges Seurat, 1859-1891, French

84. SUNDAY AFTERNOON ON THE ISLAND OF LA GRANDE JATTE, 1884-86

Oil on canvas. Height 81¼". The Art Institute of Chicago

Seurat was a postimpressionist, a term covering painters who, in different ways, departed from fading impressionism to seek new means of expression. Three of these men have already been discussed: Van Gogh, Gauguin, and Cézanne.

Cézanne once said that he wanted to make impressionism "something solid and durable like the art of the museums." Seurat could have said the same thing and it would have been even more strictly to his point than Cézanne's. Impressionist painters applied color in short strokes of variegated tones and tints to increase the luminosity of the over-all color. Although these painters thus approximated the vibrations of light and air, frequently they did so at the expense of form, which in extreme cases dissolved into rainbowed mists. Seurat stuck to the idea of using many individual bits of color, but he built these bits into forms that were uncompromisingly defined. The color itself was applied with great precision instead of freely as in impressionism. A Seurat painting is composed of thousands upon thousands of individual flecks of a few colors, each fleck the size of a piece of confetti, or smaller, combined in semiscientific proportions with others that will be blended by the eye into a final one.

Sunday Afternoon on the Island of La Grande Jatte, a huge picture, is Seurat's masterpiece and one of the masterpieces of modern painting. His Sunday strollers on an island in the Seine near Paris, whether we read them in two or in three dimensions, are designed into geometrical shapes so pure that they approach abstraction; they are disposed with such absolute nicety that the composition of this, among all pictures, can be tested by trying to imagine it with any shape changed, omitted, or moved in the slightest degree. Its relationship with Poussin's *Funeral of Phocion* and Degas's *Rehearsal* as discussed in this portfolio should be apparent. Also, if *Sunday Afternoon* is compared with Picasso's *The Studio* (Plate 38, Portfolio 4) it becomes a mid-point between the classical organization of Poussin and the abstract shapes of Picasso, which are arranged with a precision even more spare than Seurat's.

Seurat died at the age of thirty-two, leaving only a handful of pictures, a not surprising fact in view of his laborious technique, for which the word "pointillism" has been coined.

THE MIDDLE EAST

Text by
LUCIENNE LAROCHE

Foreword by
HENRY MOORE

MONUMENTS OF CIVILIZATION
THE MIDDLE EAST

GROSSET & DUNLAP

Publishers   New York

Specific acknowledgments to page-referenced quotations and to drawings are given on page 190 at the end of this volume. Here we offer our special acknowledgment to the following publishers for their kind permission to quote from the works indicated:

Selections from *Ancient Near Eastern Texts Relating to the Old Testament*, ed. by James B. Pritchard, 3rd edn., with Supplement (copyright © 1969 by Princeton University Press): pp. 265 and 267, transl. Leo Oppenheim; pp. 356 and 393, transl. Albrecht Goetze. Reprinted by permission of Princeton University Press.

Selection from *History of the Persian Empire*, by A. T. Olmstead, Copyright © 1948 by The University of Chicago Press.

Selections from *Kingship and the Gods*, by Henri Frankfort, Copyright © 1948 by The University of Chicago Press.

Selections from *Persepolis*, I (Vol. LXVIII of the University of Chicago Oriental Institute Publications, 1953), by Erich F. Schmidt. Copyright © 1953 by The University of Chicago Press.

Selections from *History Begins at Sumer*, by Samuel Noah Kramer. Doubleday-Anchor Edition published in 1959 by Doubleday & Co., Inc.

Selection from *Chronicles of Chaldaean Kings (626–556 B.C.) In The British Museum*, by D. J. Wiseman. Copyright © 1956 by Trustees of the British Museum. Reproduced by courtesy of the Trustees of the British Museum.

Lines from the inscription at Bisitun, by George G. Cameron. Reprinted from *Archaeology*, Vol. 13, No. 3, Copyright © 1960, Archaeological Institute of America.

First published in the United States in 1974
by Grosset & Dunlap, 51 Madison Avenue, New York 10010

English translation copyright © 1974 by Mondadori, Milano-Kodansha, Tokyo; originally published in Italian under the title *Grandi Monumenti: Dai Sumeri Ai Sassanidi* copyright © 1971 by Mondadori, Milano-Kodansha, Tokyo; copyright © 1971 by Kodansha Ltd., Tokyo, for the illustrations; copyright © 1971 by Mondadori, Milano-Kodansha, Tokyo for the text.

Editorial Director
GIULIANA NANNICINI
American Editorial Supervisor
JOHN BOWMAN

Frontispiece:
Bishapur: The Triumph of Shapur (third century A.D.). This detail of the rock-relief sculptures shows the Roman prisoners of the Sassanian Persians.

CONTENTS

FOREWORD

It is my profound conviction that the testimony of the past must not be ignored. A knowledge of our history can be of great use in our life; all human activity is conditioned by this past, without which man would have to start all over again from the beginning. We all owe something to our parents, as they do to their parents; this debt goes back to the beginning of man. Human history is of immense value through the light it sheds on our nature and character. The more we know about man's past responses to life, his customs, habits, efforts, achievements, and failures, the better off we are. Today we have at our disposal the most diverse technical means to gain a more profound knowledge of the world around us, as well as of the world of the past. Improved means of communication, greater possibility of travel, archaeological excavations carried out with the most advanced techniques, the development of photography — all facilitate the relationship between man and his world while opening up unlimited horizons. Certainly direct contact with nature and the monuments of the past can never be substituted by films or photos, but then neither can we see everything in a lifetime. Thus, films, books, and photos help us enormously to establish a relationship with works and countries which would otherwise be inaccessible.

I have never been to the Grand Canyon, for example, but through films and photographs I can get, all the same, a deep emotional impact from this marvel of nature. The same holds true for me over Mesopotamia, which I have never visited. My first contact with Mesopotamian art occurred when I saw the works exhibited in the British Museum. I was fascinated and moved by the monumentality of the tiny statuette of a Sumerian woman (page 6), in which the tiny head and tensely held hands seem to contrast with the large body. It is just this relationship of proportions (or disproportions, to be more exact), between parts and the whole, which produces the sense of monumentality.

When I discovered this small figure I was very excited, because at that time I was struggling to get this difference in size of the parts of the sculptural whole in my own work. For if a work is just as it is in nature,

Sumerian woman. Alabaster statuette; height 8⅔ inches; circa 3000 B.C. (London, British Museum).

one part is not more important than another. But if, for example, the head is very large, then the expression is concentrated there; and if it is small, the body becomes more important in the meaning of the sculpture. (Michelangelo always reduced the heads of his pieces.) This realization of a Sumerian woman taught me much. Certainly the tiny hands make the head important, but they also give a soft feminine quality to the piece: they are the spirit of the work.

The great architectural and monumental remains, as well as the small sculptures of Mesopotamian civilization, all have the same emotional impact, the same force; I get a similar feeling of grandeur from large and small forms alike. In Mesopotamian art there is a unity of sculpture and architecture, a strong relationship between the two; both arts are fused. The great masses that man has sculptured or organized in architectural space cannot but strike all men in some way. I think that deep in all of us there still exists something primitive which is impressed by large monumental blocks of stone, as also by mountains. In fact, in ancient civilizations we find an almost religious reverence for large boulders of stone isolated in the desert or projecting out from the sea. An example of this is Stonehenge in England. Nobody knows for certain how or why it was built, and we do not understand its "meaning," but its mysterious, monumental presence fascinates us.

This same sense of awe of the grandiose is to be found in Mesopotamian art. It reveals a richness of feeling for life, welded to a direct plastic statement born of a real creative urge. There is a bigness and simplicity about it, with no decorative trimmings. But for me its greatest achievements are its freestanding pieces — sculpture in the round. These pieces have tremendous power combined with great sensitivity. Much of the sculpture of ancient periods, even when carved from blocks and not from a slab, is not in fully realized form; often it is a relief carving on the surface of a block. But the Sumerian figures have a full three-dimensional existence. And in Sumerian art (as perhaps in all the greatest sculpture and painting), along with the abstract value of form and design, inseparable from it, there is a deep human element.

Architecture and sculpture both deal with the relationship of masses. In practice, architecture is not pure form expression; it also has a functional or utilitarian purpose, which limits it as an art of pure expression. And sculpture, more naturally than architecture, can use organic rhythms. Aesthetically, architecture is the abstract relationship of masses. If sculpture is limited to this, then in the field of scale and size, architecture has the advantage; but sculpture, not being tied to a functional and utilitarian purpose, can attempt more freely the exploration of the world of pure form. It seems to me that a perfect synthesis of sculpture and architecture is expressed in the picture of the corridors of Yazilikaja reproduced in this volume (pp. 56–57). In the procession of figures sculptured in the rock, the rhythm of men walking is wonderfully portrayed. I can imagine myself among these stones and sensing a marvelous natural life force. This is beautiful architecture, real stone architecture, where the material, the stone, has contributed to the form, so that it becomes sculpture — or rather, sculptured architecture. It also strongly expresses the importance and seriousness of ceremony and ritual. The Lion Gate at Boghaz Köy (p. 49), in particular, gives me the monumental sense that large works in stone can give. It reminds me of Stonehenge: it has the same power.

I hope I have succeeded in at least partially transmitting my emotions and feelings upon seeing the Mesopotamian world, both directly at the British Museum and through the photographs in this fine volume. Above all, I want the reader to see in these great works the testimony of a distant past which belongs to all of us, since it is an integral part of human history.

Henry Moore

INTRODUCTION

Although a book should not be judged by its cover, the fact is that it has been most difficult to know what to title this volume. On the one hand, there is the relatively simply defined, if immensely varied, geographic territory that we know as the Middle East — a term that includes the present-day states of Turkey, Lebanon, Syria, Israel, Jordan, Iraq, and Iran. But given the limits of the volume, it is impossible to furnish an exhaustive analysis of the complete histories of all these countries: even the ancient history of each would merit a volume all to itself.

So the book has had to confine itself to a somewhat more selective version of the Middle East, one that concentrates on the area known as Mesopotamia and then traces the sequence of peoples, cultures, and states that, although sometimes flourishing on its perimeter, centered upon this nuclear area. Chronologically, this means we start with a sketch of the Paleolithic hunting people and move on to the first villagers of the eighth through sixth millennia B.C. (that is, 8000 to 5000 B.C.), and then to the extraordinary achievements both in architecture and pottery in the fifth millennium B.C. We then focus on the Sumerians, who first appear as an historical people in this part of the world during the fourth millennium B.C. Following the Sumerians come the great "classic" Mesopotamian civilizations of the Babylonians and Assyrians, who extended their dominion well beyond Mesopotamia proper. Meanwhile, various peoples in neighboring regions — the Hittites, in particular — overlap the Mesopotamian civilization; and eventually new peoples — the Achaemenids of Persia, the Hellenes of Alexander the Great, the Greco-Romans — usurp the territory and dominion of the Mesopotamians, so that virtually the whole of the Middle East did become a unity, from the Mediterranean Sea to the Indus River. Then came the Sassanians, and with the end of that dynasty in A.D. 651, we have also arrived at the end of antiquity in the Middle East and the beginning of what can be called its Middle Ages.

But having satisfied this need for a panoramic view that includes the various peoples and states that flourished in such places as Anatolia (Turkey), Persia (Iran), and certain cities on the fringes of the nuclear area, the book does in fact concentrate on that area known as Mesopotamia. Yet even Mesopotamia does not have geographical unity in the strict sense of the term. In the north are the rocky hills of Assyria; in the center, the fertile plain of Babylonia; in the south, a swampy area; in the west, the desert or steppes; and in the east, the Zagros Mountains. And because the nuclear area has no natural defensive boundaries, it has proved especially inviting to invaders from the mountains and nomads from the steppes and deserts. Its constant attraction has been its rich agricultural land, which in turn is due to the Tigris and Euphrates Rivers, "the vital arteries of Mesopotamia," as the archaeologist Max Mallowan has rightly put it. Its subsoil is so poor and its terrain so lacking in raw materials — in particular, metals — that its inhabitants have always depended greatly on trade and imports. These and other factors help to explain Mesopotamian history and the struggles that every dynasty had to undergo in order to hold onto its domain and keep its commercial activities viable.

The flatness of the land also says much about the constructions of its inhabitants. Accustomed to the essentially horizontal, almost immutable countryside, "Mesopotamian" architects not surprisingly conceived largely horizontal structures, while the sculptors worked with reliefs, in which the scenes are set in ranks, or with cylinders whose engraved subjects could unfold infinitely. The exception — the vertical motif that is so obvious — are the *ziggurats*, those multistoried steppyramids: but it is no coincidence that these supported temples and thus evince the Mesopotamians' aspiration to the divine.

At first encounter, Mesopotamian art may appear difficult to appreciate; in museums, particularly, certain remains may disturb the uninitiated. This is not true of individual works such as "The Lady of Warka," or the Superintendent Ebih-il of Mari (p. 20), or the bronze head of Sargon of Agade: like all true masterpieces of art, they have their own autonomy. But there is no denying that the layman may be baffled by other works from this region until they are set in their proper religious and historical context. That, of course, is one of the aims of this book. Even a visit to the ancient cities of Mesopotamia can be rather disappointing for the layman, because aside from a few sites — the city of Ur, still so alive that one expects to run into a caravan led by Abraham; or the palace of Mari, where one is surprised not to meet a nobleman or servant, so splendid is the state of preservation of this monument — aside from these, at most sites only brick walls, abused by the ages, remain of what were once grand temples and palaces.

The study of Middle Eastern civilization can thus be difficult, often austere; but it can become passionate, if not outright inspiring. I have never understood this better than when writing this book. I shall feel I have succeeded in communicating at least some of this passion if this volume evokes the desire to seek out other, more complete and more specialized, books about the ancient Middle East — a world, after all, where so much of what we today know as human civilization had its beginnings.

MAP OF ANCIENT MIDDLE EAST

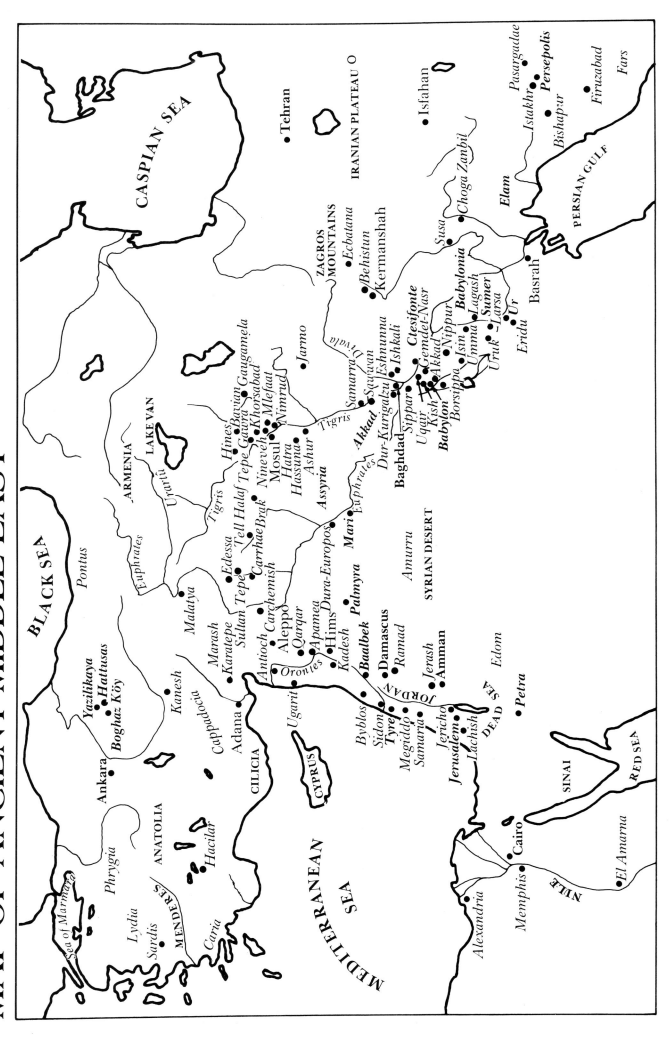

FROM THE VILLAGES TO THE KINGDOMS

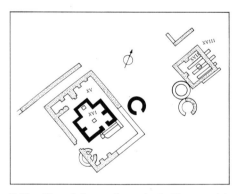

Hassuna: Reconstruction of a house. Fifth millennium B.C. In this early epoch, the rooms are already grouped around a courtyard.

Eridu: Plan of the temples on levels fifteen to eighteen. Fifth millennium B.C. The temple of level sixteen is divided into three parts.

Susa: Mound (or tell) of the acropolis and proto-Elamite level. In the foreground are some tombs.

The First Inhabitants

Since Herodotus, the history of the Middle East has always fascinated people of the Western world. Yet until the nineteenth century only its most recent periods were known. Today, thanks to the patient work of archaeologists and historians, knowledge of the early periods of human life and civilization in the Middle East increases every year.

The area was settled at a very ancient date. The first settlements, dating from the Paleolithic era were discovered in caves or in the open, in Israel and elsewhere in the Levant, northern Iraq, and Iran. The settlers were hunters who probably — in the seventh and sixth millennia B.C. — became farmers and cattle-breeders and lived together in groups. The oldest known villages are Mlefaat and Jarmo in northeastern Iraq; Tell es-Sawwan near Samarra in north-central Iraq; and Hacilar and Catal Hüyük in Turkey. The villagers lived in huts or mud and stone hovels; their tools were also made of stone. Some important findings have been made in these villages: in Jarmo clay female or animal figures, which already show the existence of religious or magical beliefs related to fecundity and fertility; in Tell es-Sawwan, Iraqi archaeologists have discovered alabaster statuettes, small crockery pieces, and vases. These are the first sculptures and they also represent some of the earliest manifestations of funerary customs. These settlements are very important in the history of man; they show him no longer trusting to the risky business of hunting and food-gathering, but producing for himself what he needs for his own sustenance, with varying degrees of success.

In the different cultural phases of the fifth millennium — called Hassuna, Samarra, Halaf, from the names of the sites where they were first recognized — this progress was confirmed. At Hassuna a more elaborate architecture appears: rooms are grouped around a courtyard, a distribution of interior space to be seen in all later Middle Eastern architecture. The typical temple plan, too, is one drawn along these lines; its interior organization is also set at this time, by division into three parts. In pottery also there are masterpieces from these sites that are unequaled in later periods.

The greatest inventions took place in the fifth and fourth millennia, however, during the so-called Ubaid and Uruk-Gemdet Nasr phases. Important technical changes date from the Ubaid period, which is characterized by the appearance of the potter's wheel, the fusion of metals, the seal, and the brick mold. These innovations did not stop man from perfecting forms earlier realized: the temple plan was definitively set down in the Ubaid period. With the exception of pieces found at Susa, in Iran, however, pottery production was less brilliant.

In the succeeding so-called proto-urban or Uruk-Gemdet Nasr period, from the fourth to the third millennium, named for two Mesopotamian sites — the first in the south, the second in the center — there were changes of a different nature. In ceramic forms, handles and mouths made their appearance, and pottery was no longer painted, at least in the Uruk period. Some containers dating from the Gemdet

Uruk: Remains of a mosaic column. Decoration was provided by inserting clay cones with colored bases into the columns.

Below:
Uruk: This close-up reveals how the clay cones were pressed into the columns while the latter were still soft.

THE SUMERIAN KING LIST

When kingship was lowered from heaven, kingship was first in Eridu. In Eridu, Alulim became King and ruled 28,800 years. Alalgar ruled 36,000 years. Two kings thus ruled it for 64,800 years.

I drop the topic of Eridu because its kingship was brought to Bad-tibira. In Bad-tibira, Enmenlu-Anna ruled 43,200 years; Enmengal-Anna ruled 28,800 years; the god Dumuzi, a shepherd, ruled 36,000 years. Three kings thus ruled it for 108,000 years.

I drop the topic of Bad-tibira because its kingship was brought to Larak. In Larak, Ensipazi-Anna ruled 28,800 years. One king thus ruled it for 28,800 years.

I drop the topic of Larak because its kingship was brought to Sippar. In Sippar, Enmendur-Anna became king and ruled 21,000 years. One king thus ruled it for 21,000 years.

I drop the topic of Sippar because its kingship was brought to Shuruppak. In Shuruppak, Ubar-Tutu became king and ruled 18,600 years. One king thus ruled it for 18,600 years.

These are five cities, eight kings ruled over them for 241,200 years. Then the Flood swept over the earth.

After the Flood had swept over the earth and when kingship was lowered again from heaven, kingship was first in Kish.

Pritchard: *Ancient Near Eastern Texts* (p. 265)

INSCRIPTION REGARDING STRUGGLE BETWEEN LAGASH AND UMMA

Enlil [leading deity of the Sumerian pantheon], the king of all the lands, the father of all the gods, marked off the boundary for Ningirsu [the patron deity of Lagash], and Shara [the patron deity of Umma] by his steadfast word, and Mesilim, the king of Kish, measured it off in accordance with the word of Sataran, and erected a stele there. But Ush, the *ishakku* of Umma, violated both the decree [of the gods] and the word [given by man to man], ripped out its [the boundary's] stele, and entered the plain of Lagash.

Then did Ningirsu, Enlil's foremost warrior, do battle with [the men of] Umma, in accordance with Enlil's straightforward word; by the word of Enlil he hurled the great net upon them, and heaped up their skeleton piles in the plain in their various places.

Kramer: *History Begins at Sumer* (p. 86)

Nasr period, however, have a monochrome or polychrome decoration with simple motifs. The first real masterpiece of sculpture, the head of a woman, found in Uruk, dates from this time. But the most important fact about the period is the appearance of writing, an invention attributed to the Sumerians.

The Sumerians are still a people relatively unknown. It is not known who they were, but it is known that they were neither Aryans (that is, Indo-Europeans) nor Semites, two of the major populations of the ancient Middle East. Their origin is also unknown: it is likely that they came from the East, but any further statements in this regard, given present knowledge, would only be rash. They came to Mesopotamia during the fourth millennium, but the exact date of their arrival is still an unsolved problem. Most scholars think it was during the Uruk period, but others maintain it was during the Ubaid era. One thing seems sure: the Sumerians were not the first inhabitants of Mesopotamia; they found a population there from which they quickly assimilated a civilization already in an advanced stage. The Semites were already living in the area, having come from the northeast at the end of the fourth millennium. There seems to have been a true coexistence between the two ethnic groups: the Sumerians occupied the south of the land, called the land of Sumer, and the Semites lived in the northern area; between them lay central Mesopotamia, the region of the Diyala River.

The City-State

When writing was born, history was born with it. If tradition is to be believed, "after the Universal Flood, the royalty descended from the heavens." In fact, the dynastic lists recorded by second millennium scribes give information that is today judged less severely than before, since names once considered merely legendary have been found engraved on clay tablet texts brought to light by excavations. Such is the case, for example, with Mesannepadda, king of Ur. It is certain that cities like Uruk and Ur were the seats of dynasties and controlled the country on various occasions. The same holds true for Kish, Akshak, Lagash, and Mari. Unfortunately, the order of succession of these dynasties is uncertain and much more difficult to establish; some of them must in fact have been contemporaneous. Mesopotamian cities were independent principalities, but each attempted to extend its hegemony over the largest possible territory, probably because of economic needs. Various cities succeeded in doing this for a certain period. They were each forced to yield in time to another stronger power. The phenomenon has resulted in various names being given to this period at the beginning of the third millennium (2800–2450 B.C.): city-state, heroic, dynastic, archaic, or even the pre-Sargonic age, in reference to the succeeding period, in which Sargon, king of Akkad became ruler of the entire area. It is worth noting that such loose, contested, and shifting structures of power should have nonetheless led to the flowering of a civilization which was homogeneous from north to south. It was a civilization with numerous cultural centers; the cities of Nippur, Uruk, Ur, Eridu, Lagash and Mari have furnished copious documentation of every kind. Lagash is the city best known at present, thanks to texts discovered there which permit a reconstruction of the organization of a city at the dawn of the third millennium.

The Temple and Religious Power

The temple and the palace were the two poles of the economic, political, and religious life of the Mesopotamian city. The precise relationships between these aspects of life are not known. At Lagash, however, there was a growing religious power — above all, of the clergy of

Uruk: The ziggurat and the Eanna quarter. This was the heart of the Sumerian city, first consecrated to the god Anu, and later to the goddess Ishtar. A wall, altered many times, separated the sacred zone from the rest of the city.

MARDUK CREATES THE WORLD

The sacred house, the house of the gods, in a holy place had not yet been built.
The reed had not yet grown, the tree had not been created,
The brick was not yet in place, its mold was not yet created,
The city was not built, living beings did not yet exist . . . .
Uruk was not built, Eanna was not yet created. . . .
Marduk, on the surface of the waters, assembled a raft,
He created the dust and with the raft he gathered it together,
In order to install the gods in a residence of satisfaction.
He created humanity. . . .
He created and put into their places the Tigris and the Euphrates,
He created grass, straw, reed, and forests,
He created the verdure of the plains,
The farmlands, the marshes, and the canebrakes,
The cow and her young one, the calf,
The sheep and her young one, the lamb in the sheepfold,
The gardens and the forests also. . . .
He put in place the brick for which he had created the mold,
He built the house, he created the town,
He built the town, and he placed in it the living beings. . . .
He built Uruk, he created Eanna.

Labat *et al.: Les Religions du Proche-Orient*
(pp. 74–6)

HYMN TO ISHTAR

I beg of you, sovereign of sovereigns, goddess of goddesses,
O Ishtar, queen of all inhabitaed places, who maintains order among all peoples,
Thou, thou art the clarity of the heavens and of the earth, heroic daughter of Sin,
Who makes armaments to clash and provokes combat,
Who concentrates within thee all powers, and bears the sovereign crown!
I ask mercy from you, o sovereign of the heavens and of the earth, shepherdess of human beings who live beneath the clouds;
I ask mercy of you, o sovereign of sacred Eanna, the holy receptacle,
I ask mercy of you, o sovereign of the indefatigable feet and the quick-bending knees,
I ask mercy of you, o sovereign of all battles and of all insults.

O dazzling Ishtar, who assembles the flock,
Goddess of men, Ishtar of women, of whom no one can know her purpose,
Where thou lookest, the dead person revives, the sick person rises;
Whoever wandered astray, regains the right road, upon seeing your face!

Labat *et al.: Les Religions du Proche-Orient*
(pp. 253–54)

Mari: The superintendent Ebih-il. Detail. First half of the third millennium B.C. Alabaster; height 20.4 inches. This statue, found in the temple of Ishtar at Mari, illustrates Mesopotamian sculpture of the city-state period, when various schools distinguished themselves. The Mari school is characterized by a sure realism and a smile that gives life to many of its statues. (Paris, Louvre Museum)

the god Ningirsu, lord and protector of the city. Priests ascended the throne, but the kings also took over ecclesiastical possessions. In reality there was no separation between sacred and profane: the true king of the city was the god, and the king who reigned was his representative, his administrator. In this post he was responsible for the maintenance of the sanctuaries and the canals, which were essential sources of life. The country also had to be defended from attacks of every kind. For this the king was aided by a permanent army — phalanxes of soldiers with heavy helmets, enormous shields, spears, and axes — reinforced in time of war by troops recruited from neighboring cities or from among the farmers. Besides the central power, there existed an elders' council, an assembly whose powers were only deliberative. Land in the city-state was divided between royal fiefs, private property, and lots belonging to the temples. One of the most important temples in Lagash — there were about twenty of them — was the one dedicated to the goddess Bau, wife of the god Ningirsu, "the Mistress of Abundance," which controlled some 11,000 acres of land. A quarter of this land was used to meet the needs of the cult and temple. The remainder was either divided among tenants or served for the maintenance of the sanctuary personnel, some 1,200 persons representing all the occupations necessary for an independent organism: farmers, artisans, bakers, butchers and many others. The administration of this property was entrusted to superintendents, under the direction of the priests, aided by numerous assistants.

INSCRIPTION ENGRAVED ON THE STATUE OF EBIH-IL

Statue
of Ebih-Il
The Intendant
To Ishtar brave
They have dedicated it
                        Temple of Ishtar, Mari

THE VICTORIES OF SARGON OF AGADE

Sargon, king of Agade, overseer of Ishtar, king of Kish, anointed priest of Anu, king of the country, great ensi of Enlil; he defeated Uruk and tore down its wall; in the battle with its inhabitants of Uruk, he was victorious. Lugalzaggisi, king of Uruk, he captured in this battle, he brought him in a dog collar to the gate of Enlil. Sargon, king of Agade, was victorious in the battle with the inhabitants of Ur, their town he defeated and tore down its wall.
Pritchard: *Ancient Near Eastern Texts* (p. 267)

The last Sumerian attempt at unification was that undertaken by Lugalzagesi, prince of Umma, who succeeded in conquering Lagash. A sentence that recurs like a motif in the texts describes at what cost "the men of Umma set fire to Temple X . . . set fire to Temple Z." Lugalzagesi then conquered Uruk, Ur, and Kish. His campaign was brutally interrupted by Sargon, a Semitic official in the court of Kish, who took Lugalzagesi prisoner and exhibited him, confined in a cage, on the threshold of the temple at Nippur.

Sargon of Akkad

Very little is known about Sargon. According to legend he was the son of a priestess, who abandoned him, putting him in a basket of rushes, which she left to float in a river, much like Moses. A water-drawer saved him and raised him as his son. Noticed by the goddess Ishtar, he was sent by her to enter the court of the king of Kish as a cup-bearer. While there Sargon rebelled. Once in power, he founded a capital, Akkad, or Agade — not yet discovered, but almost certainly situated in central Mesopotamia — and in a short time came to reign over a rather extended empire. This is reported to have reached Elam on the east and touched the Mediterranean on the west, where his soldiers reportedly "wash their weapons in the sea." Strengthened by his victories, Sargon took the title of "king of the four parts of the

Lagash: Genealogical relief of Ur-Nanshe (also called Ur-Nina). First half of the third millennium B.C. Alabaster; height 15.7 inches. This monument shows the erection of a temple. In the upper register Ur-Nanshe, carrying a basket of bricks on his head, is about to lay the first brick in the presence of his daughter and sons. In the lower register Ur-Nanshe, seated, and his sons, during the consecration cermony of the temple. (Paris, Louvre Museum)

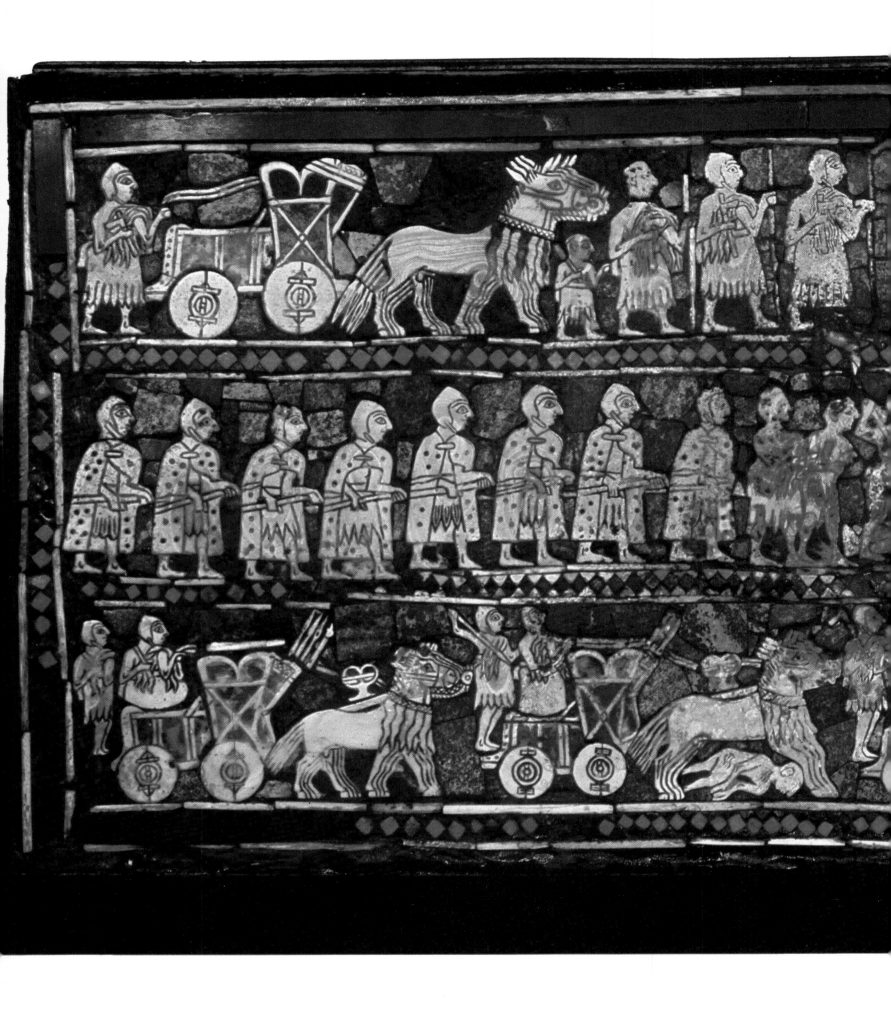

Ur: The "royal standard," showing the side with a war scene. First half of the third millennium B.C. Mosaic, made of red limestone, lapis lazuli, and shells; length 29.1 inches. Found in one of the "royal" tombs, it is in the form of a lectern, decorated on all four sides. On the face shown here, chariots, soldiers, and prisoners are depicted. The other principal side shows the victory banquet, with musicians, and servants carrying both beasts' heads and other products, which may be either booty or food for the banquet. (London, British Museum)

world," or even "king of battles," which is hard not to compare to the "god of the armies," a title later used by the Jews.

There were numerous revolts against domination of Sargon; the conquered regions remained so only for a short period. The Elamites were particularly restless, nomads were always dangerous, and the kings of Akkad had to wage several wars, in which successes alternated with defeats. Sargon's sons, Rimush and Manishtusu, who succeeded him in turn, were both assassinated. His grandson Naram-Sin, who had himself called in inscriptions "Naram-Sin the strong," also had to put down revolts, thwart invasions, and fight battles, in which he was not always victorious, despite the fact that his army had a light infantry armed with a new weapon, the bow. Naram-Sin's son, Sharkalisharri, enjoyed no more tranquil a reign, and this first Semitic hegemony ended under the blows of the Gutians, a people from the Zagros mountains, in an extremely confusing situation. An oft-quoted text describes it eloquently: "Who was king? Who wasn't?"

Too many facts are missing for any profound assessment of the Akkadian dynasty. There are some official inscriptions, but since the capital of the kingdom has not yet been brought to light, there are no archives to consult. Documentation for this period remains basically "external." The kingdom was, however, a centralized state, the first in the history of the Middle East. Moreover, the king assumed the title of "king of the four parts of the world," rather than "King of Kish" or "King of Ur." Nor did the sovereign, as in the case of Naram-Sin, hesitate to wear the horned tiara, the divine emblem par excellence.

The Gutians, conquerors of the Akkadian kingdom, were nomads from the mountains and were responsible for a period of anarchy whose duration is evaluated differently by scholars — from thirty to a hundred years — which indicates how little is known of this phase of history.

Lagash and Ur

These uncertain times and disorders were ably exploited by some southern cities, whose activity gives a name to the last years of the third millennium: the neo-Sumerian period. The city of Lagash enjoyed an extremely splendid period under the reign of Gudea, but the part played by Utu-hegal, king of Uruk, was even more important, for he liberated the land from the Gutians, the "dragons of the mountain." The governor of Ur, perhaps one of Utu-hegal's sons, then made his city the seat of royalty. Founding the third dynasty, one of the most famous in Ur, he carried out works whose plans may have been drawn by his father. Indefatigable, he ordered the construction of numerous monuments and issued a code of laws. His immediate successors continued his work, and the territory under their control was at least as important as the land which had belonged to the Akkadian empire.

Ur was an important trade center at the end of the third millennium, situated on the banks of the Euphrates near the Persian Gulf (much nearer than the site is today, for over the centuries the river waters have deposited a vast delta). Ur was a natural stopping-place for goods coming from the Indian Ocean and going to the Mediterranean. The fine geographic position partly explains the power of the city and its third dynasty, which marked the apex of the Sumerian bureaucracy. The territory controlled by the monarchs of Ur was divided into districts in which the power was in the hands of two persons, the first representing the civil authority, the second the military authority; both were assisted by overseers. High functionaries lived off tax collections, while their subordinates lived off the land given them by the palace or the temples; they also received agricultural produce. The centralized administration was further strengthened by its control of the carriers used for the supply of raw materials of every kind and of agricultural

Cylinder seals:
1 and 2. Impressions of cylinders from Uruk. End of the fourth millennium B.C.

3. Impression of a cylinder from Tell Billa. Diorite; 1.1 inch high. Beginning of the third millennium B.C. (Baghdad Museum)

4. Reconstruction of the decoration on a green stone vase. Beginning of the third millennium B.C. (Khafage)

The architecture seen on these cylinders aids modern archaeologists in understanding the facades and superstructures of Mesopotamian monuments. The first two cylinders most certainly represent brick architecture; the other two probably represent cane or reed architecture.

THE STELE OF NARAM-SIN

You who shall come in later times, read for yourself this stele,
That I, Naram-Sin, who am the son of Sargon, have written
And have left here for future times!

The Umman-manda shall arise and span the country.

Warriors with bodies of ducks, humans with faces of crows,
Such as the great gods created them.

Having pillaged the Gutians, they arrived at Elam;
Having pillaged Elam, they arrived at the edge of the world,

I would call the officer and I would give him these orders:
Employ against them both the stock and the point of the sword,
Hit them with the stock, pierce them with the point.
Labat et al.: Les Religions du Proche-Orient (p. 309)

Susa: The stele of Naram-Sin. Second half of the third millennium B.C. Red sandstone; height 6 feet, 6¾ inches; width 3 feet, 4 inches. Found at Susa, this is a monument from Babylon, which Shutruk-Nahhunte brought to his city in the twelfth century B.C. In a magnificent ascending composition, the Akkadian king leads his soldiers in battle. Mountains and woody countryside are suggested by undulating lines and trees. Symbols of astral gods crown the stele. (Paris, Louvre Museum)

products. The power of the palace, which also assured a part of the provisions of the temples, was very strong; as a result the temple, primary at the dawn of the third millennium, became less and less important in public life. Despite their rather efficient organization, however, the last monarchs of the third dynasty had to face numerous problems. There was increasing agitation by the Amorites of the west, and a revolt of the Elamites to the east. And so, despite their best efforts, the kings were unable to prevent the fall of the third dynasty, which occurred in 2006 B.C. The capital was destroyed. The famous text entitled *The Laments of Ur* gives an idea of the destruction: "In the bastions breaches are opened; in the streets once so lively the dead accumulate." The third millennium ends with a scene of desolation.

The Architecture of the First Millenniums

This brief sketch of the first millennia in the Middle East should permit a better understanding of the evolution of Mesopotamian architecture, its religious life, and its literary productions. Manifestations of these elements in each of the civilizations of the Middle East will be discussed throughout this survey.

Mesopotamian architecture developed amid a great number of difficulties. In the southern zones of the country there were various types of chalky limestone and alabaster, but there were no stone quarries worthy of the name. The local timber could at most be used for the framework of walls or as a kind of trestle for terraced roofs; its limited size forced the architects to conceive rooms of narrow, rectangular form. The only truly abundant materials at the disposal of the builders were clay, reeds, and bitumen. Clay produced the fundamental element: bricks. The most ancient bricks were simple blocks, more or less regular, shaped by hand. The invention of the brick mold in the Ubaid period — a modest open wooden frame still used today — permitted the production of bricks of regular form, although the forms differed according to period, region, and the uses to which they were put. Such bricks were "flat-convex," square, and rectangular; there were also half-bricks, quarter-bricks, and even bricks in the shape of segments of a circle, used in the construction of columns or wells. Once shaped, the brick was set in the sun to dry; this was "crude brick," as distinguished from the oven-baked brick, which appeared only at the beginning of the third millennium. Baked brick, as hard as stone, was used in more precise constructions or at points more exposed and more subject to erosion.

Reeds, of which there are many types, grew in the swampy land and in the irrigation canals, which had therefore to be continually cleaned. They had many uses: used alone for the building of huts, or *zarife* (typical habitations still to be seen in southern Iraq), reed was also a support material used in the formation of reinforcement framework in walls. It was used in the construction of roofs as well, after being transformed into matting, which was set on the trellis-work to serve as a support for beaten earth. Bitumen, in which the soil of the Middle East is very rich, acted as a lime, mixed with sand or ground straw; and as a sealer protecting the floor, walls, and roof from humidity and water.

Despite these poor materials, or perhaps thanks to them, Mesopotamian architecture has a very distinct character and is one of the most impressive of the artistic achievements of the Middle East. Although the first dwellings and temples date from the fifth millennium, it was only in the Ubaid period, in the fourth millennium, that the genius of the architects manifested itself. In the south, at Eridu — the holy city "loved by the god Enki," the water god — a temple erected on a terrace testifies to this genius. Rectangular in form, its walls are decorated on the outside with projecting corners, a detail characteristic of Mesopotamian architecture. Originally the projecting corner was built in order

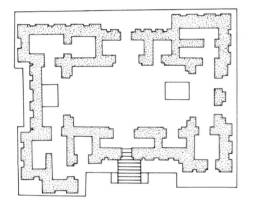

Eridu: Plan of the temple built on a terrace. Decorated with buttresses and projecting corners, it consists of a vestibule, ante-cella, and cella, and has many entrances. Fourth millennium B.C.

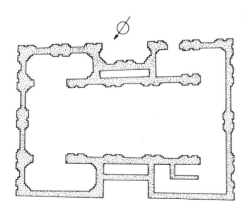

Tepe Gawra: Level thirteen. Plan of the southern temple, decorated both inside and outside with buttresses. This is a new type of construction, composed of a vast nave flanked by low lateral naves. Fourth millennium B.C.

to reinforce the construction, much like a buttress; but it soon became a decorative element, since it broke up the monotony of the facades, creating areas of light and shadow. The temple had several openings; two on one short side, which was probably the facade; one on each of the longer sides, doubtless in order to facilitate the circulation of the faithful. The double entrance in the facade probably indicates that one door was reserved for men and the other for women, while the side doors served as exits. It is also possible that the priests used a door reserved for them; it would probably have been the one rendered more majestic by a stairway. The worship area proper is a long nave divided into three parts: a vestibule; an ante-cella with an altar for offerings; and the cella proper, where a sort of podium must have served as a support for the statue of the god. On both sides of the temple are halls, sacristies, storerooms, or rooms for the priests.

The northern architecture, represented by the temples of Tepe Gawra, is not inferior to that in Eridu. Tepe Gawra is the first really large complex known in that region. Three sanctuaries are set in a vast open space; they are different, but equally majestic. The "north temple" — thus named by archaeologists for want of texts — is made up of a large nave (forty feet by twenty-eight feet) flanked by lateral naves. This temple is decorated inside and outside by projecting angles.

The architectural skill of the proto-urban period is amply demonstrated by the complex discovered in the Eanna district of Uruk, at the heart of the city. Separated from the rest of the city by a wall, this sacred zone, or *temenos*, was at first consecrated to Anu, the god of the sky with supreme power; then to Ishtar, goddess of war and love. The architectural complex includes a number of temples — which unfortunately remain anonymous, since once more texts which might identify them are lacking — as well as a large hall whose roof is supported by eight columns connected to a courtyard at a lower level. Both courtyard and columns are decorated with cone mosaics, made of small earth cones whose visible round base is colored black, white or red. These are placed together to form geometric compositions: zig-zag lines, diagonals, triangles, Greek frets, and rhombuses. Perhaps the most spectacular temple is the "calcareous temple," christened by German archaeologists because the foundation is of irregular stone blocks. It was found in a very bad state of preservation, but it was possible to reconstruct its plan by referring to the plan of a slightly more recent sanctuary called "temple C."

The calcareous temple, its exterior decorated with projecting angles, is rectangular in form. Its size is impressive: 262 feet by 98 feet. A large central hall (203 feet by 37 feet) opens out into two branches. On both sides of this long hall are various rooms, two with stairways that give access to the terraces. At one end of the hall is an apse-like section containing three rooms, which might correspond to a chapel and two sacristies, or to three chapels. The number of doors, four on each longer side, indicates a great number of worshipers.

Another edifice in Uruk is worthy of mention. Situated in the sector sacred to the god Anu, west of Eanna, it rises on an artificial platform some forty feet high; smaller than the temple discussed above (seventy-three feet by fifty-seven feet), its form — a large hall (sixty-one feet by sixteen feet) flanked by little rooms — is similar to that of the temple at Eridu. This edifice is particularly interesting because it testifies to the fact that in the same period two separate building types existed: the sanctuary as a meeting place for worshipers — such as in the calcareous temple — and the temple as the house of the god. The latter conception eventually prevailed.

The sanctuary at Uqair, built on a two-step terrace, is worthy of mention because it bears traces of badly damaged painted decoration. The facade of the podium was embellished with rhombuses and square patterns, and on the two sides there were two animals, probably leopards, which must have been considered guardian or protective animals. This is not the most ancient known painted decoration (that

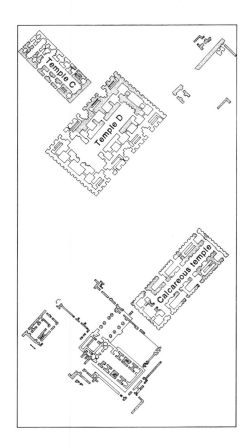

Uruk: Area of Eanna. Above, plans of Temples C and D (so named because of a lack of texts), splendid constructions decorated with buttresses and projecting corners. Below, plan of the "calcareous" temple with its courtyard and hall with columns decorated by clay cone mosaics. Second half of the fourth millennium B.C.

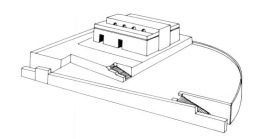

Uqair: Fourth reconstruction of the temple built on a terrace, with two stairways, predecessor of the later ziggurat. This is the temple where workers found a podium decorated with paintings. Beginning of the third millennium.

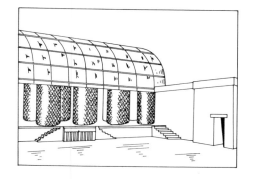

Uruk: Area of Eanna. Reconstruction of the hall with mosaic columns. Second half of the fourth millennium B.C.

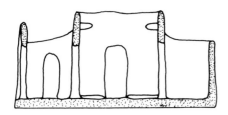

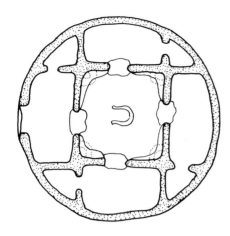

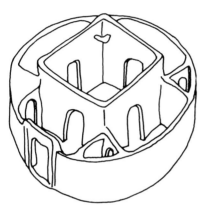

Mari: Section, plan, and reconstruction of the "round house," a small terra-cotta model of an edifice from the beginning of the third millennium; diameter 20.9 inches. Found in a street in Mari, it is now at the Damascus Museum. It may well be a model of a habitation, with eight rooms set around a courtyard. When it was found, there was pottery in the rooms, some of it miniature.

COMMERCIAL BARTER IN THE
SUMERIAN CITY OF LAGASH

Twenty-nine bushels, fifteen measures of pure silver, the inspector Shulmesharragub had weighed out under his own eyes; of the total amount, the inspector had consigned, under his own eyes, to Utulushagga, the commissioner, forty-five measures of silver, merchandise to be exchanged for a trotting ass. The inspector had consigned, as merchandise for exchange, to the merchant Urningirsu, two bushels of silver; these were sent off to Der. The inspector Shulme had weighed out for them under his own eyes the silver. After which there still remained twenty-six and one-half bushels of pure silver; the intendant Enikgal brought it to the treasury. Lugulanda, prince of Lagash. In the year I . . .
    Seventy-two bushels of fine copper, for which fine copper barley had been bartered; twenty bushels of fine copper that had been bartered for cedar; ninety-six bushels of fine copper that had been bartered for scented oils; twenty-five bushels of fine copper that had been bartered for grains of starch; there are the goods exchanged from the land of Dilmun and that the merchant Urenki had brought to Dimtur, wife of the prince. In the year I . . .
    Lambert: *Textes commerciaux de Lagash*

discovered in Catal Huyuk in Turkey dates from a much more remote age), but the Uqair decoration is the most ancient discovered in Mesopotamia so far.

The exact height of these edifices is not known. This is the case with all the ancient Middle Eastern edifices, but representations found on other monuments give some idea of it. There is unfortunately not enough documentation of civil architecture from the fourth millennium to permit a discussion of its characteristics.

The architects of the city-state period introduced no architectural innovations. Certain temples were built on a platform, such as the ones at Khafage and Ubaid, both set in an oval enclosure; but at Mari most of the sanctuaries look like common houses. The one dedicated to the goddess Ninni-Zaza belongs to this type: the courtyard, which in this period becomes an integral part of the temple, is carefully decorated with projecting angles, and the floor has asphalt (bitumen) aisles, "processional streets" as it were.

The Architecture of the Third Millennium

In the third millennium another type of sanctuary made its appearance: the *ziggurat*, or multi-level temple tower, the logical evolution of the terraced temple of the preceding period. Although no *ziggurat* from the beginning of that third millennium has yet been brought to light, it is known that it existed then because of representations found on other monuments, cylinder seals, and pottery.

More is known of the civil architecture in this age. At Mari a residential complex has been unearthed, with houses grouped around streets. The dwellings were all built according to Eastern principles: with an open-air courtyard which affords light for rather irregular rooms that are generally trapezoidal in form. Particularly worthy of mention is the fact that the water was removed both by individual drains and by pipes connected to drainage canals, forming a real sewage system. Another type of house is known thanks to a small terra-cotta model found at Mari. Its plan was circular, but the central courtyard connected the various rooms. Although rare, the circular form can be verified by more ancient constructions.

The royal residences were the most beautiful creations of secular architecture. The palace at Kish has long been known. It has a thick enclosure wall, whitewashed walls, and decorative friezes that depict prisoners, farm scenes, and musicians. The palace at Mari — still under excavation — outdoes the Kish palace, because of its excellent state of preservation (its walls are still over six and a half feet high), its quality of construction, and the beauty of its proportions.

Necropolises existed in more remote periods, but they were simply earth burials or sarcophagi concentrated in a small space, to form cemeteries. Funerary architecture worthy of the name appears only with the pre-Sargonic tombs at Ur. Sixteen of these can be called royal tombs; they are real constructions, with from one to four chambers, built of stone or bricks. In some cases access is afforded by shafts. Some chambers are roofed with true vaults — that is, made from stones set one upon the other in semicircular form, without a keystone.

Akkadian architecture is little known: regrettably, since the masterpieces of Akkadian sculpture — the head thought to be of Sargon, the stele of Naram-Sin, and cylinder seals of the period suggest that the buildings may have been of the same high quality. There is, however, the palace at Tell Brak in northern Mesopotamia, not far from the present-day Turkish border. This was built by Naram-Sin, according to an inscription. The palace (344 feet by 302 feet), surrounded by a thick enclosure wall, was at the same time residence, storehouse and citadel; in fact it had only one access gate. It is logical to assume that

Naram-Sin had it built in order to protect the roads communicating with Anatolia.

The architectural art of the third dynasty of Ur, and above all that of its first sovereigns, Ur-Nammu, Shulgi (also called Dungi) and Amar-Sin (also called Bur-Sin), is illustrated by the buildings in the capital. Ur at that time lay on the banks of the Euphrates, and was probably surrounded by canals and thus protected on every side. Two gates, one to the north and the other to the east, have been discovered. They confirm (if confirmation were necessary) the commercial function of Ur. To the northeast of the city lies the sacred enclosure, or *temenos*, surrounded by a wall, where the *ziggurat* rises over the temple, the palace, and the royal tombs. The *ziggurat*, or multi-level tower, is a typical creation of Mesopotamian architecture. Its prototype is the terraced temple of more ancient times, created in order to protect the house of the god from the frequent and often violent floods of the Tigris and Euphrates.

The step tower at Ur is well known thanks to the work of the British archaeologist, Sir Leonard Woolley. Dedicated to the moon god Nanna, and still sixty-five and a half feet high, this tower rises in a large courtyard which is itself preceded by a smaller courtyard. Rectangular in form (220 feet by 141 feet), its nucleus of crude bricks is enclosed by a covering of baked bricks. On the southeast side a triple stairway affords access to the first floor, where another stairway leads to the second floor and then to the third, which serves as a base for the sanctuary, called the "temple of the summit." Here the god who descended from the empyrean stopped before going to the lower temple amid his worshipers. The goddess Ningal, Nanna's wife, has a temple south of the large courtyard. Southeast of this courtyard is a construction that has been identified as a sacred storehouse containing the wealth of the two gods. There is also a large portal corresponding with the southeast corner of the *ziggurat* courtyard; this "great gate" is really also a judgment place. Another edifice in the *temenos* has been identified as the palace of Ur-Nammu and Shulgi.

Beyond the sacred wall, to the southeast, Woolley found a hypogeum, or chamber tomb, which certain inscriptions allow to be attributed to Shulgi and Amar-Sin. The central part of this edifice, the work of Shulgi, consists of a rectangular block (124 feet by 88 feet) with rounded corners, and includes twelve rooms. This construction covers two magnificent, vaulted projecting tombs accessible by means of a shaft. Shulgi's son, Amar-Sin, added two wings, thus allowing for the construction of five more tombs. Since the hypogeum was found violated it is uncertain whose tombs these were, but it is likely they can be attributed to Shulgi and Amar-Sin, perhaps to Ur-Nammu, as well. Who else was buried here remains a mystery. It is interesting to note that the lower, subterranean part of the construction is the *domus aeterna;* the superstructures served as a place for the celebration of the funerary cult. This at least is how the monument has been interpreted up to now.

Mesopotamian Religion

To attempt a chronological outline of Mesopotamian religion is to face almost insurmountable problems. Large numbers of texts have been discovered, but there are certainly a great many more still buried in the earth between the two rivers. Those excavated cannot be dated with precision; in the first place they are copies made in the second millennium for the libraries of the Assyrian kings. Moreover, Mesopotamian religion is difficult to frame and place, so wide-ranging are its elements. This is the case with the official religion; the popular religion is almost totally unknown.

Nevertheless, the system of beliefs can be tentatively defined as a

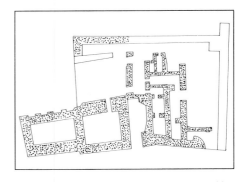

Mari: Plan of the temple consecrated to the goddess Ishtar, where numerous sculptures were found, among which were the statues of Ebih-il and king Lamgi-Mari. The inscription on the latter has made it possible to identify Tell Hariri as Mari. Beginning of the third millennium B.C.

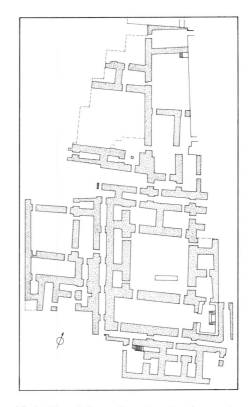

Mari: Plan of the pre-Sargonic palace (now under excavation). Beginning of the third millennium B.C. This palace lies beneath the palace of Zimrilim, which dates from the second millennium B.C.

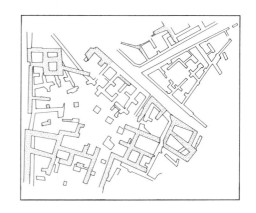

Mari: Plan of the pre-Sargonic area near the temple of Ishtar. Beginning of the third millennium B.C. The houses are set along well-marked roads. The constructions are of the usual type: an open-air courtyard from which the rooms, irregular in form and often trapezoidal, received their light.

Lagash: Statue of Gudea. Twenty-second century B.C. Diorite; height 3 feet, 5.3 inches. The king-priest of Lagash is depicted erect, hands folded, bare-footed, in the attitude of a man in the presence of the gods. His long tunic leaves his right shoulder bare. He wears a turban on his head. (Paris, Louvre Museum).

THE BUILDING OF THE TOWER OF BABEL

And the whole earth was of one language, and of one speech. And it came to pass, as they journeyed from the east, that they found a plain in the land of Shinar; and they dwelt there. And they said to one another, Go to, let us make brick, and burn them thoroughly. And they had brick for stone, and slime had they for mortar. And they said, Go to, let us build us a city and a tower whose top may reach unto heaven; and let us make us a name, lest we be scattered upon the face of the whole earth. And the Lord came down to see the city and the tower, which the children of men builded. And the Lord said, Behold, the people is one, and they have all one language; and this they begin to do; and now nothing will be restrained from them, which they have imagined to do. Go to, let us go down, and there confound their language, that they may not understand one another's speech. So the Lord scattered them abroad from thence upon the face of all the earth: and they left off to build the city.

Genesis (XI:1–8)

INSCRIPTION ON THE STATUE OF GUDEA OF LAGASH

Gudea, priest-king of Lagash, whom the *eninnu* of Ningirsu made. To the glory of Ninhursag, the lady who shines within the city, the mother of children and the city, to the glory of this woman, Gudea, priest-king of Lagash, has constructed his temple of Girsu. . . . The sublime throne of his divinity he made; in his temple sublime he introduced it. From the mountain of Magan, a stone of diorite he had brought and from it he had his statue sculptured. The lady who in the sky and on the earth determines the fate of things, Nintud, mother of the gods, prolong the life of Gudea, who constructed the temple; of this name he named her and in the temple he introduced her.

Thureau-Dangin: *Inscriptions de Sumer et d'Akkad* (p. 105)

INSCRIPTION ON CYLINDER A OF GUDEA OF LAGASH

Gudea, whose heart is fathomless, sighed in this manner: "Allow me to speak! Allow me to speak! These words that I utter them. I am the pastor: the sovereignty has been given to me at this time. Something came to me in the middle of the night: I did not make sense of it. Only to my mother was I then able to tell the story of my dream. Through the diviner, she who has the knowledge of what happened to me, my goddess Nina, the sense of it was revealed to me. . . ." To the priest-king, his mother, Nina, replied: "O my pastor, I would like to explain your dream to you. . . . It deals with my brother Ningirsu; he was ordering you to construct his house of *eninnu* . . . In order to construct the temple of Ningirsu . . . The Elamite comes from Elam; the Susian comes from Susa. Magan and Meluhha, in the mountains, assemble from the forests . . . In the mountain of the cedars, where no one had ever penetrated, Gudea, grand-priest of Ningirsu, made a road. He cut the cedars of this mountain. . . . In the mountain of the stone for cutting, where no one had ever penetrated, Gudea, grand-priest of Ningirsu, made a road. He brought down pieces of the great rocks of this mountain. . . . Like a cow who turns her eyes toward her calf, he directs all his love toward the temple; like a man who places little nourishment in his mouth, he does not allow himself to come or go . . .

Thureau-Dangin: *Les Inscriptions de Sumer et d'Akkad* (pp. 135,155)

highly hierarchical polytheism, with an attempt at simplification that manifests itself with the passing of time. A very important characteristic of the religion is its political aspect; many of the gods of separate city-states at the beginning of the third millennium were affected by political events in a very direct way. The god of the city that acquired political hegemony over its neighbors saw his prestige grow; yet the defeated god was still lord in his own home. Since power tended toward centralization, certain gods became national divinities rather than city-state divinities; such was the case with the Babylonian god Marduk in the second millennium and the Assyrian god Ashur in the first millennium. Other gods, such as Ishtar (goddess of love and war) and Adad (god of storms), remained sheltered from any political influence, however, and had a power that remained unaltered for centuries.

It is impossible to form a precise idea of the religious or magical beliefs of the periods before the historical era. One can only establish, from the sixth millennium on, at Catal Huyuk in Turkey, the existence of temples with walls embellished in high relief or paintings whose iconographic motifs — mother-gods, women giving birth, bulls' heads, dancers — are related to rites of fertility and fecundity. The human and animal figurines found at Jarmo, Tell Halaf, Eridu, and Ubaid — the representations of bulls' heads or dancers on pottery — testify to identical beliefs. Funerary rites have also been recognized in the ocher-red painted craniums found in Jericho in Palestine or in Tell Ramad in Syria, and by the funerary objects, including statuettes and stone vases, found in certain tombs at Tell es-Sawwan in Iraq. Nothing more definite than this can be said about prehistoric religious beliefs.

With the advent of the third millennium, information becomes more and more plentiful. In any panoramic view of the Middle East it is difficult to differentiate the Sumerian religion from the Akkadian religion. The Sumerian contribution to the Akkadian was considerable, however, and the Semitic Akkadians conserved a large part of it, identifying the Sumerian gods with their own; thus the sun god Utu was assimilated by the Akkadian Shamash, and the god Sin by Nanna. Sumerian remained the liturgical and religious language, and Sumerian rituals were also preserved.

The Mesopotamian gods were celestial beings who "always intervene in human affairs." Anthropomorphic in concept, they were also represented with human features; only their special attributes and the horned tiara distinguished them from mortals. They were sometimes accompanied by their sacred animal, perhaps an echo of an unknown zoomorphic stage of the religion. Their essential being was varied, but it was at most times "royal": they were called "the lord of the sky," "the lord of the earth," "of the waters" or "of the underworld"; they governed nature and only rarely represented abstractions such as Destiny or Justice. They had the same needs as man; their passions were identical, but deeper and more provoking. The basic difference between man and divinity was the gods' immortality. There were two gods who had a fatal destiny, but they were also privileged to be reborn.

Faced with such a pantheon, man is finally left with a feeling of dread. He knows that humanity, born from the blood of a god thanks to the science of Ea, lord of the waters, but also born of magic, and originated from wisdom, has been created in order to ensure the worship of the gods until they have been placated. The divine service had, then, to take place at every moment: by offerings, sacrifices, libations, and prayers. Nothing could be omitted from the rites, no portent, no incident could be neglected. It was also essential to pay attention to dreams and to deal with them, dreams being one of the manifestations through which the gods made their desires known. The king was the first of the divine servants and the destiny of the land and its inhabitants depended on his piety. He was assisted in this difficult task by divination, and ceremonies of exorcism allowed the believer to purify himself of sins that passed unrecognized, or to free himself from evil whose motives he could not understand. Another royal duty was the construction or

Sacred ship of the sky, grandeur that is made of itself,
Father moon-god, lord of the city of Ur,
Father moon-god, lord of the house of light,
Father moon-god, o great white racer,
Lord moon-god, elder son of the god Enlil,
When you navigate, when you navigate . . .
When you navigate toward Ur, in your sacred ship . . .
Lord moon-god, who can surpass you, who even equals you?
Who controls the raising of your eyes?
Your route, who triumphs over it?
Let your name be spread over the sea and the sea has fear;
Let your name be spread across the marshes and they groan;
Let your name be spread over the Tigris and the Euphrates
And the full waters, day and night, are becalmed.

La Lune, Mythes et Rites (pp. 78–9)

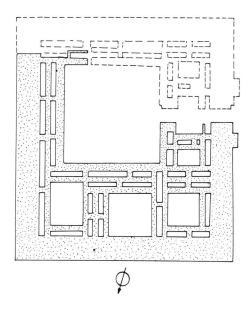

Tell Brak: Plan of the palace-citadel, and probably also a storehouse. A crude brick was found here, with an inscription giving the builder's name: "Naram-Sin, King of Akkad." Second half of the third millennium B.C.

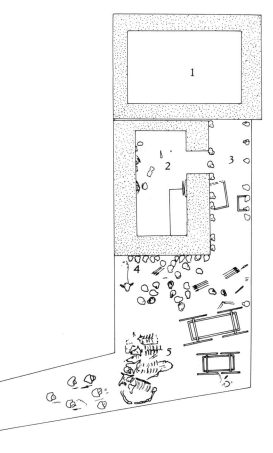

Ur: Plan of the king's tomb. Among other objects, a magnificent harp was found here, decorated with shell and lapis lazuli mosaics and adorned with a golden bull's head. As the drawing indicates, there were also the remains of the royal retinue and of animals, probably offered in sacrifice.
1. Tomb chamber (sacked in ancient times)
2. Hall of offerings
3. Dignitaries
4. Musicians
5. Chariots, cattle, and guards

restoration of sanctuaries, which were the homes of the gods. This is the reason why many times the king is depicted dressed in the clothes of a builder on monuments: Ur-Nanshe with a basket on his head containing the first brick to be laid for the building of the divine edifice, or Ur-Nammu carrying on his shoulders the bag containing bricklayer's tools, helped by a servant who holds up the burden.

Neither the king nor the simple believer was unaware of the fact that at the end of his life (despite his exemplary behavior or even when free from sin), he could not expect any consolation, since "when the gods created humanity, they gave it death as destiny and kept life in their own hands." The sole hope of the Mesopotamian people, after the failure of Gilgamesh, the Mesopotamian hero, in his search for immortality, thus consisted of living as long as possible before being condemned "to the land of no return."

Writing and Literature

After passing from a nomadic to a sedentary life, from hunting to the domestication of animals and to agriculture, man had only to discover writing to complete his passage to "civilization." The event occurred toward the end of the fourth millennium, among the Sumerians. At first the writing was pictographic, with words symbolized by images (it is interesting to note that certain signs — those for god, star, and water, for example — had already been part of the ceramic painter's repertoire for a long time). Writing soon passed into a pattern stage and then through a "linear" stage before becoming cuneiform (wedge-shaped) and abstract. This evolution is easily explained. The scribe, wishing to write more quickly, simplified the design, and then, rather than rendering a curve in one stroke, he broke it up into segments. Another factor in this change was the material used as a "support": clay was the commonly used material; it was abundant and once baked in the oven became nearly indestructible. It is quite difficult to draw on soft clay, but a good deal easier, with the help of thin cane cut in wedge-shape form, to engrave signs or combinations of signs in the form of triangular nails.

Cuneiform writing is one of the most complicated of all writing forms, because certain signs are ideograms that express an idea, while others have phonetic values, in which sign = sound = syllable. As if this were not complicated enough, one sign may have many phonetic values; furthermore, ideograms and "syllabograms" do not make up two distinct groups, but the same sign may be an ideogram and at the same time have syllabic values. Thus, while reading one must choose. Despite its complexity, cuneiform writing was used by the Akkadians to transcribe their language and in the second millennium it became an international medium; cuneiform tablets have been found throughout the Middle East and as far away as Tell el-Amarna in Egypt.

At the beginning, writing had an elementary function — markings on baskets, marks indicating numbers. The primitive signs were essentially parts of the human body, animals or parts of animals, vases, tools of every kind — in short, all the elements of daily life. Initially simple memoranda, the texts quickly became more and more complex: economic data were recorded and then sales contracts and even legal texts. Still later, writing was used for dedications to the gods and for historic inscriptions. Finally it was able to comprehend and express the great themes of religion and literature. The amount of known texts belonging to the second half of the third millennium B.C. give some record of writing's advance along this line: there are some hymns and literary texts, hundreds of dedicatory inscriptions, and thousands of tablets containing economic and administrative matters. The teaching of the science of writing is known to us mainly thanks to texts dating from the first half of the second millennium; but some tablets of the archaic period, containing lists of words and signs, lead to the belief that the educational system changed very little.

Originally the school depended on the temple, but it was eventually transformed into a private, or in any case a lay, activity. The organization must have been based on the family pattern; it was directed by a specialized teacher called "the father of the house of the tablets"; the student was called "the son of the school," and had an older pupil next to him, his "big brother." There were also other teachers: the drawing master, the Sumerian master and even an overseeing lash master. Teaching lasted from infancy to adulthood — about ten years. Although there were some women scribes at various periods, the profession was basically a masculine one. The pupils came from the upper-class families: sons of governors, military commanders, priests, and other scribes.

Archaeologists have found numerous scholastic tablets, but strange to say, these tablets — found at Nippur, Ur, Kish, Ashur, and Sultan Tepe — were discovered in domestic neighborhoods. Excavations have not uncovered any school-like structure as such. The only establishments at all like a school include that found in the palace at Mari, dating from the beginning of the second millennium. Between the royal apartments and the functionaries' quarters, two rooms were furnished with benches, arranged much like classroom desks, and next to these were earthen containers with shells, probably used to learn to count. Another installation discovered at Nimrud, the Assyrian capital of the ninth century B.C., was also perhaps a classroom. Teaching may, of course, have taken place outside. The same tradition can be found in the present-day Eastern world, where it is not unusual to find children with their books in their hands studying while walking on the side of the road.

On the other hand, the scholastic texts are well known. Exercise books were of two types: round and rectangular tablets. The round ones usually had four lines, the first two written by the teacher, the others copied by the student. The rectangular tablets were divided into two columns: the one on the left written by the teacher, often in a splendid hand, the one on the right reserved for the pupil. These tablets were not baked and could thus be "redone" once immersed in water and scratched out, that is, erased. The more advanced students exchanged their texts. There were also manuals: lists of words, grouped according to category; names of trees, animals, stones. The writing exercises consisted basically of literary compositions, most often proverbs of an edifying character, reduced to simple form.

It is difficult to mention literary texts dated with precision for this period of the third millennium. Of those that have been discovered, most are copies or posterior compilations; thus they will be discussed in the chapter concerning the second and first millenniums. One of the first historic texts can be mentioned here, however: the one engraved on the Stele of the Vultures — a real treaty made after the victory of the city of Lagash over neighboring Umma — as can the dedications engraved on statues. These dedications are only a few lines long and have almost unchangeable schemata; despite this, the texts are of inestimable value, because they often identify a temple or a site. Such is the case with Mari where the inscription on the right shoulder of a statue furnished the name of a king, a temple and a city: "Lamgi-Mari, king of Mari, his statue to Ishtar has made its vow."

Ur: In the background, left, the ziggurat (restored by the Iraqi Director-General of Antiquities). Right, E-Dub-lal-Makh, a monument consecrated to the god-moon cult; originally it was a monumental gate giving access to the ziggurat terrace and also served as the judgment place. In the foreground, the deep excavation that brought to light a layer of clay from a flood of the kind that might well have inspired the story of the Universal Flood.

SUMERIAN ESSAY: A SCRIBE'S ADVICE TO HIS WAYWARD SON

"Where did you go?"
"I did not go anywhere."
"If you did not go anywhere, why do you idle about? Go to school, stand before your 'school-father,' recite your assignment, open your schoolbag, write your tablet, let your 'big brother' write your new tablet for you.

Come now, be a man. Don't stand about in the public square, or wander about the boulevard. When walking in the street, don't look all around. Be humble and show fear before your monitor. When you show terror, the monitor will like you."
Kramer: *History Begins at Sumer* (pp. 55–6)

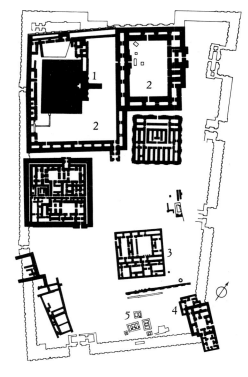

Ur: Plan of the temenos and its monuments in the third dynasty of Ur.
1. Ziggurat
2. Courtyards
3. Palace of Ur-Nammu and Shulgi
4. Hypogeum of Shulgi and Amar-Sin
5. The most ancient "royal" tombs

Ur: The ziggurat. Detail of the access stair-way.

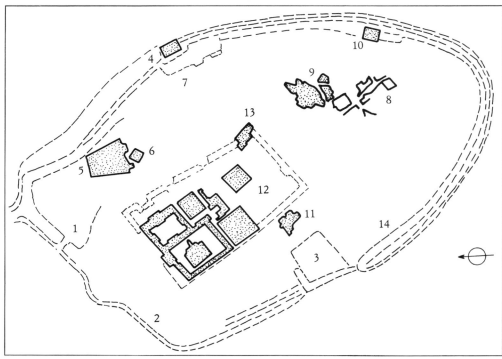

Ur: Plan of the city
 1. Northern gate
 2. Wall
 3. Western gate
 4. Fortress
 5. Palace of the High Priestess
 6. Temple of the gate
 7. House of the third dynasty
 8. Neo-Babylonian residential quarter
 9. Quarter of the Larsa epoch
10. Temple of Enki
11. Quarter of the Larsa epoch
12. Temenos (see plan, page 34)
13. Shulgi and Amar-Sin's hypogeum
14. Probable former bed of the Euphrates

THE MESOPOTAMIAN EMPIRES

Babylon

The fall of the third dynasty of Ur marked the return to a situation reminiscent of the city-state period in the third millennium, with the difference, however, that the wars no longer took place between cities but between kingdoms. Although the kingdoms might be of greater or lesser importance, they had definitely replaced the city-state as a political unit. This period of struggles was exploited by the nomadic Amorites from the west, who penetrated Mesopotamia whenever they could, and by the Elamites from the east, who took advantage of weak moments to make their own incursions.

Among the Mesopotamian kingdoms that rose to power at the beginning of the second millennium was one with its capital at Isin and whose first king, from Mari, had begun as an official, like Sargon of Agade. There was the kingdom of Larsa, with its already ancient dynasty founded by Naplanum. And then there was Mari, which, thanks to its strategic position in the northern part of the country, played an important role of its own. For some time, Mari had to submit to the occupation of a powerful neighbor, Shamshi-Adad I, king of the rising Assyrian power, who set his son Iasmakh-Adad on the throne of Mari. After this interval, however, Zimrilim, with the help of the king of Aleppo, was able to ascend the "throne of his fathers." There was also, of course, the kingdom that, if last in chronological order, was certainly not least in importance: Babylon.

In the alliances, antagonisms and coalitions that made up Babylonian history, almost none of the protagonists abandoned hope of succeeding to supreme power. Only Hammurabi was able to take and retain this power for long, however, and to do so, he was forced to eliminate, one by one, both friends and enemies. As the sixth king of the first Babylonian dynasty — which has been founded by Samuabum, a Semitic nomad from the west of the country, in Amurru — Hammurabi enjoyed a long reign (1792–1750 B.C.). His achievements were considerable in all fields: he unified the land, centralized the administration, transformed Babylon's city religion into a national religion, and encouraged the development of literature.

In unifying the country and centralizing its administration Hammurabi was patiently, tenaciously, and prudently extending the empire. It is known that the organization of the various states was already more or less the same, through the study of the archives of other capitals, particularly Mari, so this may not have been too difficult to do. Throughout its length and breadth, land was held in the same way. It was divided between the state, the sanctuaries and private owners. All had certain obligations, relative to the land they controlled, however, such as the drawing of water and the maintenance of the canals. The central power saw that the obligations were respected. The royal estates were worked by tenant farmers; certain lots were also donated to functionaries. The king supervised the economic activity of the country, the amount of salaries, and the price of goods.

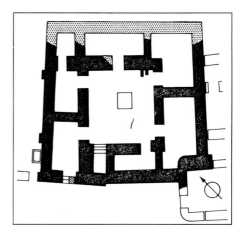

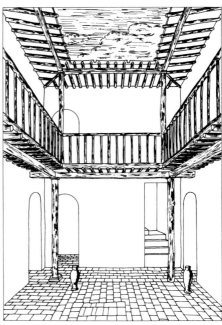

Ur: Plan of a private dwelling of the second millennium B.C. and drawing of an open-air courtyard. A stairway found in one of the rooms makes the idea of an upper floor plausible.

Mari: Sacrificial scene. Detail. Eighteenth century B.C. Paint on plaster; length 5 feet, 5 inches; height 2 feet, 7½ inches. Found in a courtyard of the palace of king Zimrilim, the entire painting shows a bull being led to the sacrifice. Seen here are the two men preceding the bull and, in the lower left hand corner, the animal's nose and ring. (Paris, Louvre Museum).

Larsa: Detail of a bronze statuette with gold covering on the head and hands. Eighteenth century B.C. Height 7.7 inches. An inscription on the pedestal states that this statuette is an ex-voto for the life of Hammurabi, king of Babylon. (Paris, Louvre Museum).

EPILOGUE TO THE CODE OF HAMMURABI

So that the strong do not harm the weak, in order to do right to the orphan and the widow, in Babylon, city in which Anu and Enlil have raised their head, and in Esangila, residence where the foundations are as firm as those of Heaven and of Earth, I have inscribed my precious words on my stele, and I have set up that before my image of the king of right, in order to judge the trials of the land, in order to make the decrees for the land, and in order to do right for the oppressed. I am the king eminent among all kings, my words are most select, my intelligence has no equal. Let the oppressed man who has some problem come before my image of the king of right, let him read my stele as written, let him hear my precious words, let my stele explain to him his problem, let him accept its judgment, let his heart relax. Let him say in addition: "Hammurabi, in truth, is a lord who is like a father of children for all people! He has obeyed the word of Marduk and he has obtained the triumph of Marduk on high and on low. He has satisfied the heart of Marduk, his lord, he has prepared good meat for people forever, and he has directed the land onto the right path...."

Hammurabi, king of right, it is to me that Shamash has presented the laws. My words are most select, my works have no peer; it is only in the eyes of the foolish that they appear vain; for the wise, they have been productive of fame.

Pirenne: *Les Hommes d'Etat célèbres* (I, p. 125)

It is in the legal field, however, that Hammurabi's work is most celebrated, although again he was more an organizer than an innovator. The oldest known legislative work, which can be dated to the middle of the third millennium, is that of Urukagina of Lagash who, by suppressing certain privileges, attempted to instill a stricter sense of justice in his state. One text says that he "cleansed the houses of the inhabitants of Lagash of usury, monopolies, famine, and theft." Moreover, Urukagina "had the god Ningirsu seal the declaration that he would never abandon widows and orphans to the mercy of the rich." Codes promulgated by Ur-Nammu at Ur, Lipit-Ishtar at Isin, and Dadusha at Ashnunnak (Tell Asmar) are also known, although unfortunately only in part.

Hammurabi's Code

These first legal texts were written on clay tablets. Although Hammurabi may have gotten his inspiration from them, he was nonetheless

the first to create an organic and masterful monument by which to preserve his legal code. It is engraved on a magnificent balsalt block over six and a half feet high, decorated at the top with a relief in which the god-judge Shamash is shown bearing the divine emblems, the circle and staff. He is seated, with his feet set upon a mountain symbolized by overlapping curves cut in the stone and is in the act of receiving king Hammurabi. (The scene is somewhat reminiscent of Moses receiving the tablets of the Law on Mount Sinai.) Should one doubt that the 282 "lay" laws were inspired by the gods, the texts that precede them would eliminate any hesitation in this regard: "Then the gods Anu and Enlil, for the prosperity of the people, called me by name, me, Hammurabi, attentive and fearful prince of god, to make justice appear over the land, to eliminate evil and perverse persons, to stop the strong from oppressing the weak, so that I can rise over the black-headed people and thus give light to the land." Found in Iran — at Susa, where it had been brought as war booty — this monument was originally preserved in the temple of Shamash at Sippar. Its fame was considerable and many copies of it were made.

Hammurabi's code was not a legal code in the modern sense of the word, since it is not a collection of all the existing rules, but merely indicates only those laws that were being changed or confirmed. It also furnishes precious information about the social structures of that time. Society was evidently divided into three classes, each with different rights and duties. Free men were the largest class; these included landowners, farmers, artisans, merchants and, naturally, functionaries and priests. The second class, the *mushkenu*, are known rather by the rights they possessed than by the characteristics that differentiated them from the free men. They were probably those who had gained their freedom rather than being born free. The third class was made up of slaves: prisoners of war, babies sold by parents who could not support them, persons incapable of paying their debts. Theirs was an inferior position, but it was protected by the law. Slaves could marry women of the free class, have a legitimate family, follow a trade, possess goods, pay a ransom for their liberty, or be freed by their masters.

The code of Hammurabi also reveals that the women of Babylonia enjoyed a good deal of liberty. They could, in fact, initiate legal proceedings, practice a profession, and hold public posts, but they could not start divorce proceedings; this was the husband's right. Marriage implied a contract. The fiancé had to make a gift, either in money or land, to his future father-in-law. The latter, in turn, gave his daughter a dowry whose benefits she alone could enjoy.

Finally, Hammurabi's code offers an interesting comparison with Old Testament laws, particularly those concerning adoption, and retaliation ("an eye for an eye and a tooth for a tooth"). This codified justice was administered by civil or religious courts, and included testimony under oath. Fines, torture, and death were the sentences allotted, and sentences varied according to the social position of the accused.

Susa: Hammurabi's code. Eighteenth century B.C. Basalt; height 7 feet, 4 inches. Discovered at Susa, this monument was orginally placed in a Babylonian temple, probably the sanctuary of Shamash at Sippar. Above the splendidly engraved 282 laws, there is a relief showing Hammurabi standing before the god of the sun and of justice, Shamash. He is holding the circle and staff, signs of his power, and his feet are placed on a mountain, indicated by the overlapping-scales. The scene is reminiscent of the episode of Moses receiving the tablets of the law on Mount Sinai.

Following pages:
Dur-Kurigalzu: The ziggurat. Fourteenth or thirteenth century B.C. The beds of reeds set every eight or nine layers of brick can be seen. (The Iraqi Director-General of Antiquities has restored the base of the monument). The ziggurat is almost 188 feet high in its present state.

The Cassites, Elamites, and Mitanni

Samsu-iluna, Hammurabi's son and successor, continued during his long reign the noteworthy administrative work begun by his father, but he had to face many difficulties. Revolts broke out in the south; moreover the Cassites, a group of nomads from the Zagros mountains, made an attempt to conquer Babylon. Although they were unsuccessful in this, they did settle in the Mesopotamian plain, where they worked as mercenaries or laborers. Then, taking advantage of the expedition made by the Hittite Mursilis I, king of Anatolia, who not only destroyed Aleppo in Syria but marched on Babylon to sack it, the Cassites again attempted to take Babylon. This time they were successful and founded a dynasty that lasted for centuries. The Cassite phase of Meso-

potamian history marks the end of the political equilibrium reached by the Amorite dynasty in Babylon. The breakup of power that followed gave rise to a complex historical situation.

Babylon was ruled by the Cassites from about 1600 to 1240 B.C., yet little is known about them except that they assimilated and perpetuated the civilization of their predecessors. We also know that they were able to resist the incursions of the Elamites. In fact, Elam (present-day Khuzistan in Iran and the mountains that dominate Babylon from the east and northeast), which appears and disappears many times in Middle Eastern political history, passed through a short but brilliant period from the thirteenth century to the late twelfth century B.C. Several Elamite kings brought the country to power: Untash-Huban (also Untash-Gal), the great builder of Choga Zanbil; Shutruk-Nahhunte, who overthrew the vacillating Cassite dynasty; Shilhak-Inshushinak, who pursued an expansionist policy. This dazzling rise of the Elamites passed into an equally rapid decadence and fall, due to Nebuchadnezzar I, then king of Babylon.

During the second millennium, the Syrian-Phoenician coast, a cross-roads of commercial routes, was divided into small independent Canaanite states, or states subject to the great empires of the time: Egypt and the Hittite empire in Asia Minor. The port city Ugarit was famous among other things for having given birth to alphabetic cuneiform writing using only thirty signs. In Byblos, another Canaanite site of this period, archaeologists have discovered one of the most ancient examples of alphabetic writings, an inscription on the sarcophagos of king Ahiram (thirteenth century B.C.).

Northern Mesopotamia in the latter half of the second millennium of the country was occupied by the Mitanni, evidently an Indo-European warrior caste. The kingdom of the Mitanni, which extended from the Zagros mountains to the Mediterranean, played an important part in history in the fifteenth and the beginning of the fourteenth century B.C.; it was later destroyed by the Hittites.

The Hittites

As has been aptly said, the Hittites are a conquest of modern science. Despite the journeys through their territory made by various curious

Above:
Choga Zanbil: Inscription of Untash-Gal in cuneiform characters. Thirteenth century B.C.

Right:
Choga Zangil: The southwestern gate of the ziggurat. Thirteenth century B.C.

THE KING UNTASH-GAL

I, Untash-Gal, son of Hubannumena, king of Anzan and of Susa, I have obtained a long life, my health prospers, I should have no end of descendants. That is why I have constructed a temple with brick vaults, a sublime sanctuary; to the god Inshushinak, Lord of the holy place, I have made a gift of this temple. I have also raised a *ziggurat* to heaven. May the god Inshushinak accept as an offering my efforts and my works!

I, Untash-Gal, son of Hubann, I have engraved on golden bricks, I have constructed there this residence; to the gods Gal and Inshushinak, lords of the holy places, I have made a gift of them. May the gods Gal and Inshushinak, lords of the holy place, accept as an offering my efforts and my works!

In the temple that I constructed, in the course of years of numerous days, may I obtain the favor of the gods Gal and Inshushinak. Whatever enemy or hostile king destroys and knocks over the temple, whoever digs up the gold and who, having erased the name of Untash-Gal, places his own there, may the wrath of the gods Gal, Inshushinak, and Kiririsha be upon him! May he have no descendants beneath the sun! As for the king of Elam, when he falls into ruins, may he be restored and place there the name of Untash-Gal.

Steve: *Tchoga Zanbil* (III, p. 15)

travelers in the eighteenth and nineteenth centuries, a systematic exploration of Hittite sites began only in 1906 with the excavations undertaken by Hugo Winckler at Boghaz Köy, while the deciphering of tablets in Hittite cuneiform characters, for the most part done by B. Hrozny, was begun only in 1917. Of Indo-European origin, the Hittites made their appearance in Anatolia at the beginning of the second millennium and clashed with the indigenous population, the Hatti (who had been there for centuries and whose culture is still relatively unknown) as well as with the Assyrian trading colonies established in the third millennium at Kadesh and Hattusas (the ancient name for Boghaz Köy). The assimilation of these groups by the conquerors was swift and total, so much so that the Indo-European invaders even took on the name of the original population, becoming the Hittites.

In the nineteenth and eighteenth centuries B.C. small independent Hittite states were formed, governed by kings, some of whose names are known. In the seventeenth century, Labarnas succeeded in gathering under his wing the entire central part of Anatolia; his achievement marks the real beginning of the first of two great Hittite historical epochs: the Old Kingdom. But this unification was a difficult one to maintain; the first kings, Hattusilis I and Mursilis I, had to suppress revolts and confront intrigues within their own families. The Hittites also undertook a policy of expansion, above all in Syria. Mursilis I took Aleppo, as mentioned earlier, and with a swift incursion he penetrated as far as Babylon, which he conquered in 1595 B.C. The expedition was futile and inexplicable. It may have been the outcome of an alliance with the Cassites or possibly a punitive expedition, since the Babylonians had helped Aleppo during the revolt there against the Hittites. Mursilis I returned home victorious, but was assassinated, probably shortly afterwards. As the ancient texts state: "Hantilis was chief cupbearer. He had married Harapsilis, Mursilis's sister. Zidantas intrigued with Hantilis and together they committed a foul deed: they killed Mursilis."

Mursilis' death marked the beginning of a period of anarchy among the Hittites which lasted for about sixty years, during which numerous assassinations weakened the already vacillating Hittite royalty. Invasions on the east by the Hurrians, a population of uncertain origin, and on the north by barbarians, further contributed to their decline. Paradoxically, it was a usurper who restored authority: Telipinus. As if that were not enough, he issued an edict, the "Edict of Telipinus," addressed to "the great, the body guards, the palace servants, the cupbearers . . .," which set down the succession and ended all dynastic dispute: "The first-born prince will be king. If there is no prince, the son of second rank will become king. If there are no male heirs, a husband will be chosen for the first-born daughter, and he will be king." This constitutional text was almost always respected; when it was not, an appeal was made to the will of the gods. (Hattusilis III did this, for instance, in dethroning his nephew about 1275 B.C.)

The second period of Hittite history, called the Empire, lasted from about 1460 to shortly after 1200 B.C. and was characterized by an expansionist policy, which had its ups and downs. Most importantly, the Hittite kings clashed with the Egyptian pharaohs over the possession of Syria. Suppiluliumas I conquered the Upper Tigris region and "in only one year" northern Syria, where he occupied the Orontes river valley as far as Kadesh. Muwattalis, in the battle of Kadesh, led the Hittite army against Ramesses II. A celebrated and victorious battle for the Egyptian troops, if one wishes to believe Egyptian annals, in reality, it was an uncertain battle for both parties. Hattusilis III, faced with the menace of Assyria, was anxious to appease the contentious Egyptian ruler, and signed with him, in 1278, a singular treaty in which there is no mention of frontiers. This treaty is known both through a copy in Babylonian-cuneiform, found in the archives at Boghaz Köy (the original, engraved on a silver tablet, has disappeared), and also through

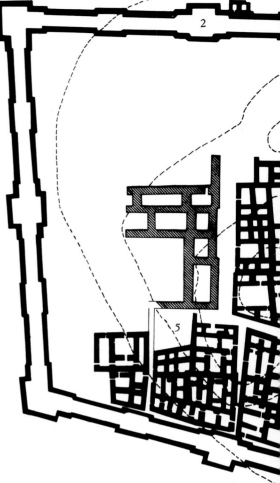

Tell Harmal: Plan of the city, which seems to have been the result of some town-planning. Beginning of the second millennium B.C.

1. City gate — 4. Temple of Nisaba
2. City wall — 5. Habitations
3. Small temples — 6. Administrative buildings

Tell Harmal: Reconstruction of the principal temple consecrated to the god of grain, Nisaba. The entrance was flanked by terra-cotta lions.

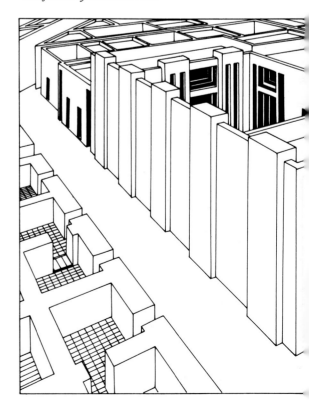

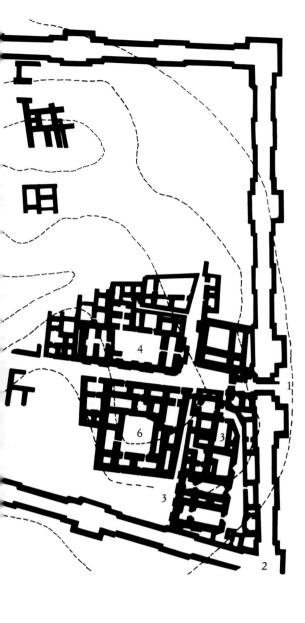

the Egyptian version, engraved in the Ramesseum in west Thebes and in the temple of Ramesses II at Karnak. A few years later, one of Hattusilis III's daughters married Ramesses II.

Hittite relations with the neighboring state of Mitanni fluctuated between war and alliance. The Assyrians coveted the kingdom, but in the end it was annexed by the Hittites.

During the Empire period of the Hittites, Asia Minor was invaded many times, in particular by the Kaskans, barbarians from the north. Amid a profusion of palace intrigues and plots, the Hittite empire grew decadent. Their decline corresponds to the rise of Assyrian power, but it was probably the pressure and attacks of the so-called People of the Sea (the biblical Philistines and others) that caused the sudden fall of Hittite power, and after 1200 B.C. no traces were left of the Hittites' empire. Their civilization did survive for a certain period, though, in the small states of Malatya, Carchemish, and Marash, where it lasted until the ninth or eighth centuries B.C., when these states became Assyrian provinces.

The Social Organization of the Hittites

The organization of the Hittite empire was of a feudal type; that is to say, the aristocracy enjoyed a privileged position and great power. The king entrusted fiefs to those faithful to him and gave them subject lands for their own revenue. The relationship between king and vassals was governed by written rules. Provinces were administered by governors appointed by royal decree, whose powers are military, civil, and judicial. They were partially responsible for worship practices as well. The king kept the direction of foreign affairs for himself, demanding not only tribute but military assistance from all his subjects. In the official records the king was called "great king." He personally gave himself the title of "my sun," and as in Egypt, the royal symbol was the winged disc. Although the king did not directly administer the empire, he was still the supreme military chief, had charge of diplomacy, and was also the supreme judge in a judicial system whose workings are still somewhat obscure, since the private proceedings are lacking and the legislative collections that have been discovered are still difficult to interpret. The principal function of the sovereign was, however, in the religious realm.

As the head of the state religion, the king became a god upon his death; while alive, he acted as the high priest. For this reason he had to keep himself from every impurity in order to carry out his sacred function, on which the prosperity and security of the country depended. All the known representations of the Hittite king show the sovereign in the act of making a ritual gesture. Contrary to the habit in other Mesopotamian civilizations, he is never depicted carrying out military activities. Moreover, it is known that the monarch could actually abandon a military campaign in order to fulfill his religious duties.

The role of the queen in the Hittite empire is exceptional compared with practice in the rest of the Middle East. Her function was independent from that of the king; even when she became a widow she remained queen. The fact that Puduhepa, wife of Hattusilis III, signed along with her royal husband the treaty concluded with Ramesses II of Egypt, demonstrates the importance of her position. Her functions in the religious field were as important as those of the king. She carried them out either alone or together with the king, but playing a specific role in every ceremony.

Aside from its feudal aspect, not too much is known about Hittite society, but it seems to have differed little from Mesopotamian society. It included free men, merchants, artisans; then, at a lower level, farmers. In the cities, authority was guaranteed by a commander, a mayor, and a council of elders. The Hittite army is worth of mention, above all for its well-organized chariot detachments and its efficient

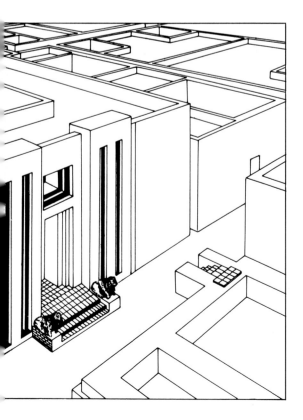

infantry. Thus, at the battle of Kadesh, Muwattalis led 3,500 chariots and 8,000 foot-soldiers. The crew of the chariot was made up of three men: a driver and two soldiers, one of whom was an archer. There were three horses for every chariot as well: two drew it while the third was kept as a spare. Soldiers were armed with long lances and protected by shields whose form was like an 8: round and broad at the top and bottom, and narrow in the middle. If the word "strategy" seems a bit exaggerated, it is fair to say that military technique evolved somewhat in this period: rapid actions and approach marches were Hittite novelties, used to take the enemy by surprise.

Mesopotamian Architecture in the Second Millennium

The architecture of the second millennium is rather well-known, though the most important capital of that period, Babylon, reveals almost nothing. Only a few private habitations have been discovered, some of whose facades have "sawtooth" decoration, an architectural effect meant to break up the monotony of the brick walls. The scarcity of findings in Babylon is explained by the fact that the city was continuously inhabited. It has, therefore, been changed many times, and the successive reconstructions have damaged the older edifices. Moreover, the Euphrates, which in ancient times passed through the center of the urban complex, has moved to the west, a shift that has provoked disorder and confusion in the interpretation of the remains.

Fortunately the excavations carried out on other Mesopotamian sites have yielded monuments from the second millennium. The architecture, whether sacred or secular, always has the same basic plan: an open-air courtyard surrounded by rooms. Not all the buildings uncovered can be discussed, of course. Ishkhali and Tell Harmal in central Mesopotamia, Ur in the south and Mari in the north provide good examples, though, and evoke quite satisfactorily the sacred and civil architecture of the first part of the second millennium.

Ishkhali, in the Diyala river region, is known above all for the architectural complex there in which three temples are joined, probably attesting to the worship of a divine triad. These sanctuaries were built according to the principles in force during the first dynasty in Babylon: monumental portals, large courtyards, magnificent perspectives through the halls, in which all the entrances are on the same axis. The main sanctuary was dedicated to Ishtar-Kititum, the local form of the great goddess of love and war, Ishtar. The other two temples are still anonymous. One of them has a cella built lengthwise, which was a novelty for that time, but later became one of the characteristics of Assyrian architecture.

Tell Harmal, about six and a quarter miles east of Baghdad, is a town whose layout of straight roads seems to respond to a certain preoccupation with town-planning. A thick wall, reinforced by pillars, protected it quite well. The protection was made even more effective by the fact that there was only one access gate. Many temples have been discovered at Tell Harmal. The most important is made up of a wide vestibule followed by a large rectangular courtyard that one must cross to reach the ante-cella and the cella, both quite wide. There are some steps, which were flanked by two guardian lions in terra-cotta, before the ante-cella. North of the courtyard a small sanctuary has been identified. The main temple was dedicated to the goddess Nisaba, goddess of grain, but also of the science of numbers (which is easily explained, since grain is a unit of weight). The secondary temple was probably that of the god Khani, lord of the seal. Khani was also god of writing before being deposed by the god Nabu, the son of Marduk, the great god of Babylon. Set into a wall in the northeast corner of the city there has been discovered a double temple — or rather two large rooms and two cellas, set together, but not communicating; at the moment they are anonymous.

Opposite page. Above:
Boghaz Köy: Ruins of the temple of the Hittite storm-god at their capital, Hattusas. Fourteenth century B.C. The temple proper is situated in the middle of the architectural complex, which measures 535 by 450 feet. Around the temple were long, narrow rooms, probably used as storerooms.

Below:
Boghaz Köy: The lion gate. Many monumental gates have been found in this city. This one is adorned with sculptured lions looking over the countryside, evidently guardians of this entrance to the city.

CORRESPONDENCE FROM THE ROYAL ARCHIVES OF MARI

To my master say this:
"Here speaks your servant, Kibri-Dagan.
On the subject of beams of three canes
And of the reeds ordered by the Palace,
To be taken to Mari,
My master wrote to me.
Now then, fifty beams that I am saving for the
Roof of the house and for the squares of the
     terrace,
I have just placed on the water.
I have just looked over the problem,
But there are absolutely no more reeds.
The reeds, at least those at my disposition,
For the making of this house,
With the bricks I have stacked them up."
     Kupper: *Archives royales de Mari* (III:25)

Ishkhali: Reconstruction of the temple consecrated to Ishtar-Kititum, the local form of the goddess Ishtar. Beginning of the second millennium B.C.

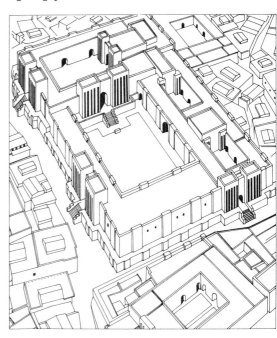

Boghaz Köy: Detail of the lion gate. The animal seems to be emerging from the stone; his jaws are open; the mane is suggested by short undulating lines. Originally there were undoubtedly colored stones inserted to represent eyes.

INSCRIPTION FROM THE PALACE OF MARI

To Zimrilim
Say this:
Thus speaks Hammurapi
Your Brother:
The man of Ugarit
Has just written me
What follows:
"Show me the
Residence of Zimrilim;
I want to see it.
And now, with this same courier,
I am sending along your son."

Mari: Plan of the palace, beginning of the second millennium B.C.
1. Entrance
2. Courtyard
3. Audience chamber, decorated with paintings
4. Small rooms where most of the royal archives were found
5. Courtyard decorated with paintings (Investiture, Bull being led to sacrifice)
6. Room where the statue of "the goddess with the spouting vase" was discovered
7. Throne room
8. Royal apartments

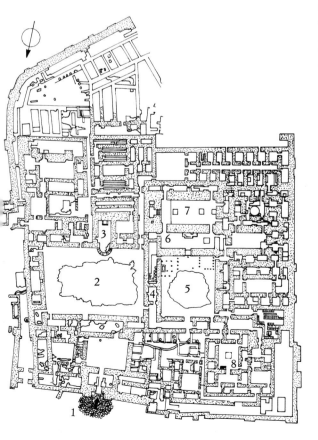

At Ur a group of private dwellings has been excavated, the first to appear in the history of Mesopotamian architecture. The work of Leonard Woolley uncovered a residential neighborhood in the southeastern part of the city. Unlike Tell Harmal, there seems to have been no plan involved in its construction. Habitations are heaped one against the other, or even set one into the other. The unpaved streets and alleys, flanked by gloomy walls, are narrow and curved. At the crossroads the corners are sometimes rounded off, probably in order to facilitate the coming and going of men and donkeys. Since the excavations in 1930–31, erosion has badly damaged the ruins; yet this quarter is still surprisingly alive. And when one has the pleasure of walking through it, sauntering through the streets that the archaeologist has christened "straight" street, "Pater Noster" street, and so forth, one gets a most vivid impression.

The houses, made of baked and unbaked bricks, covered with a layer of mud, are built according to the traditional principle of the open-air courtyard surrounded by rooms. Comforts are not neglected either; drainage systems and sanitary installations have been found. It was possible to identify kitchens, thanks to the hearths and grindstones that were found still in their place. Some houses had a private chapel, recognizable because of brick altars and the niche in the wall. In certain cases stairways were found, so there were probably upper floors. Burial took place in the houses; the adults were buried in a brick sepulcher or a ceramic sarcophagus, while the children were simply placed in a vase. This quarter of the city does not consist of private dwellings alone: public chapels, workshops, and laboratories have also been identified.

Palace architecture at the beginning of the second millennium is well known, particularly due to the palace at Mari. This splendid complex of almost three hundred elements — including rooms, courtyards and corridors — and covering over six acres, has been preserved in a surprisingly fine state. When discovered, the walls still stood over sixteen feet high; only the southwestern corner had disappeared because of erosion. The construction, although certainly executed at various times, is quite precise. The plan is typically Mesopotamian: an enclosure wall of varying thickness surrounds the usual courtyard-room blocks. For obvious safety measures, a single gate located to the north affords access to this royal residence, which was at the same time the administrative center for Mari. Not far from the entrance, archaeologists discovered a hall for guards and a section thought to have been for the monarch's guests. The private apartments were found in the northwest corner, where the outside wall is particularly thick. They consist of twenty-three rooms grouped together around a courtyard; the king's and the queen's bedrooms, two bathrooms with bath and a toilet — altogether a most complete complex.

Near the royal apartments are two rooms that have been identified as classrooms; there are also sections reserved for functionaries and superintendents, who were thus at the king's disposal. The official precinct, in the heart of the edifice, surrounds two large courtyards. One, the largest in the palace (158 feet by 105 feet) precedes the audience chamber, which is reached by means of a majestic semicircular staircase. The other courtyard, of quite harmonious proportions, affords access to the throne room, which had a sort of gallery. Since the king was the earthly representative of the gods, it is quite logical to find a chapel in a Mesopotamian palace; the one at Mari is situated in the eastern part. Finally there are also workrooms and storerooms in the southwestern zone of the complex.

Some rooms were decorated with wall paintings. In the royal apartments the motifs are mostly geometric: polychrome stripes, friezes consisting of braids in the form of an S turned sideways. At the foot of the walls were chalk plinths with false marble decorations. In the king's bedroom a decorative piece was found, made up of shell elements and red paste, whicn was probably set in a wooden frame. Finally, on the courtyard floor there was a game much like quoits, probably a diversion

Yazilikaya: A group of rocks one and a quarter miles northeast of Boghaz Köy. They form two natural gorges whose walls, after being smoothed over, were decorated with reliefs varying in height from 3 feet to almost 6 feet. Thirteenth century B.C. The large gallery: the sculptures represent two processions of gods; male on the western wall, female on the eastern wall. The two processions meet on the northern wall (center).

MESSAGE FROM IAQQIM-ADAD FOUND AT PALACE OF MARI

To my lord,
Say this:
"Thus speaks Iaqqim-Adad, your servant.
The valet who is near me is sick.
Above his ear an abscess is running. The two doctors who are with me are attempting to treat it, but his malady does not go away. Now the doctor of Mardaman or an expert doctor would be appreciated if my lord would send one. Such a doctor could examine the valet and treat his illness so that it would no longer bother him."
Finet: *Annuaire de l'Institut de Philologie* (XIV)

MESSAGE FROM IAQQIM-ADDU FOUND AT PALACE OF MARI

To my lord,
Say this:
"Thus speaks Iaqqim-Addu, your servant.
Previously I wrote to my lord
In these words:
A lion was captured in the barn
Of the home of Akkaka.
If this lion should be kept in the barn
Until my lord comes, let my lord write me so.
But if I should bring the lion to my
lord, let him write me that.
Now I have delayed while awaiting letters from my lord.
But the lion has been kept in the barn for five days.
A dog and a pig have been thrown to him
So that he might eat. But I have been thinking to myself: what if the lion escapes?
I am afraid of that. So I have put the lion in a wooden cage, and then I have put the cage on a boat, and I am having the lion brought to my lord."
Jean: *Lettres diverses* (II, 106)

Yazilikaya: Plan of the rock sanctuary
1. *Large gallery*
2. *Small gallery*
3. *Monumental entranceway leading to the temple*
4. *Main building of the temple*
5. *Entrance gate to the small gallery*

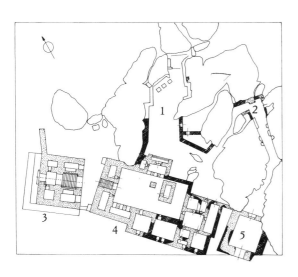

for the king and his family. The decoration of the official part of the complex, of a figurative type, was of religious inspiration. In the audience chamber one can still see scenes that are difficult to interpret, in which there are religious ceremonies with the king present; in the courtyard that precedes the throne room scenes of sacrifices or investiture are painted.

Other treasures were found in the palace at Mari: the statue of "the goddess with the spouting vase," royal statues, and also more than twenty thousand tablets that permit a detailed view of palace life and the occupations of its inhabitants. Particularly we get to view the king, whose multiple activities — diplomatic, legal, economic — did not prevent him from attending to a broken dam or from sending a doctor for a consultation sixty-two miles from Mari, or from taking care of other such matters. The king was aided by high functionaries, of whom the most important was the palace prefect. His responsibilities included the direction of the eight hundred persons who worked in the palace.

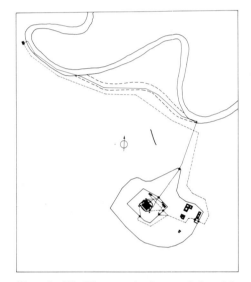

Uruk: Plan of the temple of Ishtar erected by king Karaindash. Fifteenth century B.C. The facade was decorated with pillars and niches, embellished with representations of gods and goddesses bearing the vase of spouting water.

Cassite and Elamite Architecture

Cassite architecture differs little from the type that preceded it, which once again confirms the fact that in this field as well as in others the Cassite dynasty merely carried on the work of its predecessors. The capital at that time, Dur-Kurigalzu (Aqarquf), not far from Baghdad, is dominated by a *ziggurat* whose ruins, some 188 feet high, are still impressive. It is a magnificent construction made of unbaked bricks with a casing of baked bricks; just as in Ur, a triple staircase leads to the top. Every eight or nine layers of brick, a thick layer of cane was inserted; it helped to maintain the solidity of the edifice; cordons of the same material, about four inches in diameter, were used as supplementary framework. At the foot of the *ziggurat* and close to it, temples were found, dedicated to the god of the earth, Enlil; Ninlil, his divine female counterpart; and Ninurta, god of war. A palace has also been brought to light, built, once again, according to the principle of the courtyard-room blocks; it is above all interesting for its wall decoration. In fact, series of paintings decorated some rooms: flowers or geometric motifs and processions of men dressed in a long tunic and with a kind of tarboosh on their heads, which foreshadow the painted processions in Assyrian palaces.

The Cassites also left their stamp in some ancient Mesopotamian metropolises. The little temple dedicated to the goddess Ishtar, erected at Uruk by king Karaindash, has a new type of decoration on its facade. The well-known pillars and niches occur, but the latter are embellished with depictions of the gods, made of molded bricks. The proportions of these figures are immense, at least as regards the lower part of the body. Gods and goddesses alternate. They all bear the vase of spouting water, which gushes from one niche to the other and decorates the pillars as well. The molded bricks, which were used three centuries later by the Elamites in Iran, were also very popular in the Neo-Babylonian and Achaemenian period.

The loveliest Elamite architectural complex is the one found at Choga Zanbil, the modern name for the city of Dur-Untash, built by Untash-Gal eighteen and a half miles southeast of Susa. This royal residence and religious center was never completed, since Untash-Gal's successors did not worry about carrying on the work, which was thus brusquely interrupted, as the unused bricks found there demonstrate: hundreds of them bear the founder's name, and there are about two thousand with no inscriptions.

The city has two concentric walls. The first (3,937 feet by 2,625 feet) encloses the city proper, four palaces, and a small temple dedicated to the fire god, Nusku, with an open-air cella. One of the palaces is particularly interesting because five vaulted tombs were discovered in its subsoil; these were built of crude bricks, bitumen, and chalk plaster. Built in front of the palace, which covers them, they were probably

Choga Zanbil: The processional way and plan of the city, built in the thirteenth century B.C. by king Untash-Gal. Two concentric walls surround the city; in the center is the ziggurat *complex.*

royal tombs (unfortunately long ago violated for the most part). The pulverized remains of eight persons were found in two rooms of one of the tombs, while another tomb contained the skeleton of a woman and the ashes and bones of two other persons on a funerary bed. The violations at Dur-Untash are recalled by the account of the eighth campaign of Ashurbanipal of Assyria, who boasts that he violated the tombs of the Elamite kings at Susa, dragging the bones of the princes as far as Ashur "so that the ghosts of the dead ones would find no rest, nor would the dead ever receive offerings and libations."

The second wall (1312 feet on each side) marks off the holy quarter, dominated by the sole *ziggurat* yet discovered in Iranian territory. This *ziggurat*, protected in turn by a wall, was constructed in two phases. First a large courtyard, faced by rooms and a sanctuary, was built; later the courtyard access gates were built; the upper landings were built on these gates and were set one into another. Square in form (344 feet on each side), the *ziggurat* still has three stories and is eighty-five feet high, but once it must have been five stories and over 170 feet. Each side has a monumental portal. The edifice is dedicated to the god Inshushinak, as the engraved bricks, found every eleven layers, repeat again and again.

Various temples were found in the *temenos* quarter. Their plans differ: one cella only; cella and ante-cella in the same axis; an ante-cella that forms a right angle with the cella; or ante-cella and cella parallel. Such variations demonstrate the rich imagination of the architects.

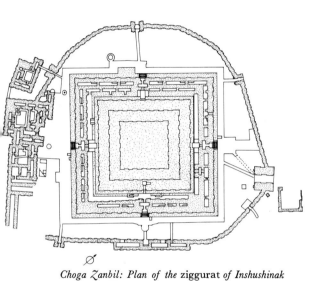

Choga Zanbil: Plan of the ziggurat *of Inshushinak and its temples.*

Choga Zanbil: Reconstruction drawing of the royal quarter with its four palaces and, to the left, the small temple dedicated to the fire god Nusku.

Hittite Literature

The components of Hittite architecture differ substantially from those so far seen in Mesopotamian architecture. The geographic framework — severe countryside and rough climate — certainly influenced the builders in Asia Minor. More fortunate than their colleagues from the "land of the two rivers," they had stone at their disposal. The architecture is quite surprising, mostly because of the edifice plans, especially those for the sanctuaries, which are mostly asymmetrical. Another novelty is the widely used columned vestibule, the *bit-hilani*, which was taken up again by the Assyrians. Lastly, the large windows looking out from the edifices attest to the need for light and follow concepts that are foreign to the Mesopotamians. Hattusas (Boghaz Köy), the capital of the empire, and Yazilikaya, a rock sanctuary, provide the best examples of the Hittite tradition.

Hattusas was already inhabited in the nineteenth and eighteenth centuries B.C., but it reached its maximum size of about 412 acres only in the Empire period. Certain of the city's fortifications existed in the Old Kingdom period, but these were considerably developed in the course of the succeeding centuries. This defensive system, a real masterpiece that foreshadows certain constructions of the European Middle Ages, takes the utmost advantage of the particularly rough, varied terrain at Hattusas, which is a mountain city. The city wall is three and three-quarters miles in perimeter and, at least on its southern side, is doubled, since to the east and west the city is protected by a natural declivity. The two walls are parallel; the inside one is much higher and much more important than the outer wall. Both are reinforced with towers or bastions. Built on an artificial embankment, the walls had a cyclopean foundation, built of thick blocks of irregular stone almost twenty feet high, and a brick superstructure. Three gates, flanked by towers, give access to the city. The King's Gate and the Lion Gate, to the east and west respectively, show the same architecture; two enormous monolithic oblique stones form the jambs, above which large blocks were set to complete an ogive arch.

The King's Gate owes its name to the sculpture in high relief that decorates it. (This has been removed and transported to the Ankara museum to protect it from the elements.) This personage — bare-footed and bare-chested, dressed in a short skirt or girdle held up around the waist by a broad belt — has alternately been identified as a king, a warrior, or an amazon. Nowadays this figure is thought to be a god or a warrior-god rather than a king. This divine interpretation is backed up by one detail: the horn that decorates the helmet with its cheek and neck covers. The warlike aspect of the god is seen in his weapons: the ax held in his right hand and the curved dagger set in the left side of his belt. Long hair falls loosely over his shoulders, a war ritual common to the Middle East, as various monuments and Deborah's hymn (Judges V, 2) demonstrate. Although this relief is not pictured here, it is discussed because it is one of the masterpieces of Hittite art, an art which often appears severe and inhospitable; but it is just this severity that renders more interesting the quality of this Hattusas sculpture, whose body is in high relief and whose head is sculptured almost completely in the round. The vital force that bursts from this monument is due both to the face, in which the eyes are in profile (Hittite artists were familiar with real profile, an exceptional thing in the whole Middle East) and in the step suggested by the legs, the right one facing the spectator, the left in profile. There is also the precision with which the artist has represented certain details of the body and dress: the chest, the headdress, and the texture of the shirt.

As the name suggests, the Lion Gate is flanked by guardian lions, which can also be seen on the doors of certain third- and second-millennium temples in Mesopotamia and which are found again in the Assyrian period. The Lion Gate is decoration, but more important, it functioned as a guarantee for the protection of the edifice. The third gate, protected by sphinxes, is to the south. The postern gate passes under the south entranceway. This is a vaulted subterranean tunnel, almost 230 feet long, which allowed rapid sorties and surprise attacks to be made against the enemy.

The city, which is still under exploration, extends over a number of hills. On the highest point rises an acropolis, with many monuments, among which the archives building has been identified. This is a lovely architectural complex with five large rooms, four of which had two rows of stone pillars, almost certainly used to support an upper floor. More than three thousand tablets were discovered in this edifice. In the acropolis there are also administrative buildings; the royal palace; another edifice decorated with upright slabs made of granite and limestone and with wall paintings, a complex that may have been the private dwellings of the royal family; a small temple; and a large square that seems to have played a prominent part in public and official meetings.

Hittite Religious Architecture

The sacred architecture of the Hittites is known to us through Yazilikaya, with its open-air sanctuary, but also through the temples uncovered at Hattusas. If one wishes to give credence to the text, the Hittites did not consider themselves worthy enough to build the divinity's habitation: "It was the gods who were their creators; Telipinu laid down the foundations; Ea, the king of wisdom, erected the walls; the mountains produced the wood and the stones; the goddesses made the plaster." Considering the splendid architecture at Hattusas with its imposing size, we are almost tempted to believe this.

Of the five temples found in the capital, the largest is almost certainly dedicated to the storm god. This is a gigantic complex, 525 feet long and 446 wide, which has three access gates. Seventy-eight storerooms — narrow halls used for provisions (some halls contain large jars), for the temple treasury, and also for the archives (as many tablets were also found there) — surround the rectangular sanctuary. This consists of a monumental entranceway to the south, followed by a large tiled courtyard surrounded by rectangular rooms. To the north is a wing of nine halls, which is properly speaking the section dedicated

to the cult; this wing was preceded by a three-columned portico. It is interesting to note that this sacred wing is made of granite, while the rest of the edifice is of limestone. In the northeastern corner of the courtyard there are the remains of a kind of wash-house. The arrangement of this wing is reminiscent of a Hittite account of religious ceremonies; the text speaks of the king going through a door, crossing a courtyard and washing his hands before penetrating the "holy of holies," the most sacred area, where he officiated.

In the largest hall in the sacred wing, a stone pedestal was used to hold up the cult statue. Unfortunately, no such figure has been found in its entirety. Each hall had at least one window, and in the hall with the pedestal the light came through four windows. Contrary to everything known about the ancient architecture elsewhere in the Middle East, this need for a lot of light in the sacred edifices can perhaps be explained simply as a carrying over of cult habits from an earlier period. In fact the Hittites worshiped the mountains and springs, and there are numerous open-air places of worship, marked by rock reliefs; it can be surmised that when they built the houses of one of their gods, they respected the natural atmosphere as much as possible.

The loveliest example of an open-air sanctuary is the one at Yazilikaya, the construction of which is attributed to Tudhaliyas IV (circa 1250 B.C.). Yazilikaya is situated a mile and a quarter northeast of Hattusis, in a rocky enclosure. Two natural galleries, their walls decorated with reliefs, were used from early days. Later, a temple in which three architectural phases have been distinguished was built, blocking the entrances to the galleries.

The larger gallery is decorated with reliefs of sixty-three gods, divided into two processions that seem to be going toward each other. On the western wall, the gods are represented; on the eastern wall, the goddesses. This arrangement, however, is not rigorously respected, since three goddesses are to be found in the gods' procession, while one god is depicted among the goddesses. The meeting of the two processions is on the northern wall. Here Teshub, the storm-god, standing on two mountains with human forms, Namni and Hazzi (Mount Casio), is depicted opposite the goddess Hepat; she is seated on a lion and followed by her son Sharruma on a panther. The gods are all depicted in the same way. The sculptor, perhaps adhering to imperative rules, has repeated the same face on each, with no variants. The gods all make the same gesture: one arm is bent against the body, the other slightly stretched out. The goddesses keep both arms in an attitude of offering and are often depicted in profile. These divinities (identified by Emmanuel Laroche, who succeeded in deciphering the inscriptions) are actually Hurrian divinities, whose names have been written in Hittite hieroglyphics. Yazilikaya thus proves that the Hittite pantheon was profoundly influenced by the gods of the Hurrians.

The smaller gallery has a separate entrance, protected by two hybrid winged creatures with lions' heads. At the end of this gallery there is a base for a statue that has disappeared; but it is known that it represented Tudhaliyas IV, thanks to an inscription nearby. The same king is found again further on in the same gallery, in company with the god Sharruma, who holds him tightly in his arms. This interpretation is borne out by the inscriptions. The decoration of this gallery is completed by two independent panels oriented to the north — that is, toward the statue of Tudhaliyas IV. Twelve gods bearing tall tiaras and carrying a large-bladed sickle on their right shoulder, are depicted running on the first panel; the second, called the "dagger-god," poses identification problems. It may be an important divinity, or, more simply, a monumental representation of a dagger or sword of a type that is known. Such a weapon may have belonged to Tudhaliyas himself and may thus here be a symbol of his power. Finally, there are three rectangular niches that were perhaps used as royal funerary urns, since in the Empire period it was the custom to cremate the dead of the royal family.

The purpose and use of the Yazilikaya sanctuary are unknown. Cer-

Yazilikaya: The small gallery. Detail of the panel showing the "running gods."

tain scholars think it served the same purpose as the Mesopotamian *Akitu* house (discussed below). Others think it may have been a royal necropolis; in this case the "god-sword" and the twelve gods would be related to the afterlife. The two hypotheses may be connected, since we know that there is a relationship between the worship of the dead and the spring feasts, which were assemblies of the gods.

Mesopotamian Religion in the Second Millennium

Mesopotamian religion in the second millennium was distinguished by Hammurabi's code, which made Marduk, the god of Babylon (probably of agricultural origin as his symbol is the shovel), a national god and the supreme divinity in the pantheon. This reform was shaped by events: since Babylon had become the capital of the kingdom, it was logical that the fortunes of its god should be connected to the nation and that Marduk should take on a dominant role. However, political considerations had a great deal to do with this promotion: Hammurabi hoped he could strengthen the nation's unity.

The change had repercussions in religious literature: Ancient myths were adapted and rewritten according to the new divine hierarchy, in which Marduk takes precedence over Enlil, the god of the earth. The most famous of the myths that exalt Marduk is the poem of the creation called *Enuma Elish*, "When on high," which are the words with which the poem begins. It includes one of the numerous Mesopotamian traditions about the creation of man. The primitive Universe is evoked: a vast aqueous chaos in which salt water (*Tiamat*) and fresh water (*Apsu*) are mixed, a chaos that gives rise to various couplings. The upper and lower worlds give birth to Anu, who creates Ea in his image.

But the young gods plot against their fathers. Tiamat shouts for revenge, and prepares for battle. The great gods are afraid and search in vain for a champion to set against him. Ea and Anu refuse, and only Marduk, the son of Ea, accepts, not without setting conditions, however: "If I must be the one who subdues Tiamat and secures peace for you, then meet and proclaim that from now on I will be your chief and that nothing can change what I will establish and lay down." The gods therefore meet and eat and drink. In high spirits they consign all their powers to Marduk, who is proclaimed king. Marduk then gets ready and goes before Tiamat armed with bow and arrows, thunderbolt, net and the four winds. When face to face Tiamat and Marduk begin to provoke each other, just like the heroes of classical antiquity. Tiamat casts a spell and Marduk takes advantage of this moment and hurls the four winds into his mouth. At the same time, Marduk shoots an arrow into Tiamat and then cuts his swollen body in two. With one half suspended on high, Marduk creates the sky, and with the other half he creates earth, symmetrical to the sky. He later organizes the world and finally creates man "with the purpose of installing the gods in a dwelling-place dear to their hearts."

This poem was recited every year during the New Year's, or *Akitu*, feast, which was celebrated on different dates in different cities. It could be in autumn or in spring, as at Babylon, where the ceremonies lasted twelve days. Nabu, Marduk's son, the god of Borsippa, had a prominent place in these festivals. As the scribe of the gods, Nabu was responsible for writing on the tablets the annual destinies established during the assembly, which brought together the gods who had come to Babylon. One part of the rites took place in Marduk's temple. The king participated in this most actively; among other things he had to make the gesture symbolic of "taking the god's hand" to invite him to open the great procession. This took Marduk, and all the other gods to the chapel, outside the city, called the *Akitu* house. The gods stayed there for three days, then in the nighttime returned to Babylon. There, in the Chapel of Destinies, the divine decisions were registered, and the next day each god returned to his own sanctuary.

HITTITE PRAYER TO THE SUN-GODDESS

To the Sun-goddess of Arinna, my lady, the mistress of the Hatti lands, the queen of heaven and earth.

O Sun-goddess of Arinna, queen of all countries! In the Hatti country thou bearest the name of the Sun-goddess of Arinna; but in the land which thou madest the cedar land thou bearest the name Hebat. I, Pudu-hepas, am a servant of thine from of old, a heifer from thy stable, a foundation stone upon which thou canst rest.

Thou, my lady, rearedst me and Hattusilis, thy servant, to whom thou espousedst me, was closely associated with the Storm-god of Nerik, thy beloved son . . .

Pritchard: *Ancient Near East Texts* (p. 393)

An essential aspect of Babylonian religion is deification, but it is a difficult and complex matter to touch on in the vast panorama of civilization that is the concern of this book. A reference to the hypothesis put forward by J. Nougayrol must suffice. According to this, deification "had in a certain sense the function that in other religions was taken on by the fundamental notion of salvation."

Hittite Religion

It has been said that studying Hittite religion is like penetrating a forest. This is by way of saying that knowledge of Hittite religion is at best imperfect. The complexity of this religion is due in part to the great number of gods, even if the mention of "the thousand gods of Hatti" found in the texts is not taken literally. Many of them were only diverse local forms of a single divinity. Moreover, the Hittites never rejected a god, so their pantheon was a vast mixture. Besides the very ancient gods of the Hatti group, who are the great gods of the state (for example, the solar goddess of Arinna, Wurusemu, and her husband, the weather god), there was a host of divinities of foreign extraction, belonging to both the Babylonian and the Hurrian pantheons. The latter exerted an evergrowing influence. The gods were arranged in divine families, which normally included the god, his counterpart (that is his goddess-wife), their children and their court. Naturally the temples were their homes. And the temples were closely guarded, even at night, because only a privileged few were allowed to pass over their threshold.

The sacerdotal class consisted of priests, of "mothers of god," and the anointed. Assistants helped the clergy in their many tasks; there were also religious musicians and cantors. Rules were severe: Each gesture was codified not only for the priests but also for all those who had any job in the sanctuary. The following text demonstrates this: "Those who prepare the daily bread shall be clean. They shall wear clean clothes. If they are not clean, they shall not prepare the bread and it shall be prepared by those who are acceptable to the soul and the person of the gods." From this we can conclude that priestly rule was also a rule of hygiene, as is the case with almost all religions.

In Anatolia, therefore, as in Mesopotamia, everyone attempted to please the gods and respect their will. Divination was a means to discover the gods' will. No one was unaware of how much it cost to transgress the will of the gods: "If anyone provokes the wrath of a god, will the god revenge himself only on that person? Or will he not rather revenge himself also on his wife, and children, his descendants, his parents, his men and women slaves, his cattle and sheep, his crops? Therefore pay attention to the words of a god." On the other hand, it was possible to be a model worshiper and at the same time not neglect one's own interests. A whole series of prayers demonstrates this, and even the king himself did not supplicate in a disinterested manner: "God of storms, my lord, make the rains fall in abundance on the black earth so that the bread offerings given up to you shall be plentiful."

The fulfillment of religious duties also included pilgrimages to numerous sanctuaries and feasts that had to be celebrated at the proper time: thus, one must not "celebrate the spring feast in autumn or the autumn feast in spring." Many texts describe the ritual of these feasts. There were also cults given over to the statues of the kings and queens, and perhaps to the other members of the royal family as well, since upon death they were deified.

Mesopotamian Literature of the Second Millennium

The second millennium marked the apex of Mesopotamian literature. There was, first of all, intense literary production. Sumerian had be-

Yazilikaya: The small gallery. The eastern wall with the reliefs of the dagger-god (left) and of the god Sharruma holding king Tudhaliyas IV. The dagger-god relief is a complicated composition: a human head with the divine tiara crowns a blade set into the earth; the hilt is decorated with four lions.

HITTITE RITUAL FOR THE ERECTION OF A HOUSE

When they rebuild a house that had been destroyed or build a new house in a different place and they lay the foundations, they deposit under the foundations as follows: 1 mina of refined copper, 4 bronze pegs, 1 small iron hammer. In the center, at the place of the *kurakki* he digs up the ground. He deposits the copper therein, fixes it down on all sides with the pegs and afterward hits it with the hammer. While doing so he speaks as follows: "Just as this copper is secured, as moreover it is firm, even so let this temple be secure! Let it be firm upon the dark earth!" He mentions the name of the sacrificer: "He who built this temple, let him be firm before the gods likewise! Graciously let him draw upon himself before the gods the potency of this temple for enduring life!

"Just as the four corner stones of the house are firm on the ground and as they will not be overturned, even so let the sacrificer's well-being not overturn in future before the gods! Graciously, god, let him draw upon himself before the gods the potency of this house for life, good health and vigor on the part of the lordship over the Hatti land and on the part of the throne of kingship!"
Pritchard: *Ancient Near Eastern Texts* (p. 356)

HITTITE PROVERB

When one has finished the construction of the palace, and when one has plastered the exterior, then one will recover long years of life, well-being, majesty, and magnificence.
Le monde du sorcier (VII, p. 107)

AN IMPRECATION AGAINST THE SPIRIT OF DEATH

O Gilgamesh, perfect king . . .
Powerful, wise, great among men, . . .
Thou art judge, thy regard is that of a god,
Thou keepest thyself on earth, thou overseest the judgment.
Thy judgment cannot be changed, nor thy word forgotten.
Thou interrogate, thou evaluate, thou judge;
Thou art a seer and go straight along thy way.
Le jugement des morts (IV, p. 91)

come an erudite language, reserved for the clergy, while Akkadian had attained the purity of a classical language. In the palace and temple schools, the scribes collected and translated the works of the past, wrote and even edited dictionaries in order to facilitate their work (and the work of modern Assyriologists as well, it might be added). This ordering of ancient texts in no way obstructed the writing of new texts, however, or hindered research in the most diverse fields. Tablets discovered at Tell Harmal reveal the mathematical knowledge of the time. Numerical tablets show multiplication and division, square and cube roots, and collections of geometry problems (solved by means of algebra) and algebra problems (already third degree equations were known). Royal lists were compiled. Hymns were written, some of which have flights of lyricism: "Sing of the most august of the goddesses/May the queen of the peoples, the greatest of the Igigi be honored,/Sing of Ishtar, the most august goddess,/May the queen of women, the greatest of Igigi, be honored./She who is all joy, is bedecked with love,/Is filled with seduction, with enchantments and with voluptuousness."

But the epic and epistolary literature is perhaps more immediately interesting: the epic because of its stirring qualities, the latter through their eternal human appeal. The master work of the Mesopotamian epic tradition is the story of Gilgamesh. It is a long poem, thought to have had originally about three thousand verses, half of which have been preserved. Although the text is undisputably of Sumerian origin, the most ancient known version dates only from the age of Hammurabi. It was quite popular in the entire area, though, even in Asia Minor, and fragments of it have been found both in Anatolia at Boghaz Köy, and in Megiddo in Palestine. The dynastic list included in the poem relates that at Uruk, Gilgamesh was the fifth king of the first dynasty that followed the Universal Flood. This would mean that Gilgamesh was active in Uruk in the first half of the third millennium. After his death the legend and epic were born.

Although "he is two-thirds divine and one-third human," Gilgamesh reigns despotically over Uruk, and his subjects, tired of his tyranny, ask the gods to do something about the situation. Enkidu is created, half-man and half-beast, in order to fight against the king. But contrary to all expectations, the two, equally strong, far from killing each other, "embrace and strike up a friendship." To seal their relationship, they decide to go together to subdue Humbaba, the guard of the cedar-forest; victorious over the giant, they then return to Uruk. The goddess Ishtar asks Gilgamesh to marry her, but he, enumerating the goddess' many lovers and the fate that she had reserved for them, concludes: "If you love me, you will treat me like them!" Outraged by this crude refusal, Ishtar asks her father to give her the celestial bull to kill Gilgamesh. But her hopes are dashed as Gilgamesh and Enkidu succeed in killing the bull; then, not content with this feat, Enkidu insults Ishtar. This offense to the goddess is unpardonable, and Enkidu dies.

Gilgamesh weeps bitterly for his friend. Unwilling to undergo an equally grim fate, he decides to ask for advice from Ut-Napishtim, a survivor from the Flood to whom the gods have granted immortality. After a long journey, the hero finally meets Ut-Napishtim, who first narrates his adventure and then tells Gilgamesh that if he wants to secure immortality he has to get a plant growing at the bottom of a lake. Gilgamesh succeeds in doing this, and returns to Uruk. But on his way back to Uruk, a serpent takes the miraculous plant from him and immortality eludes the hero forever: "That day Gilgamesh is motionless, and cries. The tears run down his cheeks." On this sadly resigned note the poem ends. It is the story of friendship, human anguish, and resignation before the inevitable.

The many letters found in the Mesopotamian cities give a clear idea of the human beings of the second millennium B.C. They seem, in their concerns not to differ so much from those of this era's twentieth century. The private correspondence found at Mari is most valuable in this regard. One letter of the king's shows him as a worried father, anxious about his son's actions: "How long must we guide you incessantly?

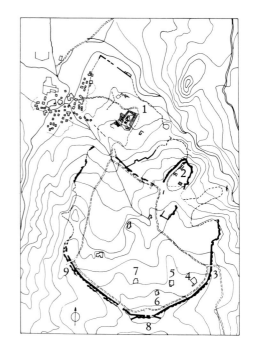

Boghaz Köy: Plan of the city.
1. *Temple of the storm-god*
2. *Acropolis*
3. *King's gate*
4.–7. *Temples*
8. *Sphinx gate*
9. *Lion gate*

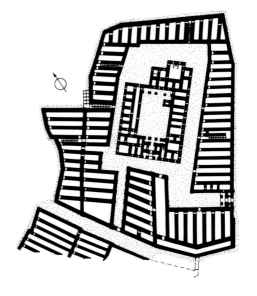

Boghaz Köy: Plan of the temple of the storm-god. Sixteenth century B.C. Bottom of page, schematic drawing of the central nucleus of the temple.

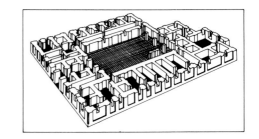

Boghaz Köy: Plan of one of the city gates, and reconstructions of the inner and outer sides of this gate.

Boghaz Köy: The southern stretch of the city walls. The inside wall is higher than the outside wall. Under the gate in the middle the "postern" tunnel passed.

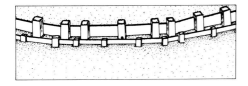

Following page:
Yazilikaya: The small gallery. The god Sharruma and king Tudhaliyas IV. Hittite hieroglyphs engraved on the god make it possible to identify him. Tudhaliyas, held by the god, is depicted in very small scale. The name of the king is to be found in the group of hieroglyphs next to the god's head.

You remain small, you are not a man, you have no beard on your chin! How long will you continue not to take care of your house? Do you not see your brother commanding armies?" Or there is the queen's letter full of solicitude for her royal husband: "May my lord defeat his enemies, and then, safe and sound and his heart brimming with joy, may my lord return to Mari! With this messenger I send him a gown and cloak, which I have made with my own hands. May my lord put them on his shoulders."

Hittite Literature

Before giving a brief account of Hittite literature, something should be said about the type of writing used for it, as distinct from that in use in Mesopotamia. In Anatolia two types of writing existed contemporaneously; one was cuneiform, the other hieroglyphic. In the cuneiform system, the Hittites used some Sumerian-Akkadian signs in order to transcribe various indigenous dialects. The hieroglyphic system was more complex. It was invented by the Hittites and probably corresponds to a need for a national writing form as well as to preoccupations of a religious nature. It was used mostly in official and monumental inscriptions. Deciphering began in earnest in 1930, and has proceeded quite successfully, especially since the discovery, at Karatepe in 1947, of bilingual Phoenician-Hittite inscriptions. The known texts written in hieroglyphics are of local or private interest; there is no writing of an historical nature, but there are temple or palace construction dedications. The hieroglyphs also appear — next to cuneiform characters — on the seals that served as the king's or the functionaries' signatures.

Hittite literature is essentially composite in character, since the Hittite scribes copied, translated, or imitated their Babylonian colleagues. Hymns, writings on astrology and liver divination, the Gilgamesh epic — the Hittite versions are almost identical to the Mesopotamian original. The scribes also used Akkadian, since the Hittite kings wrote in this language to the kings of Babylon and to the Egyptian pharaohs. But the personality of the Hittites is revealed in their annals and "practical" writings. The royal chronicles and the annals of Suppiluliumas, Mursilis, Tudhaliyas, and Telipinus' edict are really the earliest historical documents known. Among "practical" writings, there is a "hippological" treatise, written by a Mitanni veterinarian called Kikkulli. It discusses, in more than a thousand lines, the daily regimen of horses, what their food should be, the length of horse races, and their proper training and necessary equipment.

Hittite myths are also recorded. For example, there is the story of Telipinu, the god of vegetation, who disappears — the incomplete text fails to explain why. The god, angry, "puts his left shoe on his right foot, his right shoe on his left foot, and abandons the Hittite nation. . . . The mountains and trees dried up, the springs became arid, famine struck the land. Men and gods died of hunger." The sun god sends the eagle in search of the missing god, but in vain. The storm god, who in turn goes to find Telipinu, has no better luck. The mother-goddess then sends the bee, a sacred insect, who succeeds in finding Telipinu. Only magic can placate him and convince him to return to his temple, but as with most gods of the Middle East, he soon again becomes angry with his land.

THE MEETING OF EAST AND WEST

The Assyrians

The history of the first millennium in Mesopotamia is the history of great international empires. In this period, Assyrians, Neo-Babylonians and the Achaemenian dynasty ruled the Middle East in turn. The Assyrians were not new on the historical scene. They had lived in northern Mesopotamia from the beginning of history, passing in time from a nomadic to a sedentary life, and from submission to independence. During the third millennium they were vassals of the Akkadian power and then of the second Ur dynasty. The fall of the latter allowed them to free themselves. As early as the nineteenth century B.C., the Assyrians had begun to establish commercial colonies in Anatolia; in the eighteenth century B.C., Shamshi-Adad laid the basis for what was to become the Assyrian empire, but Hammurabi soon opposed its emerging power. The Cassites did likewise, at least at the beginning of their hegemony. From the fourteenth century B.C. on, however, Assyria was, for all practical purposes, an independent state.

This early phase of Assyrian history is perhaps best illustrated by the figure of Tukulti-Ninurta I (1244–1208 B.C.). He was certainly a powerful ruler; he was victorious over the Hittites and succeeded in defeating Babylon, and went on to set himself up as successor to these empires. But his reign ended with a rebellion, and the period that chroniclers term the "time of confusion," began, a period also distinguished by the invasion of the "People of the Sea."

Tiglath-Pileser I (1115–1077 B.C.) attempted to keep the Assyrian frontiers intact. He also made incursions toward Lake Van, the area of Palmyra, and the Mediterranean. He reached the Mediterranean, but his conquests were short-lived, for the Aramaeans, nomads from the Syrian steppes, attacked and sacked both Assyria and Babylon. In order to defend itself, Assyria was forced to change from an essentially agricultural nation to a military nation, a reconversion that marked the beginning of its domination over the Middle East. This hegemony was won at a high price, and it was often put to the test by Assyria's neighbors: to the north, the reign of the kingdom of Urartu, situated in the Lake Van region, whose history is still little known; to the south, Babylonia, favored by the religious prestige of its capital. Although subject to the direct and indirect authority of the Assyrian kings, Babylonia — sustained by the Aramaeans or the Elamites — rebelled frequently; the Aramaeans themselves, having become sedentary and having established numerous states in Syria, also resisted Assyrian rule.

Not all the Assyrian monarchs warrant discussion, of course, but some account must be given of those who played a prominent part in Mesopotamian history. Assyrian power in the area waxed and waned in relation to the quality of its kings. Thus, Ashurnasirpal II (883–859 B.C.) conducted numerous campaigns, some to extend his kingdom, others to exact tribute from subject areas or even to cut down timber in Ammon (north of Antioch) for the construction of the city of Calah

A TEXT OF TIGLATH-PILESER I CONCERNING THE ZIGGURAT OF ANU-ADAD AT ASHUR

Two great *ziggurats*, as they befit the ornamentation of their sublime divinity, have I constructed. . . . A sanctuary as a dwelling place of their pleasure, as a seat for their celebrations, which radiate like the stars of heaven, I would imagine, I made these *ziggurats*, raised unto heaven.

Dombert: *Der Sakralturm* (I)

ASHURNAIRSPAL II TO THE GODDESS ISHTAR

I was born amid mountains which no one knew.
I did not recognize thy might and did not pray to thee.
The Assyrians did not know of thy godhead and did not pray to thee.
But thou, O Ishtar, fearsome mistress of the gods,
Thou didst single me out with the glance of thine eyes;
Thou didst desire to see me rule.
Thou didst take me from among the mountains.
Thou didst call me to be a shepherd of men.
Thou didst grant me the scepter of justice.

Frankfort: *Kingship and the Gods* (p. 239)

THE POWERS OF THE ASSYRIAN KING

I am Ashurnasirpal, the devotee of the great gods, the destroyer of evil . . . the king whose word destroys the mountains and seas, who by his power has forced his supremacy to be recognized by those powerful kings without mercy who rule from where the sun rises to where the sun sets.

A palace of cedar wood, a palace of cypress, a palace of juniper wood, a palace of boxwood, a palace of mulberry wood, of pistachio wood, of tamarisk wood — this have I raised for my royal residence and for my pleasure.
I made to be sculptured in the white limestone and in the alabaster images of animals and of mountains and of seas, and with these I ornamented the gates. I had them affixed with braces of brass. And I had placed there doors of cedar, of cypress, of juniper, of mulberry wood. Silver, gold, tin, bronze, and iron — the plunder that I took from the lands I conquered — I stored here.

Vieyra: *Les Assyriens* (pp. 135, 171)

Nimrud: Winged bull with human head. Detail. Ninth century B.C. A guardian animal that decorated one of the gates of the northwestern palace.

(Nimrud). He distinguished himself above all as a gifted administrator. He was also one of the first to organize the Assyrian army.

His son, Shalmaneser III (858–824 B.C.) carried on his father's expansionist policy, concentrating on an attempt to conquer Syria. Although he at first met with defeat, he also gained a number of victories. Facing a coalition of his antagonists he defeated them in the battle of Qarqar, if his annals are to be believed: "With the sublime force given me by the lord Ashur, with the mighty weapons granted me by Nergal who marches before me, I fought against them. . . . I had a flood rain down on them; I heaped up their cadavers . . . . With their bodies I filled up the Orontes river as if it were a shallow ford. In this battle I took their chariots, their knights, horses, and harnesses." The continual military campaigns weakened Assyria, however, and as a result the state passed through a difficult period of rebellion, and even civil war, during the course of which the upper and lower nobility fought against each other, each party led by their own prince. After prolonged conflict, the lower nobility gained the upper hand, thanks to Tiglath-Pileser III (745–727 B.C.), one of the greatest Assyrian kings.

As an administrator, Tiglath-Pileser III consolidated the structure of the empire, by controlling the growth of the too powerful provinces; as a strategist, he moved to create a permanent army, so that, as one authority has written, "incursions are replaced by wars." From the time he ascended the throne, he faced threats from all sides — from the Aramaeans, the Medes, and even the Babylonians. Tired of the nest of intrigues that was Babylon, he deposed its king and became king himself. As such he took another name, Pulu; the Assyrian and Babylonian kingdoms were thus kept separate. In a certain sense, Babylonia was thus not made subject to Assyria, perhaps for religious reasons.

The reign of Sargon II (721–705 B.C.) corresponds to one of the apexes of Assyrian power. He was above all the great conqueror of Samaria, capital of the kingdom of Israel: "I surrounded the city of

Left:
Khorsabad: Winged human-headed genie. Detail. Eighth century B.C. Alabaster. These genies, who hold a pine cone and a metal vase, were generally found — in Khorsabad — behind a human-headed bull in the passageways of the decorated gates; their task was to purify the visitor, whom the bull had allowed to enter the city.

Right:
Nimrud: A winged genie with a pine cone and a metal vase; before him is the sacred tree, in stylized form. Ninth century B.C.

Samaria and conquered it. I took into captivity 27,290 persons who lived there; I took possession of fifty chariots that were there. I allowed the rest of the inhabitants to resume their former life. I set up a general over them and imposed on them the same tribute the preceding king had demanded." Sargon II also reached Cyprus. King Mita (Midas) of Mushku (Meshech) sent an ambassador to him. Elam continued to back Babylonia, however, and Egypt gave considerable help to the Aramaean states in Syria. In his seventeen years of rule, Sargon II enjoyed only two years of peace. Appropriately, he died in battle.

His son Sennacherib (704–681 B.C.) succeeded him. He had already ruled the nation during his father's absence. It was in Sennacherib's reign that the bloody battle with the Elamites took place. He also crushed the continuous rebellions in Babylonia, not hesitating to commit a sacrilege in the process: he absolutely destroyed the holy city, carying away the statues of the gods and diverting the course of the Euphrates River in order to flood it (689 B.C.). He declared: "I treated it worse than a flood." Eventually, Sennacherib was assassinated, probably at the hands of the pro-Babylonian faction.

He was succeeded by his son Esarhaddon (680–669 B.C.) who may have been involved with his father's death. He ordered the reconstruction of Babylon and its temples. Like the kings who preceded him, Esarhaddon had to intervene on all fronts, but the main object of his reign was the conquest of Egypt. He penetrated the kingdom of the Nile as far as Memphis, taking the city. Within Assyria, his decision to divide the kingdom between his two sons proved disastrous. Ashurbanipal set himself up in Nineveh, then the Assyrian capital, while his brother Shamash-shum-ukin went to Babylon. Although the division of power held for a time, Shamash-shum-ukin eventually rebelled against Ashurbanipal, who reacted by besieging Babylon. Shamash, defeated, perished in its flames. A number of kings succeeded him, but in 626 B.C. Nabopolassar, taking advantage of Assyrian weakness, proclaimed Babylon independent.

Ashurbanipal was the last great Assyrian king. He continued to fight in Egypt, taking Thebes; he gained victories in Elam too, sacking Susa in 648 B.C. He boasted of such accomplishments in these words: "In one month I cast the entire nation of Elam into ruins. With these campaigns I eliminated the voice of men, the tread of oxen and small cattle, every shout of joy." But these brilliant Assyrian successes were short-lived. The death of Ashurbanipal in 631 B.C. marked the beginning of the decline of Assyrian power. Weakened by continual wars and the intrigues of the court and the dignitaries, shaken by the Scythian invasions that had been threatening the nation for a long time, the huge empire fell to the Babylonians and Medes. Nineveh was conquered in 612 B.C. and, as the prophet Nahum wrote, "all those who know of its fate applaud its fall." Definitively annihilated by 605, Assyria gave way to the Neo-Babylonian empire.

Assyrian Society

The Assyrian king, earthly representative of the national god Ashur, was really legitimate sovereign only after his coronation. He reigned as an absolute monarch, assisted at first by functionaries chosen from among the ranks of the upper nobility; from Tiglath-Pileser III on, these functionaries were chosen from the lower nobility. He was supported by a powerful administration and by a well-organized system of control in the provinces that made up the empire. In Sargon II's time, there were more than seventy of these provinces. They were directed by governors, also chosen from among the nobles, who probably exercised every aspect of power: military, legal, and financial. The governors' financial control was extremely important and it was also a little dangerous to the governor. A letter to Tiglath-Pileser from one of the governors of the western regions informs the king that the exaction of taxes in Tyre and Sidon has given rise to serious incidents; at Tyre the

Khorsabad: Gilgamesh. Eighth century B.C. Alabaster; height 15 feet, 5 inches. The Mesopotamian hero is here depicted taming a lion cub. (Paris, Louvre Museum)

PRAYER OF KING SARGON OF ASSYRIA

O Ea, lord of wisdom, creator of all things, to Sargon, king of the universe, king of Assyria, viceroy of Babylon, king of Sumer and Akkad, builder of thy abode — open thy fountains; let his springs send forth the waters of plenty and abundance; give water in abundance to his fields. Quick understanding and an open mind decree for him; prosper his work; let him attain unto his desire.

Frankfort: *Kingship and the Gods* (p. 310)

THE ORACLE OF ISHTAR

Ashurhaddon, king of the land, fears nothing!
The wind that blows against you,
Have I not broken its wings?
Your enemies everywhere will fall at your feet

I am Ishtar of Arbela,
O Ashurhaddon, king of Assyria!
In the cities of Ashur, of Nineveh, of Kalah,
and of Arbela,
I shall give to Ashurhaddon, my king,
Long days and eternal nights.

Labat *et al.: Les
Religions du Proche-Orient* (p. 257)

TEMPLE INSCRIPTION OF ESARHADDON

The earlier temple of Assur, which Shalmaneser, son of Adad-nirari, king of Assyria, a prince who lived before me, had built, fell into decay.... That temple, the place of its site I did not change, but upon gold, silver, precious stones, herbs, and cedar oil I established its foundation walls and laid its brickwork. I built and completed it, I made it magnificent to the astonishment of the peoples. For life, for length of days, for the stability of my reign, for the welfare of my posterity, for the safety of my priestly throne, for the overthrow of my enemies, for the success of the harvests of Assyria, for the welfare of Assyria, I built it.

Frankfort: *Kingship and the Gods* (p. 267)

ASHURBANIPAL'S HYMN TO PROSPERITY

After Assur, Sir, Shamash, Adad, Bel, Nabu, Ishtar of Nineveh, queen of Kidmuri, Ishtar of Arbela, Urtu, Nergal, and Nushku had caused me to take my seat, joyfully upon the throne of the father who begot me, Adad sent his rains, Ea opened his fountains, the grain grew five cubits tall in the stalk, the ear was five-sixths of a cubit long; heavy crops and a plenteous yield made the fields continuously luxuriant, the orchards yielded a rich harvest, the cattle successfully brought forth their young — in my reign there was fullness to overflowing, in my years there was plenteous abundance.

Frankfort: *Kingship and the Gods* (p. 310)

TEXT OF TIGLATH-PILESER I

With the injunction of Ninurta, who loves me, I have shot with my powerful bow four savage bulls ... in the desert of Mitanni.... I have felled ten elephants in the region of Harran and of Habour.... On the order of Ninurta, I have shot while on foot 120 lions and from my chariot 800 lions.

Vieyra: *Les Assyriens* (p. 116)

king's representative was killed by the people, while at Sidon he was taken prisoner.

Assyrian society differed little from those that preceded it. But mention must be made of the extraordinary mixture of populations in the empire, the result of massive deportations effected by the Assyrians. They wanted to eliminate every possible attempt at rebellion in the subject nations, to obtain a necessary labor force, and probably also to repopulate Assyria, whose vital forces were often diminished by the wars. The eternal enemies of the Assyrians, the Aramaeans, were the largest of these deported populations. Their language became everyday speech not only in the provinces but also in Assyria itself, so that eventually cuneiform writing was used only for official documents.

In Assyria war was made by order of the gods, and rebels were treated as less than human. The national god Ashur is usually depicted at the center of a winged disc in the act of bending a bow, and it was to him that Sargon II addressed an account of the eight campaigns he conducted in eastern Iran, Armenia, and Kurdistan. This report — a magnificent text of over four hundred lines — is written in the form of a letter: "To Ashur, father of the gods . . . from the depths of my heart, greetings . . . . For Sargon, the holy priest, the servant who fears your great divinity, and for his following, everything goes very very well."

In such a country, the army was obviously a primary institution. Organized by Ashurnasirpal II, then reorganized by Tiglath-Pileser III, who created a permanent army to stand beside the provincial militias, the Assyrian military force consisted of various armed corps: infantry, cavalry, chariots. The infantry was divided into soldiers armed with sword and spear; archers, often accompanied by a helper to protect them; and sling-shooters who generally fought behind the archers and who were used above all in besieging a city. All these men were protected by coats of mail, by pointed ornamented helmets whose form changed from period to period, and by round or rectangular shields, either medium size or very large (and in the latter case used to protect the archers or besiegers of a fortress), made of intertwined twigs or leather. The cavalry was used mainly for battles in woody or mountainous areas; the men were armed with swords or bows. In battle the cavalry, armed with swords, would charge, while their companions with bows protected the flanks and the rear of the troops. It was difficult to protect the archers in battle, however, and the mounted archer was thus paired off with another cavalryman, who held his shield and led the two horses. The chariots were also an important element of the force and attempts were continuously made to improve them.

The Assyrian war machines necessary for sieges are well-known. These were rams set on wheels; the men who maneuvered them were protected by mobile towers. Smaller devices than these were also used, of course: ladders and flaming torches were used by defenders and besiegers alike. Various means of approach were utilized, such as earth, stone, or tree trunk ramps.

The victories were generally followed by slaughters, which presumably served as warnings against future rebellion. Men were impaled before the walls of the conquered city; their heads were heaped up at the gates; those responsible for the rebellion were mutilated. Yet not all enemies met such a grim fate; some were spared so as to "celebrate the greatness of Ashur, Ishtar and the great gods," and perhaps also for political reasons. After a victory the king would usually return to his capital "accompanied by singers and musicians" to render thanks to the gods.

Assyrian Architecture

The Assyrians built with the same indefatigability with which they made war. Every monarch wanted a new palace, built to the glory of the god Ashur and of himself. The Assyrian kings had a consistent preoccupation with historical accounts, and required their scribes to write the annals of their reign. Their sculptors and painters were likewise required to depict their accomplishments on the palace walls.

The Assyrian architectural creations are all similar in plan; they are varieties of the type used for all the Mesopotamian palaces. Each royal residence differs from the others in decoration, however, and thus furnishes us precious information about royal daily life. Unfortunately this only concerns official duties; the king is shown carrying out his religious obligations, receiving homage from his vassals, watching the payment of tribute, displaying his unusual courage and force, participating in hunting or military expeditions. These scenes all have in common the exaltation of Assyrian power, which is held to be indisputable.

The texts often to into detail about the construction of a new palace: "The palace that had been erected by the kings, my fathers . . . had become too narrow for me," Esarhaddon relates. "The people of the nations my bow had conquered, were made by me to bring the mattocks and die casts, and they made bricks . . . . I assembled the kings of the Hittites and of the other bank of the Euphrates . . . in all, twenty-two kings. I gave them my orders: beams, columns, cedar and cypress boards, . . . winged bulls and stone colossi, stone covering slabs, baked bricks, marble, stones from the mountains for the needs of my palace they had brought to Nineveh, my royal city, with difficulty and trouble. . . . Gates of pleasantly perfumed cypress wood I had covered with silver and copper . . . . I completed the work with joy and satisfaction, to the sound of music." Actually, the music must have served to give rhythm and coordination to the laborers' work.

The excavations carried out at Ashur, Nimrud, Khorsabad, Nineveh — all cities that were from time to time capitals of the kingdom — have uncovered these constructions. Most of the metropolises so carefully developed by the Assyrian kings had been in existence since the most ancient times. The first edifices at Ashur date from the dawn of the third millennium; the origins of Nimrud are set at the end of the fourth and the beginning of the third millennium: Nineveh shows signs of settlement as far back as the fifth millennium. Only Khorsabad is a "new" city.

Ashur rose up in magnificent surroundings. The city was built on a promontory that dominates the Tigris to the east and one of its canals to the north: natural fortifications that were completed with a wall as early as 2300 B.C. Often restored, this wall was later doubled from the inside by Sennacherib. In the northern part of the city lies the concentration of official buildings and sanctuaries — according to the annals of Sennacherib, Ashur had thirty-four of them (or thirty-eight; the numbers vary according to the text) — all dominated by two constructions. One was a *ziggurat* that was at first dedicated to Enlil, the god of the earth; then, in the thirteenth century B.C., it was dedicated to the god Ashur by Tukulti-Ninurta, who wished to commemorate his victory over Babylonia and give thinks to the national god.

The second edifice was of a new type, consecrated to Anu, god of the sky, and to Adad, god of the elements and storms. This edifice consisted of two identical sanctuaries separated by a narrow corridor, framed by two square step towers, like all the Assyrian *ziggurats*, and preceded by a common courtyard. The German archaeologists who excavated at Ashur also recognized various palaces, underneath one of which there was a royal necropolis containing five sarcophagi, which unfortunately had been violated. One of these might have belonged to Ashurnasirpal II. Finally, beyond the wall to the northeast, was the *Akitu* house for the New Year's feast; as in Babylon in the second millennium, this took place outside the city. Ashur, the capital city abandoned in favor of Nimrud, always remained the religious city of Assyria.

Founded by Shalmaneser I as an Assyrian city, Nimrud (Calah) became the leading metropolis in the land through the efforts of Ashurnasirpal II. It remained so until the reign of Sargon II, who lived there for some time in a provisional palace next to the temple of Nabu until

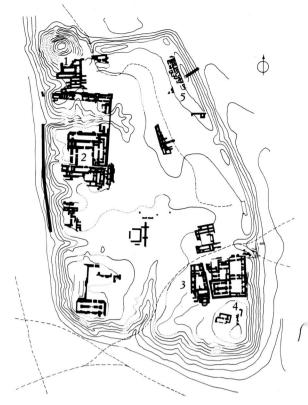

Nimrud: Plan of the acropolis.
1. The ziggurat *dedicated to Ninurta, god of war*
2. The northwestern palace
3. The "burnt palace"
4. The temple of Nabu
5. Habitations

Nimrud: Plan of the "burnt palace," where lovely ivory pieces were found in the throne room and the adjacent room.
1. Throne room
2. Large courtyard
3. Palace and temple of Nabu

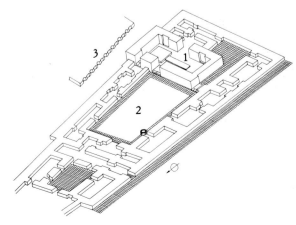

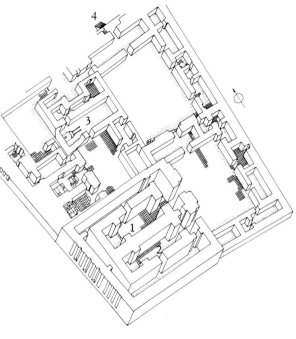

Nimrud: Plan of the temple of Nabu, the god of writing. In the throne room archaeologists found a tablet with 647 lines, a treaty between king Esarhaddon and the governor of a province of western Iraq.
1. *Sanctuary of Nabu*
2. *Sanctuary of Tashmetun, goddess counterpart of Nabu*
3. *Throne room*
4. *Main gate, flanked by two statues of fish-men*

the construction of Khorsabad was completed. Neglected in favor of Khorsabad, Nimrud was restored by Esarhaddon in the seventh century B.C. It rose up on the banks of the Tigris and was a splendid city measuring 6,890 feet by 5,478 feet, surrounded by an enclosure wall and fed by the waters of a canal cut out of the rock that carried the waters of the upper Zab River, an affluent of the Tigris. In the southwestern corner of this city rose the acropolis, where many sacred edifices were situated, among them a *ziggurat* dedicated to the god of war Ninurta, and the temple of Nabu, a god who enjoyed great favor here, perhaps because he was the son of the god Marduk of Babylon. In this way the Assyrians showed their interest in that holy city, without, however, attaching too much importance to it and encouraging any desire for independence.

Excavations made by Layard and Loftus in the last century, and those carried out by Max Mallowan a few years ago, have brought Ashurnasirpal II's palace to light. The official part of the palace, the administrative rooms, and the storerooms have been identified. The official part has a throne room, traditionally preceded by a vestibule and enclosed between two courtyards, the first public and the second private. Some lines from a long text engraved on a stele found in a room near the throne room, reveal that Ashurnasirpal put all his energies into this construction. After calling the palace "palace of Ashurnasirpal, priest of Ashur, well-loved by the gods Enlil and Ninurta," and furnishing his titles and genealogy, citing his conquests, and proclaiming his faith in Ashur, the king then speaks with pride of this edifice and goes into detail about the inauguration which he had after its completion. The festivities lasted for ten days, and 69,574 persons participated, among whom were 47,074 workmen, 5,000 officials (from "all my palaces," as the king specifies), 16,000 inhabitants of the city, and 1,500 functionaries.

Another important discovery made at Nimrud, in the southeastern corner of the outer wall of the city, is an edifice called "strong Shalmaneser," 1148 feet by 837 feet, with nearly 200 rooms that formed various blocks. The north wing seems to have been reserved for the lodgings of officers and officials, barracks, workrooms and storerooms; the south wing includes throne rooms, reception halls, the treasury, and lodgings. Some have thought this was a sort of arsenal "for the order of the field, the care of the stallions and mules, the maintenance of the chariots, weapons, war materials and booty of every kind," as a slightly later text states. Some remains of the ornaments and treasures in this building have been preserved. These include the decoration of the gates flanked by lions and winged bulls with human heads, where the doors might have been covered with bronze or gold leaf, with embossed military scenes. Also included are the vertical slabs of sculptured stone that decorated and at the same time reinforced the plinths of the walls, an architectural technique that the Assyrians almost certainly learned from the artists of northern Syria and Anatolia and which is found in most of the palaces.

Assyrian reliefs, executed in easily workable chalky alabaster, show, in consistently rigorous symmetrical composition, the royal functions; those at Nimrud are no exception to the rule. The king is represented seated, a cup in his hand; or is shown while preparing to leave for a hunt or to do battle, holding a bow and arrow in his hands; he is also depicted in action, on horseback while killing a lion with a lance, or in a chariot while thrusting his dagger into a wild bull. In Assyrian art one rarely sees sculpture in the round, but Nimrud has a statue of Ashurnasirpal and some of Shalmaneser, all of the same kind, almost stereotyped. The king is depicted standing, in a hieratic pose, and only the inscriptions allow us to identify the statues. Finally, the great number of ivory pieces, some worked with gold, support the notion that the palaces were very richly furnished. These were found, scattered in various places or in the wells and shafts, where they had been thrown by the conquering Babylonians or Medes.

The Fortress of Sargon

Khorsabad: Relief depicting servants bearing the royal table and throne.

But it is Khorsabad (the modern name for Dur-Sharrukin) that best demonstrates the qualities of the Assyrian architects. Here they had a "virgin" site and they were in no way obstructed in the realization of their projects. The short text engraved on some bricks in the city can be endorsed without reservation: "Sargon, king of the universe, has built a city, and has called it Dur-Sharrukin. He has built an incomparable palace inside it."

Dur-Sharrukin ("Fortress of Sargon"), situated about ten miles from Mosul, testifies in fact not only to the greatness of Sargon II's reign, but also to the great means at his disposal, which made it possible to build these really gigantic constructions in six years. The largest was the enclosure wall that extended for almost two miles around the four sides. It consisted of a magnificent stone base more than a yard high which supported a crude brick wall over seventy-eight feet thick and seventy-five feet high; this was reinforced by rectangular towers over forty-four feet long; they jut out thirteen feet from the wall and are set eighty-nine feet from one another. One entered the city through seven gates, three of which were decorated with winged bulls followed by winged

Khorsabad: Relief depicting servants bearing the royal table and throne.

Dur-Sharrukin (Khorsabad): Reconstruction of a part of the citadel.

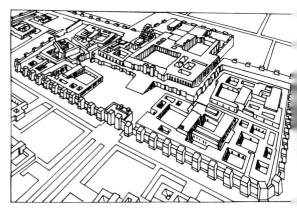

genies. One of these gates was found with its vault intact, decorated with an archivolt of enameled tile.

Not all the enclosed area (about 741 acres) was covered with constructions. Sargon built only the citadel to the northwest; a palace (probably that of the heir-apparent Sennacherib) near the southern corner; and a sanctuary consecrated to the Sibitti, the constellation of the Pleiades, discovered during the construction of a road.

The citadel, protected by a wall, was accessible by means of two gates decorated with genies and winged bulls with human heads. It included the lodgings of the high functionaries; one of these men could be identified, thanks to the inscription on the threshold, as that of the grand vizier Sinahutsur, Sargon II's brother. Another lodging, not identified, had a hall that was decorated with wall paintings. With the fragments found, it was possible to reconstruct a panel more than thirty-two feet high. On top, the king, followed by a dignitary, gives homage to a god, perhaps Ashur; the rest of the composition shows winged genies, bulls, and geometric motifs. Besides the lodgings, a temple dedicated to Nabu, built on a terrace, has been recognized; in it two courtyards preceded a vestibule that gave access to two cellas. The temple was decorated with statues of gods with spouting vases, and enameled tiles.

Built on a platform (between forty-four and fifty-seven feet high) embellished with tiles, the royal palace at Dur-Sharrukin with its majestic and harmonious proportions, took up almost twenty-five acres of space. Its courtyards formed a perfect balance in the plan of the edifice. But curiously, the palace, which had to be entered by means of a ramp, was placed directly on the enclosure wall. This palace, with its thick walls (from eleven to twenty-six feet) had few entranceways, obviously for reasons of security. The main entrance, perhaps a triple portal, was decorated with monumental reliefs: on the sides, winged bulls with human heads and a winged genie; on the facade, identical bulls and representations of Gilgamesh taming a young lion merely by grasping it with his arm. Once through the portal, one found oneself in a large courtyard surrounded by rooms that afforded access to other monumental blocks. Once again stone slabs were used for the wall decoration. The motifs of those at Khorsabad are hardly different from those at Nimrud or Nineveh: scenes of war, rows of tributaries, of servants bearing the royal chariot and furnishings, bow-hunting scenes, winged genies. Only one scene, showing the transport of timber from Lebanon, sounds a new note in this decoration.

Six sanctuaries, at one time called *harems*, were placed together and set against the royal residence. They were consecrated to Sin, Shamash, Adad, Ea, Ninurta — the gods, respectively, of the moon, the sun, storms, waters, war and hunting — and also to Ningal, the female counterpart of Sin. Like the sanctuary of Nabu, the facades of the sanctuaries were decorated with enameled tiles. On both sides of the entranceways were statues of gods holding the vase of spouting water. The decoration in the temple of Sin is the most complete. A plinth of enameled tiles runs along both sides of the door, reproducing the same scene: a procession to the temple, with the king in the lead, followed by attendants carrying a lion, an eagle, a bull, a fig tree, and a plow; a high functionary is at the end of this procession. It is evident that these motifs correspond to some symbolism, but the symbolism is difficult to interpret; perhaps the lion and eagle symbolize Assyrian power, while the bull, the fig tree and the plow evoke different aspects of the fertility necessary for the nation. To complete this sacred complex, dedicated to the god Ashur, there was a *ziggurat* with a square plan. One had to go up a spiral ramp, a new means of access (not found again in Mesopotamia until much later, at Samarra in the spiral minaret of the great Moslem mosque).

Within the citadel enclosure, there was also a second, smaller palace, whose plan almost certainly was inspired by the Hittite construction called *bit-hilani*, and characterized by a pillared portico. This palace looked out through its portico to the northeast over a landscape of nearby mountains. The columns of the portico were made of wood,

Following pages:
Nineveh: Hunting scene. Seventh century B.C. Alabaster. In the upper register, king Ashurbanipal fights a lion; in the lower register, lion-hunting on horseback. (London, British Museum)

THE MEETING OF EAST AND WEST   75

probably with a bronze or gold covering, since fragments of these metals were found at Khorsabad, with embossed decorations of scales imitating palms. Of this great city, "unrivaled in the four parts of the world," there remain only a few earth bulwarks, corresponding to the wall, and mounds that show the former location of the monumental gates.

Nineveh

Of all the Assyrian cities, Nineveh is perhaps the one whose name is most evocative. Yet a visit to this city is disappointing. The ancient remains are concentrated in two tells: Nebi Yunus and Quyungik. A cemetery and a mosque obstruct any systematic exploration of the former tell; the latter was excavated at the dawn of archaeology, but very little is now visible of the walls then brought to light. Everywhere on the soil of the capital of Tiglath-Pileser, Sennacherib, Esarhaddon, and Ashurbanipal there resounds the anathema of Nahum, prophet of Israel: "Woe to the bloody city! it is all full of lies and robbery; the prey departeth not" (*Nahum* III: 1). But before becoming a "desert, a refuge of wild beasts," Nineveh possessed treasures of every kind, among which were the decorations of its palaces, still consisting of reliefs, but with a changed style. In them personages are depicted much smaller, although the number depicted is larger; reliefs are rather chiseled than sculptured, though the motifs remain the same — hunting and war. To mention only the masterpieces of this artistic production in Nineveh, there are: the surrender of the city of Lachish in Palestine, with the losers prostrating themselves before Sennacherib, who is seated on a reviewing throne; the battle in the swamps; the defeat of the Elamites, with the extraordinary swarming movement of the soldiers and the slaughter of the men, (which corresponds to the sacrifice of the beasts in reliefs of the hunts of Ashurbanipal, depictions which include splendid bits of animal sculpture — the wounded lioness and the lion and lioness in the shade of a tree). Once again, there is no intimate scene; in fact, it is difficult to make the so-called banquet under the arbor pass for such, since next to the seated queen and to the king lying on a bed, the head of the king of Elam hangs from a tree.

Nineveh is justly famous also for its library, which Arnold Toynbee, the British historian, did not hesitate to describe as "not at all unworthy of the Athens of 405–404 B.C." Ashurbanipal, who boasted of being able to read and write, was its founder: "I, Ashurbanipal, king of the legions, king of the nations, king of Assyria, to whom the gods have given attentive ears and open eyes, have read all the writings that my princely predecessors had accumulated. In my respect for the son of Marduk, Nabu, god of intelligence, I have collected the tablets, have had them transcribed, and after having compared them, have signed my name to them for the purpose of preserving them in my palace." Fortune smiled upon the archaeologists, who found at Nineveh more than twenty thousand tablets. Inscribed on them were not only the epic of Gilgamesh but the myth of Etana, who desired to ascend to the skies to find the plant of birth and, despite the help of an eagle, did not succeed; also the myth of Adapa who, furious because the south wind had overturned his boat, broke its wings.

The account of the Universal Flood (translated by the English Assyriologist George Smith in 1872–73) was also found there. It has many similarities with the Old Testament version, describing how the gods decided to destroy rebellious man, saving only one, Ut-Napishtim, who was just and pious. The boat that Ut-Napishtim built saved him from the catastrophe, whose greatness was such that even the gods were terrified; during the six days and nights during which the destructive wind blew and the "storm crushed the earth," the gods remained "squatting like dogs." Finally "the sea became calm again and the wind silent and the flood ceased." Ut-Napishtim then offered a sacrifice

Babylon: General plan.
1. *Ishtar gate*
2. *Northern area of city, including the royal palace and hanging gardens*
3. *Temple of Ninmah*
4. *Bastion on the Euphrates*
5. *The Euphrates*
6. *Processional road*
7. *Ziggurat (E-temen-an-ki)*
8. *Temple of Marduk (Esagila)*
9. *Lugalgirra gate*
10. *Adad gate*
11. *Shamash gate*
12. *Urash gate*
13. *Enlil gate*
14. *Zababa gate*
15. *Marduk gate*
16. *Sin gate*

Babylon: Plan of the northern area.
1. *Royal palace with the "hanging gardens"*
2. *Inner wall of the city and Ishtar gate*
3. *Processional way.*
4. *Temple of Ninmah*
5. *The bastion that dominated the Euphrates*

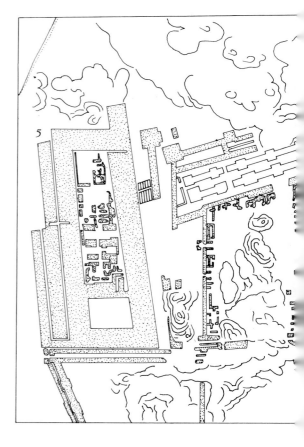

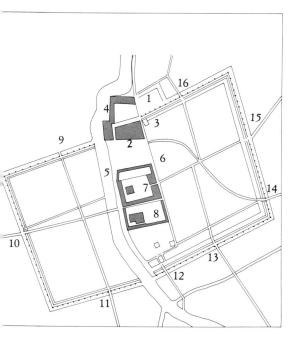

to the gods who, "scenting the pleasant odor . . . gathered like flies" around the sacrificer.

The Assyrian kings did not limit themselves to building cities. They also built roads and undertook gigantic works for the diversion of water. The most celebrated of these are the work of Sennacherib; they directed the water from Bavian to Nineveh, a distance of about fifty miles. The most spectacular part of this project is the aqueduct of Gerwan; crossing a valley, and held up by five arches, the aqueduct measures about 900 feet long and 40 feet wide. It was made of stone blocks.

There are also the enormous rock reliefs of Maltay, Bavian, and Hines. Taking up an artistic tradition that goes back to Naram-Sin, the Assyrian kings had rows of gods sculptured in the rocks, reminiscent of the Hittite sanctuary of Yazilikaya. This tradition of rock relief would be taken up again in both the Achaemenian and Sassanian dynasties.

The Neo-Babylonians

It has already been mentioned that in 605 B.C. the Neo-Babylonian empire replaced Assyrian power, which fell under the combined blows of the Medes and the Babylonians. The victors divided the kingdom; the Medes took the northern region, Assyria and the Anatolian provinces, while the southern and western provinces went to the Babylonians.

This new Babylonian empire was distinguished from its predecessor by an entirely new spirit. Military expeditions followed by deportations took place, but war was no longer the basis of the empire. The new kingdom was governed much more to meet the needs of trade, which was then in a flourishing state. By the Neo-Babylonian period, the temples had really become autonomous economic enterprises. They were able to gather a considerable number of workmen, and even had special statutes governing their conduct. This is shown by the "laborers' charter" set out by Nidniti-Bel, the administrative director of Eanna (the temple corporation) and Nabu-ah-iddin, royal governing commissar and executive director of Eanna: "Nidniti-Bel, administrative director of Eanna, son of Nabu-mukin-zer and descendant of Dabibi, and Nabu-ah-iddin, royal governing commissar and executive director of Eanna to [and here there follows a list of 29 proper names] and to the whole of the carpenters, metal engravers, goldsmiths and all the artisans of Eanna, speak thus: 'You shall execute the repairs and the work that includes the use of silver, gold, bronze, precious stones, wood, and you shall perform every sort of service. If you do not execute the work and do not make the repairs and if someone executes work or repairs at another temple, you will be severely punished by the king.' "

The export of dates, wheat, bitumen, and wool played an important part in the economy of the time, and the expansion of trade was most certainly helped by an official system of weights and measurements. However, at the beginning there was some inflation, caused by the development of credit, the growth of which was considerably facilitated by private banking organizations such as Murasho and Sons. With its seat at Nippur, this firm had about sixty agents scattered over the northern region of Babylonia and the Sealands (the southern region).

The Neo-Babylonian historic phase was of brief duration: 626–539 B.C., not even a full century, covering the reign of six kings. The most famous are surely Nabopolassar, the founder of the dynasty, who was not Babylonian but Chaldean, and his son Nebuchadnezzar II. The problems the latter had to face were the same the Assyrians had dealt with. Egypt continually intervened in the affairs of Syria-Palestine, and Nebuchadnezzar was forced to step in many times. The most celebrated of his campaigns were those directed against Jerusalem — occupied for the first time in 597 B.C., then taken again in 586 B.C. — and the siege of Tyre, which lasted thirteen years.

The death of Nebuchadnezzar in 562 marked the beginning of difficulties for the Neo-Babylonians. Four kings followed one another in six

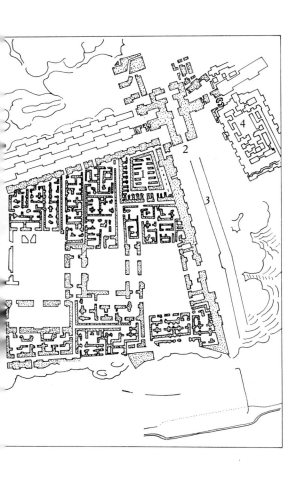

years. The last was Nabonidus (the version of his name, Nabuna'id, by which he is best known) son of a priestess of the temple of Sin, the moon god, at Harran. He was a strange man; he supported the Persian, Cyrus, in his fight against the Medes, and favored the cult of Sin at the expense of the national god Marduk. Under Nabonidus, the New Year festival was no longer celebrated in Babylon. For unknown reasons, he withdrew for eight years to the oasis of Teima, in northern Arabia, leaving the kingdom in the hands of his son Belshazar. He returned to the sacred city only to see it fall in 539 B.C. to Cyrus, a fall that was facilitated by the treachery of the priests of Marduk. The hour of Persian power had arrived.

Architecture of the Neo-Babylonians

As builders, Nabopolassar, Nebuchadnezzar and Nabonidus were hardly inferior to the Assyrian sovereigns. They did not hesitate to reconstruct temples in numerous Mesopotamian cities — in particular the *ziggurat* at Ur — but it was naturally at Babylon, their capital, that they made their greatest efforts. The city was set in a double enclosure. The outer portion consisted of two walls about eleven miles long, and enclosed a vast space used as a refuge for the people from the surrounding countryside in time of war. The second, rectangular in shape, was the city "wall" proper, and consisted of two walls reinforced by towers; the one closest to the city was twenty-one feet wide, the other twelve feet wide. Babylon was built on both sides of the Euphrates. One entered it through nine gates, each of which bore the name of a god. Of the four entranceways that have been discovered and excavated, the most imposing is the Ishtar Gate. It is one of the gates that affords access to the sector built on the left bank of the river, where the palaces and sanctuaries were situated. Still forty-one

PUNITIVE EXPEDITIONS OF KING NEBUCHADNEZZAR

In the first year of Nebuchadnezzar in the month of Sivan he mustered his army and went to the Hatti-territory, he marched about unopposed in the Hatti-territory until the month of Kislev. All the kings of the Hatti-land came before him and he received their heavy tribute. He marched to the city of Askelon and captured it in the month of Kislev. . . . He turned the city into a mound and heaps of ruins and then in the month of Sebat he marched back to Babylon.

In the seventh year, the month of Kislev, the king of Akkad mustered his troops, marched into Hatti-land, and encamped against the city of Judah and on the second day of the month of Adar he seized the city and captured the king. He appointed then a king of his own choice, received its heavy tribute, and sent them to Babylon.

Wiseman: *Chronicles of Chaldaean Kings*
(pp. 69, 73)

INSCRIPTION OF NEBUCHADNEZZAR ON THE ISHTAR GATE OF BABYLON

The two entrances having become too low because of the heightening of the street, I dug out the soil for this gate, I strengthened the foundations, on the river's side with bitumen and with baked bricks. I covered the gate with bricks of blue enamel on which were represented savage bulls and dragons. I had placed above some beams of cedar in order to cover it. I placed in the gateway doors of cedar covered with copper and some hinges and supports in bronze. I placed in the entranceway some proud bulls in bronze and angry dragons. I embellished this gate in this manner to gain the admiration of all peoples.

Rutten: *Babylone* (p. 42)

Babylon: Reconstruction of the city. From the fore-ground to the background: the bridge on the Euphrates, the city wall, the wall of the temenos, *the* ziggurat (E-temen-an-ki) *on the left, the temple of Marduk* (Esagila) *on the right, then the city proper.*

feet high, it consists of two gates, corresponding to the city's double wall. Nebuchadnezzar decorated it with enameled tiles in which blue predominates and from which there jut out friezes of dragons with serpents' heads (an animal sacred to the god Marduk), and bulls, companions of the storm-god Adad. The animals were in blue or black.

Once through the gate one found oneself on the processional road, the extension of an outside avenue, flanked by walls also decorated with enameled tiles representing lions, the sacred animal of the goddess Ishtar. Almost 3,000 feet long, this processional way was from thirty-three feet to sixty-six feet wide and was completely paved with limestone slabs sealed with bitumen. Each slab bore the following inscription: "Nebuchadnezzar, king of Babylonia, son of Nabopolassar king of Babylonia, am I. The road of Babylon I have paved with blocks of stone brought from the mountain, for the procession of the great lord Marduk. May Marduk, my lord, grant me eternal life." A pious work, but not without ulterior motive. This road began at the Ishtar gate, skirted the left side of the temple of Ninna, and the right side of the royal palace. It then led to the heart of the city, where the *ziggurat* and the temple of Marduk were situated; turning at a right angle, it passed between the two sanctuaries and ended at the bridge over the Euphrates.

The temple of Ninna, god of the infernal regions, had a classical Mesopotamian plan: vestibule, courtyard with well, ante-cella and cella. In the cella was found an elevated base evidently used for the cult statue; all around the temple were rooms that served as lodgings for the priests or as sacristies. In front of the temple, right before the entrance, was an altar.

The entrance to the royal palace was on the processional road. With a length of 1056 feet and almost 628 feet wide, this palace also adopted the typical Mesopotamian architectural pattern, with blocks of rooms surrounding courtyards. Five such blocks are set side by side. The first has been called the precinct of the royal guard; the second that of the

palace functionaries; the third housed the throne room, whose outside wall, looking out onto the courtyard, was decorated with enameled tiles with palm-tree patterns and columns surmounted by Ionic capitals and crawling lions; the last two blocks were reserved for the king's private apartments and the women's quarters. In the northeastern corner of the complex, there is a vaulted construction, 139 feet by 98 feet, closed in by a thick wall, in which fourteen halls were set along a corridor; while to the west and south lay small rooms that were annexes. This construction has been identified as the celebrated "hanging gardens," in reality terraced gardens held up by vaults. They were built by Nebuchadnezzar for the daughter of the Median king Astyages, Amiti — whom he married in order to strengthen the Median-Babylonian alliance — to remind her of the mountains and vegetation of her native land.

The *ziggurat*, called *E-temen-an-ki* ("house of the foundation of the sky and earth"), rose up in an enclosure between the processional way and the Euphrates. If the texts are to be believed, Nabopolassar personally saw to its construction: "Marduk, the lord, ordered me, as regards *E-temen-an-ki*, the step tower in Babylon that before my time had been destroyed and had fallen into ruin, to set its foundations in the heart of the infernal world and make the top resemble the sky." In order to win the god's favor, the king did not hesitate to take part in the work himself: "I took a cane and measured the dimensions [for the tower]. For Marduk, my lord, I bent my neck, took off my tunic, and

Persepolis: View of the eastern staircase of the Apadana.

carried bricks and earth on my head. As for Nebuchadnezzar, my first-born son, the dearest to my heart, I had him carry the mortar, the wine and oil offerings, just like my subjects." This *ziggurat* was a gigantic structure; an idea of its size can be given by the perimeter of the wall that surrounded it: 1332 by 1309 by 1496 by 1350 feet. As for the construction itself, it is known only through the so-called Esagil tablet, now kept at the Louvre, a tablet that is not easy to interpret. Of the actual building, which once testified to Neo-Babylonian power, there survives today only a nucleus of crude brick, surrounded by a ditch dug by those who later looked here for baked bricks with which to build their houses.

A short distance from the *ziggurat*, but outside the wall, lay the temple of Marduk, called *Esagila*, where there was a chapel consecrated to Ea, the father of Marduk, god of wisdom and medicine. It is here that one must look for the hall where Alexander the Great's generals Python and Seleucus asked the god whether they should bring their sick leader to this place.

Such was the city into which Cyrus made his peaceful entry and established "midst acclamation and joy, the seat of dominion in the Palace of Princes." As Cyrus himself says, Marduk rendered the heart of the Babylonians favorable to him, while he dedicated himself to the daily tasks of Marduk's veneration.

The Achaemenian Empire

Up to this point, Iran has been mentioned only briefly. Without underestimating either the importance of Elam in the third millennium, or Elamite power in the thirteenth and twelfth centuries B.C., it has been possible, given the limits of this volume, to mention only the events of primary importance in Middle Eastern history. It was only at

Persepolis: Eastern staircase of the Apadana. The reliefs show a procession of guards.

Following pages:
Persepolis: One of the monumental staircases of the Apadana, decorated on the inside and outside with reliefs. This is the outside of the eastern staircase, the best preserved of all. Two groups of guards, Persians and Medes alternately, face each other. This central portion also has the theme of the lion attacking the bull. In the frieze above there is a floral decoration and two winged human-headed lions on either side of the winged disc, symbol of the god Ahura-Mazda.

Persepolis: The eastern staircase of the Apadana. Detail from the reliefs, showing the royal chariot.

Persepolis: The eastern staircase of the
Apadana: Median and Persian dignitaries.
The Medes wear the dome-like headdress,
the Persions the cylindrical fretted tiara.

the end of the first half of the first millennium that Iran finally came to play a leading role. For a time, it was the very center of history, thanks to the Achaemenian dynasty.

Little is known about the early history of the Medes and Persians. The Assyrian texts of Shalmaneser III (858–824 B.C.) mention them for the first time. They were Indo-Europeans, at one time nomads, who settled on the Iranian plateau, where the Medes occupied the northern part and the Persians the southwestern part. At first simple tribes, then kingdoms, the Median dynasties were initially the stronger (their intervention in Mesopotamia has already been discussed); then the Persians gained the upper hand, thanks to Cyrus. He was probably a vassal of the Median king; rebelling, he emerged victorious over the Medes. The result was the unity of Iran and the birth of the Achaemenian dynasty, which took its name from Achaemenes, an ancestor of Cyrus. The Medes did not become vassals of the Persians. An "association on two unequal levels" was formed instead, and Medes and Persians functioned and worked side by side.

In the space of about twenty-five years, two sovereigns, Cyrus and Cambyses, built up the largest empire the Middle East had seen up to that time. Cyrus (558–530 B.C.), after unifying Iran, first conquered Lydia, then captured Babylonia and its Syrian possessions. He was received as a liberator everywhere. His generosity, his clemency toward defeated kings, his respect for the customs of the subject nations, are famous, as is the great tolerance he showed for the local religions. He restored the statues of the gods which were in captivity; he granted to the Jews the right to return to their country from Babylonia and allowed them to rebuild their temple in Jerusalem.

Cyrus was succeeded by his son Cambyses, who had already shared in the rule. Cambyses undertook the conquest of Egypt, preparation for which Cyrus had already ordered. For the first time Egypt was completely occupied by a foreign power. Upon his return from Egypt, Cambyses learned that a man pretending to be his brother Smerdes had usurped his throne; before he could do anything about it, however, he died as a result of an accident, leaving no heirs. Smerdes' rule was a brief few months; despite some popular measures he put into effect (reduction of tributes and military service), his intransigent religious views made him many enemies. A plot of the nobility put an end to his reign.

When Darius (522–486 B.C.) ascended the throne, only a few provinces recognized him as king. Two years of fighting were necessary to reestablish peace and unity in Iran. These struggles of Darius are recorded in an inscription in the rock of the mountain of Behistun, on the road connecting northwestern Iran with Mesopotamia. Not only is this the most ancient historical text left by Darius, it is also the document that helped scholars in deciphering cuneiform writing. The text is accompanied by a monumental relief, forming an immense panel fifty-nine feet wide and twenty-six feet high. In this relief two dignitaries follow Darius, who is depicted as larger than the other personages, with his left foot set on a rebel lying on the ground. In front of him other men have their hands tied behind their backs. The symbol of the Persian god Ahura-Mazda is engraved over the scene.

Once peace was reestablished in Iran, Darius reconquered the empire, subjugated some of the Aegean islands and Thrace, thus extending his conquests to Europe; but he was defeated by the Greeks at Marathon in 490 B.C. With his reign the exemplary organization associated with the Persian empire actually began. The many different populations that made up this immense kingdom preserved their institutions, languages, and religions, and enjoyed equal rights and responsibilities with the provinces of Iran — in proportion to their resources — but they were all governed by a Persian. The empire was divided into satrapies. Cyrus had created some of these, but Darius deserves credit for having extended the system; at the end of his reign there were thirty-one satrapies. Each satrapy was governed by three persons, who

Persepolis: Detail from the eastern staircase of the Apadana, showing stylized plant motifs.

Following pages:
Persepolis: The eastern staircase of the Apadana. The procession of the twenty-three nations. Separated from each other by a tree, the various delegations are introduced by an usher, alternately a Mede and a Persian.

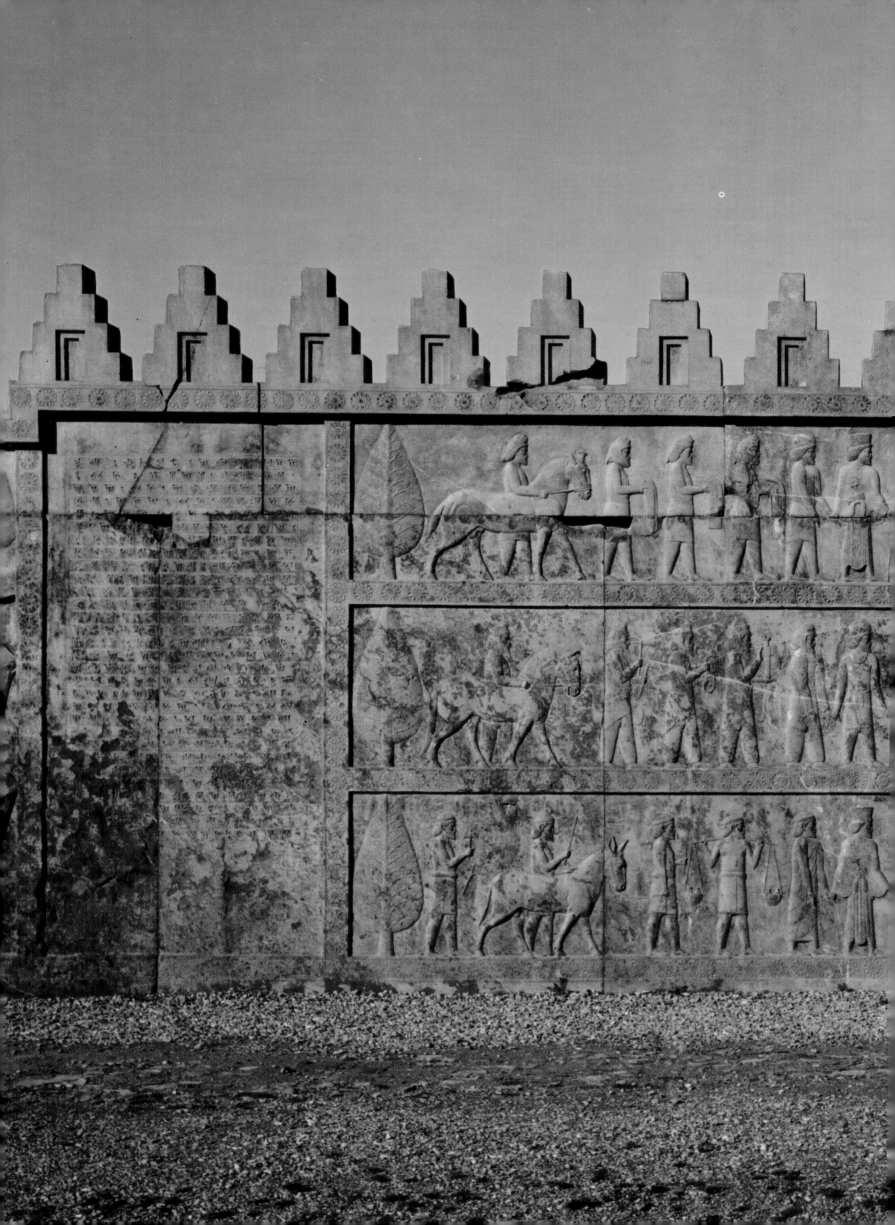

watched and checked one another. All three were chosen by the king and were directly dependent upon him. The satrap, a sort of viceroy, was normally a man of noble lineage, and sometimes even a member of the royal family, especially when the satrapy was an important one. He was appointed for an indefinite period of time, and his office could be revoked by the king. On the other hand, the office tended to become hereditary. The satrap had vast powers; he exercised legal as well as civil authority, guaranteed security, and collected the taxes fixed by royal edict. Every province was taxed according to its wealth, and the payment was made in metals. This system did not, however, exclude contributions in goods as, for example, horses and provisions of every kind for the court and troops in the region.

The Persians and Medes were exempt from taxes. Under Darius, also, silver coins were made. The satrap was aided by a treasurer, a powerful personage whose political functions were far from negligible, especially in the frontier provinces. The satrap was also helped by a secretary who answered directly to the king and who never hesitated to

Persepolis: The eastern staircase of the Apadana. The delegation from Susa, bearing a lioness and her cubs.

Following pages:
Persepolis: View of the palace of Darius, where the window and door frames, made of local limestone, are still preserved.

inform the king of the satrap's activities. To round out power and administration in each satrapy there was a commander-in-chief, who was responsible for the provincial troops. Inspectors sent by the king, called "the eyes and ears of the king" were also able to range throughout the country, thanks to a well-developed system of roads.

Besides the provincial troops, who were called up in case of war, the Achaemenians had a permanent army, composed of three corps: the cavalry, consisting of ten thousand men; the infantry, with an equal number of soldiers; and the celebrated "Immortals," the personal guard of the king, a ten-thousand-man regiment. The Achaemenian army, despite the great number of soldiers, was less efficient than it might have been. It lacked cohesion both in its arms and in its method of combat; moreover, every foreign armed corp within the army had its own way of fighting; nor did the diverse languages contribute to any unity. No truly national sentiment animated the troops.

Darius was succeeded by Xerxes I (486–465 B.C.). In his reign, revolts broke out in every part of the empire — in Iran, Egypt, and

INSCRIPTION ON FORTIFICATION WALL AT PERSEPOLIS

Great Ahuramazda, who is chief of the gods, who has established Darius as king, he has given to him the kingdom. By the favor of Ahuramazda, Darius is king.

Says Darius the king: This land Parsa, which Ahuramazda has granted me, which is beautiful, possessing good horses and good men, by the favor of Ahuramazda and of me, Darius the king, it has no fear of an enemy.

Says Darius the king: May Ahuramazda bring me help with all the other gods, and may Ahuramazda protect this land from a hostile horde, from the evildoer, and from the Lie. Against this land let them not smite, neither a hostile horde, nor an evildoer, nor the Lie! With this supplication I pray to Ahuramazda, with all the gods, this to me may Ahuramazda grant with all the gods.

I am Darius, the great king, king of kings, king of the lands numerous, son of Hystaspes, the Achaemenid.

Olmstead: *History of Persian Empire* (p. 175)

Above:
Persepolis: The staircase of the Tripylon, with reliefs of Median dignitaries.

Right:
Persepolis: The Tripylon. Persian guards armed with lances and protected by shields.

Babylonia. All were crushed with the greatest firmness by the new sovereign. Xerxes was also intransigent in the political and religious fields.

He no longer took the title of king of Babylonia and Egypt, thus giving those two nations a privileged rank; instead he divided the ancient Babylonian empire into two satrapies and destroyed the temple of Marduk at Babylon. He then resumed the expansionist war with Greece. He invaded Attica, taking Athens, which he burned. But he was defeated in the naval battle of Salamis in 480 B.C., and then on land at Platea in 479: these two blows marked the end not only of Persian influence in Europe but also the end of expansion of the empire. The kings who succeeded Xerxes were involved in court intrigues and rebellions conducted by princes and satraps. Achaemenian power declined to the point that Alexander the Great had little difficulty in defeating Darius III Codomannus at Gaugamela, not far from Nineveh, in 331 B.C. More than a military victory, Alexander's victory marked the entrance of the Occident into Eastern history.

Achaemenian Art and Architecture

Achaemenian art developed rapidly under its first kings. At first sight it seems extremely original, but upon closer examination numerous influences can be distinguished. It was evidently Mesopotamian architecture that gave the Persian architects their taste for the monumental and for terraced constructions, while in all probability Egypt inspired their columned halls. The Persians also borrowed from Egypt the molding decoration that ornaments the lower part of almost all the rooms, gates, and windows. Greek influence is equally indisputable, although much more difficult to specify. Through the report of Pliny the Elder, it is known that a certain Telephanus of Phocis worked for Darius and Xerxes; evidence of the Greek sculptor's work can be seen in the rendering of the flowing dress and in the fluting of the columns. Achaeminian architecture was above all an architecture of palaces, and this is illustrated by the constructions discovered in the three capitals of the empire: Pasargadae, where the coronation of all the kings took place; Susa, the best situated from a geographical point of view, and the political and administrative capital; and Persepolis, which, according to some scholars, was occupied only in the spring, during the New Year feasts.

Very little remains of Pasargadae: some elements from fortifications, an artificial terrace, vestiges of various palaces, a monumental entranceway decorated with winged or human-headed bulls, as well as a relief depicting a four-winged genie. Not far from these ruins is a tomb said to be that of Cyrus the Great, a simple sepulchral room set on a tall base with six steps.

In Susa the *Apadana*, or audience chamber, is worthy of mention. It was decorated with justly celebrated enameled tiles representing lions, bulls, and archers. These enamel tiles were made of a sand and lime mixture; once dried, they were baked for a short time, and the figures were then drawn with blue enamel. After a second baking process, the empty spaces were filled in with color, and finally, the last baking took place. At this point the tiles had only to be set up in order to create the decorations with the blue, white, yellow, and green tonalities that are so pleasing to the eye.

At Susa various fragments of a text written in three languages — Old Persian, Elamite, and Babylonian — have been discovered on stone

Persepolis: The hall of a hundred columns. Decoration of a door frame showing a row of Persian and Median soldiers, armed with lances and daggers and protected by shields. A floral motif separates the registers of this relief.

and on a tablet. In the text, after homage from Darius to Ahura-Mazda, the list of the king's titles, and his vocation for the royalty, there is an account of the foundation of the Susa palace. The text is important because it furnishes precious information about the materials used, where they came from, and the nations that collaborated in the building of the palace: "The cedar beams have been taken from a mountain called Lebanon. The Assyrian people brought them to Babylonia. From Babylonia, the Carians and Ionians brought them to Susa. . . . The gold was taken from Sardis, Bactria, and was worked here. The magnificent stone called lapis lazuli, and the carnelian were worked here, but were obtained from Sogdiana. The precious turquoise was obtained at Khorasnia and worked there. The silver and ebony came from Egypt. . . . The ivory, worked here, was taken from Ethiopia, Sind and Arachosia. . . . The stonecutters were from Ionia and Sardis. The goldsmiths were Medes and Egyptians. The men who worked the

Persepolis: The Tripylon. Decoration of a door. Under a canopy surmounted by the symbol of the god Ahura-Mazda, Darius and Xerxes are depicted. In the lower part of the relief, on separate registers, are the bearers of the royal platform.

baked bricks were Babylonians. The men who decorated the walls were Medes and Egyptians."

Persepolis

But it is Persepolis, the work basically of Darius and Xerxes, that is the most spectacular of the three capitals. The city is set on a mountain, and its buildings are placed on a high terrace reached by a large staircase with a double ramp of steps which has intermediate landings. Once at the top, one finds oneself facing the "Gate of Nations," built by Xerxes, a square hall over eighty-two feet on a side, its roof supported by four stone columns. This hall has three doors. The first, which faces east, is decorated with guardian bulls. Of the other two, the eastern one, decorated with human-headed bulls, leads to the hall of the

Persepolis: The hall of the hundred columns. The side of a portal, with the sculpture of a battle between the king and a lion.

Left and right:
Persepolis: Details from two zoomorphic capitals depicting a griffin (left) and a bull (right).

INSCRIPTION ON THE GATE OF XERXES AT PERSEPOLIS

A great god is Ahuramazda who created this earth, who created yonder heaven, who created man, who created welfare for man, who made Xerxes King, one king of many, one lord of many.

I am Xerxes, the great king, king of kings, king of countries possessing many kinds of people, king of this great earth far and wide, the son of Darius, the Achaemenid.

Says Xerxes the great king: By the grace of Ahuramazda, this gateway of all lands I made; much else that is beautiful was done throughout Parsa which I did and which my father did; whatever work seems beautiful, all that we did by the grace of Ahuramazda.

Says Xerxes the king: Let Ahuramazda protect me and my kingdom and what was done by me and what was done by my father, all this let Ahuramazda protect.

Schmidt: *Persepolis* (p. 65)

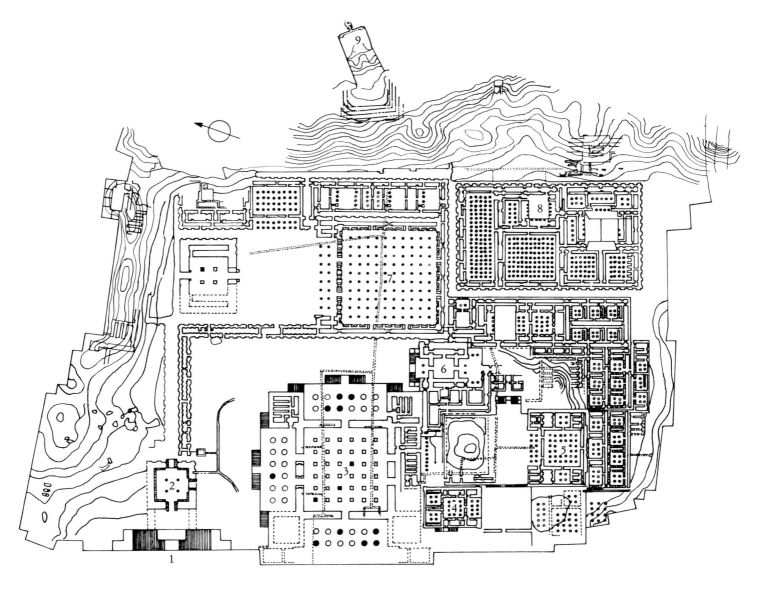

Persepolis: Plan of the terrace.
1. Access stairway
2. Gate of Xerxes, or "of nations."
3. Apadana
4. Palace of Darius
5. Palace of Xerxes
6. Tripylon
7. Hall of the hundred columns
8. Treasury
9. Tomb of Artaxerxes II

Persepolis: Palace of Xerxes. Relief showing a man carrying a kid goat.

hundred columns. The southern one, which overlooks a courtyard, leads toward the area of the *Apadana*, the audience chamber of Darius and Xerxes, and the residential palaces of Darius and Xerxes and to a group of apartments called the "*harem* of Xerxes." Finally southeast of the terrace is the treasury, an imposing complex of storerooms. The official edifices, some of which were built on a platform, all have in common a large hall with its roof supported by columns, which marked off a nave of the same width; this hall is flanked on one or more sides by columned porticoes.

Persepolis is situated near limestone quarries. Thus, although the architects used bricks for the walls, they made doors, windows, decorative niches, bases, foundations, and columns of the local limestone. The doors are decorated with reliefs. The king is shown, followed by two servants, leaving or entering a room, or seated on the throne, whose platform is held up by men representing the various nations of the empire; or the king is shown facing a lion, a bull, or some composite animal of fantastic aspect. In certain cases the king's tiara, neck, and wrists have holes in them, indicating that a gold or bejeweled covering, now missing, was once attached to the relief. The columns are set on a base that is either square or bell-shaped; the shafts are fluted and surmounted by composite capitals: bulls, human-headed bulls, horned lions, or griffins. Shafts were sometimes made of wood, plastered over and decorated with various geometric motifs.

In all this imposing architectural complex, the *Apadana* certainly deserves separate discussion. Built on a base eight and a half feet high, it is the work of Darius and Xerxes, as is confirmed by the foundation texts inscribed on gold and silver plaques found there. The main hall, its

roof supported by thirty-six columns, is 198 feet on each side. It is bordered on three sides by porticoes and flanked to the south by store-rooms. In the corners are four towers, each with a stairway to the terraced roof. To the north and east, two monumental staircases with double ramps of stairs form entrances to the construction. The stair-cases are embellished, both inside and out, with reliefs. At one time these were polychromed, a real imperial manifesto. On the center of the facade flanking an inscription there are guards, alternately Persian and Median; on each end a lion is shown attacking a bull. In the upper part

Left:
Susa: The palace of Darius. Enameled tile relief of a lion-griffin. Fifth century B.C. Length 13 feet, 9 inches; height 4 feet 6 inches. (Paris, Louvre Museum).

Susa: The palace of Darius. Enameled tile relief of the archers of the royal guard. Detail. Fifth century B.C. Height six feet. (Paris, Louvre Museum).

of the facade is the winged disc of the god Ahura-Mazda, flanked by two sphinxes and a decoration of stylized palm leaves.

On the interior of the staircases, reliefs of Persian guards formed a line of honor for those who went up the stairs. On the end wall — that is to say, on the base of the audience chamber itself — the reliefs show the procession proper: to the left, the delegations from twenty-three nations are shown, each one introduced by a Persian or Median usher. The people from Susa offer arms and lions; Babylonians present cups, cloth and buffaloes; the Lydians bring horses. On the right are the personages of the court, Persians and Medes, accompanied by horses and royal chariots. At the ends of this long three-paneled frieze there is once again the lion attacking the bull, a very ancient motif in Mesopotamian iconography, which is generally interpreted as the struggle of the forces of evil against those of good.

Aside from some topical details — a man turning to chat with another, resting his hand on his neighbor's shoulder, or two friends walking and holding hands — this decoration seems rather monotonous. Yet when this architectural complex was inhabited, there must have been a harmony between the reliefs and the scenes that were really taking place in the palace halls: the same personages depicted in the reliefs paraded back and forth, dressed in the same fashion, bearing the same objects in homage to the king, wearing the same jewels. The pieces of goldsmith's work found during excavations afford us a closer glimpse and a deeper knowledge of these objects: silver plates decorated with rosettes and ruffle designs, gold or silver rhytons ending in animal heads, vases with animal heads or winged goats, open gold armlets decorated at the end with lions or griffins.

Anyone planning to visit the palaces at Susa and Persepolis would do well to re-read the Biblical book of Esther. There is no better way to imagine the feasts that took place in those grandiose places: "In the third year of his reign [King Ahasuerus, or Artaxerxes] made a feast unto all his princes and his servants; the power of Persia and Media, the nobles and princes of the provinces, being before him; when he showed the riches of his glorious kingdom, and the honor of his excellent majesty, many days, even an hundred and fourscore days. And when these days were expired, the king made a feast unto all the people that were present in Shushan the palace, both unto great and small, seven days, in the court of the garden of the king's palace; where were white, green and blue hangings, fastened with cords of fine linen and purple to silver rings and pillars of marble: the beds were of gold and silver, upon a pavement of red, blue, white and black marble. And they gave them drink in vessels of gold (the vessels being diverse one from another), and royal wine in abundance, according to the state of the king. And the drinking was according to the law; none did compel: for so the king had appointed to all the officers of his house, that they should do according to every man's pleasure." (Esther I: 3–8).

Persian Religion and Architecture

There is little to be said about Achaemenian religious architecture, since religious architecture proper did not exist. The tower of Naqsh-i-Rustam (just north of Persepolis) must have housed a fire-worship altar, as did the similar tower at Pasargadae that is in a state of ruin; two altars at Naqsh-i-Rustam, which are perhaps from a later period, may have done the same. There is thus little to say about the religion of this period, since relevant documents are missing. It is certain that various doctrines existed, both royal and popular. There were the Magi, the traditional scholar-priests, and there was Zoroaster (or Zarathustra), the prophet-reformer.

In the official religion, the greatest (but not the only) god was Ahura-Mazda, the Creator, who demanded that men love the truth and hate lies. He is symbolically represented by a winged solar disc from which the bust of a crowned man emerges, probably in imitation of the Assyrian model. The people worshiped essentially the natural elements — water, earth, the wind, light; they also indulged in animal sacrifices, but only in the presence of the Magi. The beliefs of the Magi, of Median origin, are little known, but most certainly have very ancient roots. Their funerary customs are singular: in order not to soil the earth, they exposed corpses, offering them to dogs and birds. As for Zoroaster's doctrine, it was basically a monotheistic reform of the Iranian religion (since in fact it attempted to make Ahura-Mazda the only god). It

Susa: The palace of Darius. Enameled tile relief of a lion. Detail. Fifth century B.C. Length of entire relief 8 feet, 4 inches. (Paris, Louvre Museum).

Following pages:
Naqsh-i-Rustam: The royal Achaemenian tombs (center) of the sixth and fifth centuries B.C. and the Sassanian reliefs of the third and fourth centuries A.D.

Page 114
Naqsh-i-Rustam: Tomb of Darius and Sassanian reliefs. The relief in the lower left hand corner shows Shapur's triumph over Valerian.

THE MONUMENT OF KING DARIUS AT BEHISTUN

For this reason Ahuramazda and the other gods brought aid to me: because I was not hostile, I was not a follower of the Lie, I was not a doer of wrong — neither I nor any of my family. According to righteousness I conducted myself: neither to the weak nor to the powerful did I do wrong; the man who cooperated with my house, him I rewarded well; whoso did injury, him I grievously interrogated.

Says Darius the King: If you who behold this inscription or these scriptures shall destroy them or not protect them so long as you have strength, may Ahuramazda smite you, may you not obtain descendants, and may Ahuramazda utterly destroy for you whatever you do!

Cameron: *Archaeology* (XIII:3, pp. 163, 167)

Following page:
Behistun: Rock relief showing Darius victorious over the rebels. This relief has an accompanying text, the most ancient one concerning Darius, engraved in three languages — Old Persian, Elamite, and Babylonian — which has helped scholars to decipher ancient cuneiform characters.

enjoyed great favor, especially in the Sassanian period (A.D. 224–651), a long time after Zoroaster lived (seventh century B.C.).

Royal funerary architecture is well-known. The tomb of Cyrus at Pasargadae has already been mentioned. Darius and his successors were buried in hypogeums cut out of the mountains at Persepolis and close by at Naqsh-i-Rustam. All the sepulchers are alike and were certainly imitations of Darius's. The facade decoration is similar to a Greek cross: on the lower part a simple rectangle, then an architectural decoration (the arm of the cross) where, under a four-columned portico surmounted by capitals in the shape of animal heads, the door that gives access to the inside of the tomb is surmounted by an Egyptian type of decorative molding. In the upper part of the facade is a platform held up by twenty-eight men in two rows who represent the provinces, some of whose names are mentioned. On the stage is the king standing on a three-step base, his left hand holding a bow and his right stretched out toward an altar on which the sacred fire is burning; the symbol of Ahura-Mazda dominates the scene. The inside of the tomb includes a vestibule and a lower chamber whose soil has funerary niches cut out of it. While the other hypogeums have no inscriptions, that of Darius at Naqsh-i-Rustam bears a proud one: "Look at the image of those holding up my throne and you will understand how great a number of lands Darius the king has possessed." After such a text it is easy to understand why Darius's successors, who were unable to preserve the integrity of the empire, preferred to have no text engraved on their tombs.

THE GREAT INTERNATIONAL EMPIRES

The Breaking Up of Alexander's Empire

Having conquered the Middle East, Alexander the Great attempted to unite two worlds, the Orient and the Occident, with victors and losers working side by side, but his early death at Babylon, in 323 B.C., brought an end to this roughly sketched plan. Since his succession was scarcely guaranteed by a half-brother and by his new-born son by Roxana, the daughter of a Bactrian noble, the regency was entrusted to his general Perdiccas. But the ambition of Alexander's generals, called the Diadochi, quickly brought about the partition of the empire: Egypt went to Ptolemy, Babylonia to Seleucus, Asia Minor to Antigonus, Syria-Palestine to Laomedontus. This short-lived partition provoked only unrelenting and confused struggles among the "heirs," each of whom tried to dominate his neighbor. Twenty years after the death of Alexander, however, the political situation had been somewhat stabilized. The Middle East was then divided into two kingdoms: Egypt, governed by the Lagides, a dynasty founded by Ptolemy, son of Lagos; and Babylonia and Iran, governed by the Seleucids, a dynasty derived from Seleucus. Syria-Palestine was coveted by both kingdoms, and proved the source of almost incessant war between them.

The Seleucids, a foreign dynasty on inhospitable soil, met with numerous difficulties. These rather mediocre monarchs were unable to impose their will on their immense and scarcely homogeneous territories, which extended from the Caspian Sea to Palestine, the Persian Gulf, and Afghanistan. Nonetheless, they attempted to unify this disparate dominion by setting it up on a Hellenistic basis. To do this they created numerous cities, and populated them with Greek colonizers. In reality these were little more than Greek "islands" with little influence; many provinces and ancient satrapies soon emancipated themselves. Antiochus III, called the Great (223–187 B.C.), succeeded in rebuilding an empire as vast as that of the Achaemenians, but he was unable to stop Roman penetration of Asia Minor. Defeated by these conquerors from the west, Antiochus III was forced to accept a dictated peace at Apamea in 188 B.C.

The Seleucids were no luckier in their eastern territory, where the Iranian tribe of the Parthians, from the northeastern area of Persia, led by Arsaces, pressed them hard. Arsaces was the founder of the Parthian Arsacid dynasty and was independent from the Seleucids by 250 B.C. Caught between these two forces — the Romans and the Parthians — the Seleucids were no longer able to maintain their power. Mithridates I (174–136 B.C.), the most illustrious of the Arsacid kings and the real creator of the Parthian empire, moved to inflict a blow on the Seleucids from which they never recovered. He conquered the western regions of Iran up to the Persian Gulf, took Babylon, and established his capital at Ctesiphon, near Baghdad.

Somewhat later the Romans, under Pompey, took Damascus (64 B.C.) and settled in Palestine (63 B.C.), inflicting the *coup de grâce* to the Seleucids, with the result that two new forces faced each other — the Romans and the Parthians.

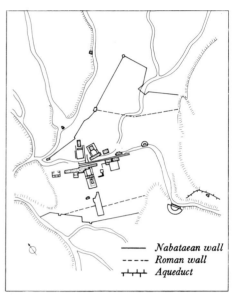

— Nabataean wall
----- Roman wall
┼┼┼┼ Aqueduct

Petra: Plan of the archaeological site.

INSCRIPTION ON A TOMB
AT PETRA

This tomb, its large room and the small room in the interior, with the sculptures that have been cut out in the form of ash-niches, the enclosure that is in front of the tomb, the gateways, the ditches that are here, the gardens, the banquet couch, the water cisterns, the terrace, the walls, and everything else contained in this place, is sacred and the inviolable possession of Dushara, the god of our Lord and his throne and all the gods, in their records relating the sacred things and according to their contents. And this is the order of Dushara and his throne and all the gods, that according to what is said in the records relating sacred matters, it must be done and nothing must be changed, nothing must be altered of all that is contained here and nothing should be removed from this tomb; in the name of him to whom this tomb has been granted, let this be forever inscribed, in the words required for acrsed affairs.

Corpus Inscriptionum Semiticarum (II, 350)

Petra: The tomb "of the obelisks."

The Parthians reigned over Iran and Babylonia from about 250 B.C. to A.D. 224, without ever moving beyond the western bank of the Euphrates. Numerous vassal kingdoms were included in this vast empire, such as Hatra in northern Mesopotamia. The Romans attempted many times to conquer the Parthians, but were disastrously defeated in 53 B.C. at Carrhae, where the army of Crassus was severely beaten and he himself was killed. After the numerous setbacks suffered by Mark Antony, Augustus, much wiser, decided to negotiate a peace treaty, which was respected for over a century. Trajan took up the offensive once again, and successfully took Ctesiphon (A.D. 115–116), but the many revolts which broke out in both Babylonia and Iran caused his successor, Hadrian, to abandon Mesopotamia. The Parthians, in turn, attacked. Vologases III (148–192) invaded Armenia, Cappadocia, and Syria. Marcus Aurelius reacted, and Ctesiphon was again conquered by the Romans. Conflicts continued, however, until a peace was made in 219, recognizing Parthian superiority in the area. At this juncture, a revolt broke out in the southeastern part of Iran, and Ardashir, grandson of Sassan, the high priest in the temple of Anahita at Ishtakhr, rose up against his lord, the Parthian king Artabanus V, whom he defeated and killed in 224. Ardashir was the first of the dynasty called the Sassanian whose power lasted until 651.

It was in this historic setting that the cities of Petra and Palmyra flourished and then disappeared. They were caravan track cities, and they had a similar fate. Both were the seats of local dynasties subject to

Left:
Petra: Entrance to the Sik, the long gorge, a mile and a quarter in length, which leads to the city.

Above:
Petra: In the Sik. In the background, visible between the two walls, is the Khazneh Firaun.

Right:
Petra: The theater, with thirty-four rows of seats cut from the rock.

Rome, Petra by A.D. 106, Palmyra by A.D. 272. Both occupied key geographical positions: Petra at the crossroads of two tracks, one between Syria and the Red Sea and the other between the Mediterranean and the Persian Gulf, while Palmyra lay on the axis which led from the Mediterranean to the Persian Gulf, across the Syrian desert. Both secured the transport of such goods as Persian Gulf pearls, spices, and perfumes from the Indies, silk from China — all highly prized by the Mediterranean Romans.

Petra

Petra, situated in the desert, in the heart of a rocky, almost impregnable massif, at first belonged to the territory of Edom, which the Nabataeans, coming from Arabia, conquered probably around the fifth century B.C. The defeat of two expeditionary corps sent by Antigonus, one of Alexander's successors, in 321 B.C., is the first certain historic fact concerning the city; but not until the date of 100 B.C. is it possible to record the names of the Nabataean sovereigns. The power they wielded was undeniable, since they even occupied Damascus. Rome at first negotiated with the Nabataean king and then, as Ammianus Marcellinus put it: "Trajan forced Arabia to submit to our laws, having often subdued the arrogance of the inhabitants when he victoriously repelled the Medes and Persians." Annexed to the province of Syria and shortly afterward to that of Arabia, Petra was no longer

Following pages:
Petra: The Khazneh Firaun, one of the most beautiful tombs in the city, perhaps that of king Aretas IV.

considered as a caravan track city, but it remained an important place, as is confirmed by Hadrian's visit there in A.D. 130 and by numerous monuments that date from the period of the Roman Antonine emperors.

Forgotten for many centuries, Petra was discovered in 1812 by Jean-Louis Burckhardt, an eccentric Swiss explorer and Orientalist converted to Islam, who visited it in particularly risky circumstances: "I found myself defenseless in the heart of the desert where no visitor had ever passed before, and a close examination of those 'works of the infidels,' as they are called, would have aroused the suspicion that I was a wizard, a treasure-hunter." Despite his brief exploration Burckhardt immediately understood the importance of the site: "Future travelers will be able to visit the place . . . and then the antiquities of Wadi Musa will be recognized as worthy of standing among the most curious remains in ancient art."

In the twentieth century there is little danger in the trip, but a visit to Petra never fails to arouse profound emotion. After a few hours' journey by car through the desert of Moab and Edom, one enters a rocky path on foot; then there suddenly appears the entrance of the Sik, a gorge cut out by the Wadi Musa. After implacable desert sun, there is only the half-light of a tortuous gorge flanked by magnificent rocks over 160 feet high, in certain places so narrow that two horses cannot pass through it. One continues in this manner for about a mile, a bit worried, as the end does not seem to be any nearer, when a vertical ray of light shows a monument nearby, the *Khazneh Firaun*, which one faces a few moments later. The gorge continues, now wider, and the more abundant light allows one to admire the rose, mallow, violet, and marble hues of the stone. There are many tombs, and then the great theater, in which the thirty-four rows of steps cut from the rock could seat many thousands of spectators.

Finally one reaches a large open space surrounded by cliffs; here the city itself rose up. Of its habitations and its temples, baths, palaces, nympheums, marketplaces, gymnasium, and monumental gate, there remain only the ruins of a sanctuary with a portico made up of two doors and four columns, and an isolated column that is the last vestige of the palace.

Fortunately the funerary architecture is intact and plentiful. The vast amphitheater of Petra, in fact, contains hundreds of tombs. These are hypogeums, cut from the rock, whose inner chambers have both compartments in various forms, and graves cut into the floor. The outside decoration is varied: the most common represents bulls surmounted by one or two rows of crenellations. But there are also facades that imitate public buildings; this is the case with one three-storied tomb, reminiscent of some Parthian architecture. However, the most beautiful tombs of all are the tomb-temples, given this name because their facades evoke sacred architecture.

The most celebrated of these is the *Khazneh Firaun*, "Pharaoh's treasure," whose terminal urn the Arabs once thought contained treasure. Therefore, as certain nineteenth century travelers recounted, "every once in a while they pass by in the gorge, stop for a moment, load their rifles, take aim at the urn and try to knock off a piece of it so as to break it and take out its treasure." This mausoleum, which perhaps belonged to king Aretas IV, has a two-storied facade; the lower part resembles a temple entrance with portico, the upper part represents a *tholos* surrounded by peristyle with its roof sloping outward. Sculptured decoration completed the monument: in the lower part, statues of the Dioscuri; in the upper part, Amazons and Victories; the center of the *tholos* was decorated with the image of Fortuna.

Another celebrated hypogeum is the *Ed-Deir* ("the monastery"), built in a style like that of the *Khazneh Firaun*, but more sober. This tomb got its name from the belief that in the Byzantine period it served as a church for monks who lived in Petra.

One cannot leave Petra without having visited the "high place," an open air sanctuary, perhaps dedicated to Dusares, the chief god in the Nabataean pantheon, which once again demonstrates man's preference

Petra: A three-storied tomb whose facade imitates that of a palace.

PETRA AS DESCRIBED BY A
FIRST-CENTURY B.C. PHILOSOPHER

The metropolis of the Nabataeans is called Petra and extends across a flat and uniform terrain, but it is completely surrounded by steep and precipitous rocks that defend it; within the interior abundant sources of water assure food and gardens. Outside this enclosure, it is virtually desert everywhere, notably in the direction of Judea.

Athenodorus (XIV: 4, 21)

for worshiping the gods in an elevated place, whether it be artificial or natural. The "high place" in Petra rises up on one of the natural high points of the city and everything there has literally been "torn" from the rock: the two obelisks at the entrance of the sacred area, the courtyard, the altar, the sacrificial table, the basin for ablutions, and the cavity for libations.

Palmyra

An oasis in the desert, thanks to the Efqa spring, Palmyra was at first a mere village, mentioned for the first time in cuneiform texts dating from the beginning of the second millennium B.C. Its favorable geographic position and the importance of trade relations between the Mediterranean, the Indies, and China, caused its transformation into a metropolis in the Hellenistic period. Once it became independent, it remained so until 41 B.C., when Mark Antony raided it, in an attempt to bolster his finances. The raid had a poor result, as Appian records: "Antony sent his knights to Palmyra, a city situated near the Euphrates, with the order to sack it. . . . Antony intended to make money for his knights. But the Palmyrans found out about his plans; they crossed the Euphrates with all their possessions and as a precautionary measure posted archers along the river bank. These were highly skilled shooters. The knights burst into an abandoned city; they returned empty-handed and without striking a blow."

Palmyra later became a tributary of Rome, under Tiberius; but it was made a free city again by Hadrian, and became a full-fledged Roman colony under Caracalla. Under the Antonine (A.D. 117–193) and Severian (193–235) emperors, Palmyra's power — especially its economic power — reached a peak, partly because of the favor of the Roman rulers and partly because Petra was no longer important for caravan traffic. Side by side with the economic development of the city there was intense architectural activity. A great number of buildings went up, and Palmyra took on the aspect of a Greco-Roman city. Its main artery was a great colonnade that crossed the town from east to west. The colonnade, whose impressive ruin can still be seen, is bordered by porticoes, whose columns display a characteristic touch of Palmyran architecture: a third of the way up corbels jut out. On these were set statues of city dignitaries; unfortunately none of the bronze statues has been preserved. The great artery ends at the western point with a funerary temple; at the eastern point with a monumental arch, the starting place for another colonnade that leads to the temple of Bel. Along its course, the second colonnade is cut into by a double arch, which serves as an intersection or connection point with a transverse road that leads to the Agora. Not far from this double arch are the two columns whose corbels held the statues of Zenobia, Palmyra's "most illustrious and pious queen," and of Odenathus, "king of kings, corrector of the East."

Through careful town-planning, the public monuments are concentrated in the area that extends from the monumental arch to the double arch. To the north are the baths, preceded by a platform that, crossing the portico, communicates directly with the colonnade. The baths are a magnificent construction in which the separate rooms — the frigidarium, tepidarium, caldarium, gymnasium, and various courtyards (some with pool or basin) — have been recognized. South of the colonnade, and near to each other, are the theater and the senate house, a small edifice with a columned courtyard and a hall with semicircular stairs, whose modest size seems to indicate that there were only a few senators, the "municipal councillors" of the city, who legislated with an autonomy that varied according to the relations Palmyra maintained with Rome.

Not far from the Senate is the Agora or public plaza, of quadrangular shape, surrounded by a portico whose corbeled columns held

Palmyra: Panorama of the city. In the background, from left to right, are the temple of Baalshamin, the monumental arch, and the temple of Bel.

PALMYRA AS VIEWED BY A FIRST-CENTURY ROMAN

Palmyra is a city remarkable for its location, the richness of its soil, and the pleasure of its waters. On all sides, the sands surround the oasis, and nature screens it from the rest of the world.

Pliny the Elder: *Natural History* (V:88)

PALMYRA AS VIEWED BY AN EIGHTEENTH-CENTURY ENGLISHMAN

In this vale, to our right and left, were several square towers of a considerable height, which upon a nearer approach we found were the sepulchers of the ancient Palmyrenes. We had scarce passed these venerable monuments, when the hills opening discovered to us, all at once, the greatest quantity of ruins we had ever seen, all of white marble, and beyond them, towards the Euphrates a flat waste, as far as the eye could reach, without any object which showed either life or motion.

Robert Wood: *The Ruins of Palmyra* (1753)

statues of dignitaries. To the north were the statues of Roman and Palmyran functionaries; to the west those of the military, who played an important part in both the local militia and the auxiliary contingents of the Roman army. On the south side, the statues honored the chiefs of the caravans, while the eastern side was reserved for the senators. This center of Palmyran public life was decorated with fountains. There is a foundation that perhaps corresponds to a stand for speeches and addresses.

Not far from the Agora is a banquet hall with benches, altar and fire-sacrifice altar, used for the liturgical meals of the religious fraternities. Those invited to the meals or to the distribution of food that followed

Palmyra: The colonnade that crosses the city. On the hill behind are the ruins of an Arab castle.

the sacrifices were allowed in upon presentation of a "membership card." This was a small terra-cotta tablet that bore on one side the image of the donor, and on the other the ration offered or the representation of the god to be honored — an ancient version of an admission ticket.

The habitations must have been set together in the western part of the city. There is also an important construction in the southwestern zone that remains enigmatic. According to certain scholars this is the palace of the Palmyran princes, which has not otherwise been recognized and identified in the city interior. The excavations now under way (conducted by the Poles) will probably shed light on this problem.

If the number (about sixty) of the indigenous and foreign (Arab or Babylonian) gods mentioned in the dedications or represented on the monuments — all of whom make up the rather syncretistic pantheon of Palmyra — is considered, the number of temples found up to the present is still quite small. In fact, apart from various halls reserved for ritual banquets, each one connected to the sacred edifices, only three sanctuaries warrant discussion in any detail. One dedicated to Nabo, the "good dispenser of rewards," was discovered recently near the great colonnade and the monumental arch. Another one, the home of Baalshamin, "lord of the skies," known since the journey to Palmyra made by Robert Wood in 1751, was excavated only a short time ago by a Swiss mission, which brought to light — besides the cella — courtyards and various halls. One of these halls has been identified as the banquet hall, further confirmation of the importance the meals had in the cult ceremonies at Palmyra.

But the most important monument is still the temple of Bel, the main divinity in the pantheon. Its architecture perfectly reveals the composite character of Palmyran civilization, which at first sight may seem to be entirely Greco-Roman, but which also has an important Semitic element. This Greco-Roman sanctuary is in fact set over a Semitic foundation. After passing through the *propylaeum*, or monumental entranceway, on the western side (which was transformed in the twelfth century A.D. by a bastion), one enters a vast courtyard (656 feet by 672 feet), paved with monumental slabs and surrounded by a double portico. At the center is the temple. In front and to the left of it there is

Palmyra: The monumental arch that marks the end of the great colonnade to the west and the beginning of the colonnade that leads to the temple of Bel.

Palmyra: The "valley of tombs," situated outside the city walls.

Palmyra: Plan of the city.
1. *Great colonnade*
2. *Funerary temple*
3. *Double arch*
4. *Temple of Bel*
5. *Agora*
6. *Theater*
7. *Temple of Baalshamin*
8. *Camp of Diocletian*
9. *Aqueduct*
10. *Reinforced wall*
11. *Valley of tombs*
12. *Efqa spring*
13. *Arab castle*

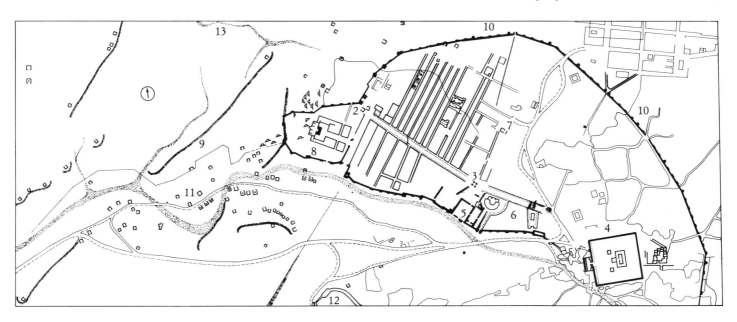

Above:
Jerash: The ruins of the nympheum, which was also a monumental fountain fed by an aqueduct.

Opposite page: Above:
Jerash: The temple of Artemis.

Below left:
Jerash: The oval forum and the main road. In the background (left), the temple of Artemis.

Below right:
Jerash: The monumental entrance to the temple of Artemis.

a large altar for sacrifices; not far away is the exit passage for a ramp passing under the western portico used to bring sacrificial animals to the altar. To the right is a ritual basin, used both for the priests' ablutions and for the maintenance of the cult instruments. Erected on a base, the sanctuary is surrounded by a peristyle of fluted columns with Corinthian capitals made of gilded bronze, of which only the core of stone remains; a row of crenellations crowns the roof. This temple has some elements unusual in sacred Greco-Roman architecture: the door opens on a long side; inside, on the short sides, two raised niches, like tabernacles, open out, one opposite the other. Their facades are decorated with inserted columns; the northern niche has a ceiling in the form of a cupola, decorated with the bust of the god Bel, representations of the various planets, and signs of the zodiac.

Besides its sacred and secular architecture, Palmyra is rich in funerary architecture. An open city, with no natural defenses, it was protected by a wall reinforced with square or round bastions. Outside the wall are the necropolises that further attest to the opulence of the city — if there were any further need of such proof. There is a great variety of tomb types. Individual tombs are marked by a simple stele that sometimes bears the representation of the dead person and always has his name followed by the exclamation "Alas!" The collective tombs consist

THE GREAT INTERNATIONAL EMPIRES 133

Baalbek: View of the ruins of the temples of Jupiter Heliopolitanus and Bacchus. The latter is now thought to have been consecrated to Atargatis, goddess counterpart of Jupiter, rather than to the god of wine.

Following pages:
Baalbek: The great courtyard of the temple of Jupiter.

LETTER FROM QUEEN ZENOBIA TO EMPEROR AURELIAN

Zenobia, queen of the East, to Aurelian Augustus: Never has anyone dared to demand that which your letter asks. Courage must decide everything in a war. You desire that I yield, as if you were not aware that Queen Cleopatra preferred to die rather than to be indebted to a master for her life and whatever honors followed. We are unceasingly awaiting the certain aid of the Persians. We have on our side the Saracens and the Armenians. Various brigands from Syria have beaten your army. Aurelian, what will become of you then once we have the reinforcements that are coming to us from all sides? Indeed, you will then abandon your proud tone with which you demand my surrender, as though your armies were everywhere victorious.

Gage: *La montée des Sassanides* (p. 355)

of tomb-towers, tomb-houses, or subterranean hypogeums. The tomb-tower is quite common. It is a heavy square construction, which can be as much as five stories high, furnished with rows of superimposed compartments, each of which is closed by a slab decorated with the bust of the deceased. Several hundred people could have been buried in these collective tombs. Of less expensive construction, the house-tomb is rather like the cella of a temple. In the numerous subterranean tombs, an inclined ramp normally led to a stone door, which was surmounted by a slab bearing a text noting the tomb's foundation. The interior was normally a simple vaulted corridor, often built in the form of a "T"; the walls of the corridor were divided by arches perforated with compartments. One of the most celebrated of this type of tomb is the one called "the three brothers," which is decorated with wall paintings. These family hypogeums did not always belong to one family alone. In fact, it is not unusual to find inscriptions that state an unused part of the tomb was given to another family.

At the end of the Severian dynasty, Rome, torn by external strife and threatened by the barbarians, suffered a diminution of its power. This weakening of Rome's sway corresponded with the growing power of a Palmyrian family of Arab origin, that of Odenathus, who received the title of Roman senator. After the Sassanians defeated the Romans at Edessa, his son Odenathus II remained faithful to the Roman emperor Valerian; he even challenged Shapur, the Sassanian king and inflicted considerable losses on him. Nominated "corrector of all the East" by the emperor Gallienus, Odenathus II proclaimed himself "king of kings." He conducted two more campaigns against the Persians, but then, while going to Cappadocia to stop the Goths, he was assassinated, together with his eldest son. His wife Zenobia lost no time in taking over the reins of power. Her son, Wahballat, was too young to reign.

It is difficult to judge the actions of Zenobia, a woman whose life almost immediately became a legend. Her conquest of Egypt and Asia Minor may have been merely coincidental to her ambition, but it might also have been the wise decision of a great strategist, who understood the profound change that had taken place in the balance of power in the Middle East after the Roman defeat at Edessa. Zenobia may have thought that the only way to save Palmyra — whose source of income (trade) was threatened by the shifting of the east-west trade route to the north — was to make it the center of imperial power. The emperor Aurelian swiftly put an end to this imperialistic design, however. He besieged Palmyra and after prolonged resistance the city surrendered. Zenobia attempted to escape to the Euphrates, but was taken prisoner. At first, Palmyra was spared, but when it revolted and the Roman garrison was massacred, Aurelian returned to burn and sack the city. Aurelian found it necessary to justify himself for his victory over Zenobia: "I understand, conscript fathers, that it will be held against me, as an action unworthy of a man, for having triumphed over Zenobia. But even those who now censure me would not refuse me their eulogies if they knew what kind of a woman they were talking about; if they knew her prudence in giving advice, her perseverance in discussions, her resoluteness toward her soldiers, her generousness when the occasion demanded it, her severity when circumstances necessitated it." Zenobia took part in the triumphal procession in 274, and ended her life "like a Roman lady of rank," but Palmyra never recovered from the disaster it had suffered.

Jerash

Petra and Palmyra were only two of the many Greco-Roman period cities that rose on Middle Eastern soil. Among the others, Jerash, Baalbek, and Tyre are well preserved, and remain quite eloquent in their effects. Once a city of Decapolis, the Syrian federation, Jerash is north of present-day Amman. Its period of splendor was the third century A.D. The city was then entirely surrounded by an irregular

Above:
Baalbek: Decoration on one of the two basins of the grand court of the temple of Jupiter.

Left:
Baalbek: Detail of the niches that give rhythm to the north and south walls of the great courtyard of the temple of Jupiter.

Baalbek: Plan of the temple complex.

1. *Propylaeum*
2. *Hexagonal ante-courtyard*
3. *Great courtyard*
4. *Altars*
5. *Basins*
6. *Temple of Jupiter*
7. *Temple of Bacchus*
8. *Arab gallery*
9. *Arab tower*

Page 140:
Baalbek: The six columns of the temple of Jupiter that are still standing.

Page 141:
Baalbek: Temple of Jupiter. A fragment of the frieze; the head of a lion also serves as a gutter spout.

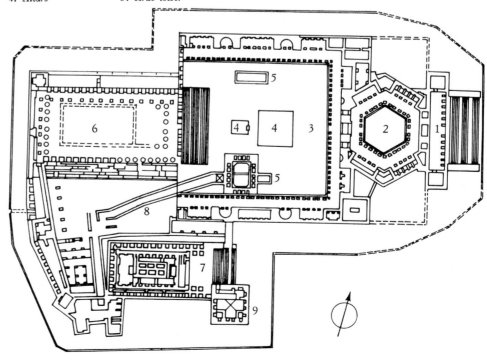

wall, reinforced by towers in which, to the north and south, there were two gates connected by a straight colonnaded road flanked by shops. Two double arches mark the intersections of the road with the eastern and western arteries. Interestingly enough, the forum — in a Roman city normally situated at the intersection of the main north-south and east-west roads — is found near the southern gate. It is surrounded by a colonnade and has an unusual elliptical shape. Between the two double arches that mark off the center of the city are amassed various thermae and a nympheum, whose monumental fountain was fed by an aqueduct and whose two floors are decorated differently — the first floor with marble and the second with painted plaster. A semi-dome covers the edifice. A very beautiful temple preceded by a *propylaeum* was consecrated to Artemis. The city also had two theaters, one to the north, not far from the temple of Artemis, and the other to the south near a temple dedicated to Zeus. Outside the city wall, and south of the city, there was a stadium where athletic events took place, and an arch of triumph with three barrel-vaults, which commemorated Hadrian's visit in A.D. 139–140.

Baalbek

At the foot of the western slope of the Anti-Lebanon mountains at the the edge of the Beqaa plain, in a splendid setting, lies Baalbek, the center of the cult of Jupiter Heliopolitanus. Of the ancient city, surrounded by a pentagonal wall with five gates, only the acropolis and

Baalbek: Reconstruction of the temples of Jupiter (right) and Bacchus (left).

Right:
Baalbek: Temple of Bacchus, now attributed to Atargatis.

Page 144
Baalbek: Temple of Bacchus. The peristyle: a detail of the coffered ceiling.

Page 145:
Baalbek: Temple of Bacchus. The entrance portal.

the temple complex, a colossal group dominated by the temple of Jupiter, have been preserved.

The construction of the temples was not only a work of piety, it had important political motives underlying it as well. Rome was engaged in continual war in the Middle East, threatened on its frontiers by the barbarians and disturbed by the development of Christianity. Rome thus undertook the construction of the temples as a means of giving prestige to its military presence in the east. Work began under Antoninus Pius (A.D. 138–181), was continued by Septimus Severus (193–211), and was finished by Caracalla (211–217).

The entrance to the sanctuary consecrated to Jupiter is marked off by a monumental staircase that gives access to the *propylaeum*, preceded by a portico framed by two towers. Three doors, whose raised thresholds emphasize the boundary between the sacred and the secular, lead to a hexagonal ante-courtyard decorated by a portico and four *exedrae*, each of which is preceded by four columns. To the west, three doors communicate with the courtyard proper, an immense open space (443 feet by 370 feet) decorated on three sides (south, east, and north) by *exedrae*, alternately rectangular and semicircular, among which there are niches for statues. Along these three sides there also ran a colonnade. In the middle of the courtyard are the two altars used for worship: one was reserved for the priests; the other, erected on an enormous base with sides over sixty-five feet long and more than fifty-five feet high, was used for public ceremonies and was accessible to pilgrims. On both sides two oblong basins, one of which was richly decorated with Tritons, Nereids, Medusa heads, Cupids riding on dolphins, and genies bearing garlands. To the west, a majestic staircase led to the temple of Jupiter, which dominated the courtyard from a height of twenty-three feet. The temple (288 feet by 56 feet) was built on a base and surrounded by a portico. Only six columns of the south side remain of this grandiose architecture; they are surmounted by a frieze ornamented with bulls and lions and a frame in which lions' heads served as gargoyles.

Next to the temple of Jupiter, but independent from it, lies the so-called temple of Bacchus; today it is thought that the sanctuary was dedicated to Atargatis, Jupiter's female counterpart. Less grandiose than the other temple, but nonetheless imposing (226 feet by 118 feet), this smaller temple was built on a podium. A thirty-three-step stairway divided into three ramps led to the *pronaos* with fluted columns, then to the cella through a majestic portal (42 feet by 24 feet), with jambs decorated with vine-leaves, poppies, and ivy; the architrave had an eagle that held a caduceus in his talons and garlands holding up genies in his beak. The cella is decorated with fluted columns and niches with rectangular and semicircular pediments, and ends with the "holy of holies" (the innermost sacred chamber) preceded by a staircase. The temple is surrounded by a peristyle where at certain points there is still a splendid coffered ceiling richly sculptured and embellished with groups of gods: Mars, Diana, Victory, Bacchus, and others. Not far from these grandiose temples, on a podium surrounded by a colonnade, is the enchanting circular sanctuary consecrated to Venus, a temple of much more human proportions.

Tyre and Dura-Europos

Tyre, also in Phoenician territory, was a celebrated city long before Roman times. Its thirteen-year-long resistance to the assaults of Nebuchadnezzar's armies, and its surrender to Alexander the Great

Tyre: **Remains of a colonnade of the Roman period. First to third centuries A.D.**

Following pages:
Tyre: **The baths of the Roman era.**

after a seven years' siege, were famous. What is now being brought to light is really from the period of the city's decadence after centuries of its indigenous prosperity and glory — the monuments of the Roman era: an arena, thermae, a marketplace, a gymnasium, a hippodrome and a road highlighted by a monumental arch, flanked by tombs and sarcophagi, and set off to the south by an aqueduct. All this is nothing compared to the prosperity and splendor of what had been one of the greatest ports in the Mediterranean world.

The number of cities built on Middle Eastern soil in the Greco-Roman period is truly impressive. Many could be mentioned but there is space to discuss only the most important or representative. Among those not yet noted, but one of the most significant, was Dura-Europos, founded during the Seleucid period and utterly destroyed by the Persians in 256 B.C. Situated on the edge of the rocks that dominate the Euphrates, it was both a trade center and a military outpost, inhabited by a very mixed population that included worshipers of numerous religions, a fact testified to by the temple "to the gods of Palmyra," the Christian chapel, the synagogue, and the underground sanctuary consecrated to the god Mithras.

Parthians and Sassanians

It is a difficult task to define the Parthian civilization, since original texts are lacking, and those of the Roman and Greek historians and geographers furnish very little information. However, it is possible to understand its institutions and beliefs by referring to those of the Sassanians, who most certainly retained much of their predecessors' way of life. For this reason the two civilizations are considered together here.

Parthian art also poses many problems. For a long time it was considered a local expression of Greco-Roman art, yet more is being discovered every day of the force and influence Parthian art had on Sassinian art. Daniel Schlumberger, in a recent work, calls it an original "Hellenistic type" of art that originated in Mesopotamia and then spread out toward East and West. The sculpture in the round or in relief, of rock or other materials, is characterized by a rigid frontal attitude that preserves "an archaic sentiment of the 'presence' of the frontal figure." Parthian architecture, known above all through monuments in Mesopotamia, also has original features. The plan of its buildings was profoundly changed thanks to the invention of the *iwan*, a large rectangular room entirely open on one of its shorter sides and covered with a vault.

The vault is not a Parthian creation — in fact, it was already in use in the ancient Middle East — but the Parthians were the first to use it to cover large spaces. As the Parthians were originally nomads, it is reasonable to suppose that the *iwan* got its inspiration from the tent of their ancestors, which was always open on one side. The invention enjoyed great favor during the Sassanian and Islamic periods that followed the Parthians. The decoration of the edifices, although inspired by Greece, is peculiar as it does not emphasize the architecture, but rather masks it. Plaster was much used and was to be used even more by the Sassanians.

Not many Parthian monuments are presently known. Of the examples in Iran, there is little to say. The most beautiful architectural specimens of this period are in Mesopotamia — especially at Ashur and Hatra. The Parthian and Sassanian capital, Ctesiphon, has not yet revealed anything related to this period. At Ashur many temples were discovered, grouped around the same place where the earlier Assyrian sanctuaries were found; these are colonnaded temples of Greek inspiration, or temples that resemble the sacred architecture of the Babylonians. The Parthian palace excavated by the German mission reveals a mixture of these diverse influences. The open air courtyards

OLD ARABIC SONG

Do you not see Hatra whose inhabitants lived in prosperity?
But he who is happy — is he also eternal?
Sapor al-Djanoud attacked the city; during two years he dug up the earth.
But his God did not add anything to his forces and he was not able to equal his adversary.
And when his Master saw how affairs went, Then he fell upon him and he was not avenged.
The cry of the people was: To your duty! It is written!
Die courageously with your swords!
I see that he who is brave courts death.
  Gage: *La montée des Sassanides* (p. 223)

Hatra: One of the entrance gates to the sanctuary.

surrounded by chambers, the outside false facades, the single access —
all are evidently typical of Mesopotamian custom; but the entranceway
— a large room in peristyle form — resembles Greek architecture. A
more distinctive note is given by the various *iwan* and by a room with
pillars that support a vault. The decoration of the facades that frame
the *iwan* also are a novelty, not because of its elements (pillars, columns
that support the lintels, niches distributed on various levels) nor because of the decorative motifs (tendrils, foliage, Greek frets), but rather
because of its proportions, more slender than those of the Greco-
Roman world, and the fact that the ornamental themes are treated in
rather low relief.

Hatra

Hatra, about thirty-one miles west of Ashur, was also an important
city during the Parthian era. Its origins are unknown; it was the seat of
a local dynasty that recognized the dominion of the Parthians. Early
second century A.D. texts record that it was besieged many times by the
Romans — in 117 by Trajan, in 200 and 201 by Septimus Severus —
but the Roman assaults were thwarted every time. Dion Cassius states
that the inhabitants "cast bottles of burning oil, crossbow arrows, and
jars full of scorpions at the aggressors." Later, when menaced by the
Sassanians, the kings of Hatra established ties with Rome. But the
Sassanian Shapur I took the city around 250; according to the Arab
historian Tabari, this conquest took place only after a siege that lasted
four years and thanks to the treachery of the king's daughter. The city
was later abandoned.

According to some scholars Hatra was a caravan route city; according to others, it was first of all a holy city — "Hatra of Shamash," as it
is called on the coins. Its commercial activity was considerable, in any
case, thanks to the pilgrims who visited the sanctuaries there. The city
is surrounded by two concentric circular walls. The outside wall perhaps protected only the suburbs and gardens, the resting place of the
nomads; the inside wall, reinforced by towers and having four gates,
was the bastion proper of the city. In the heart of the latter enclosure
wall there is a rectangular open space (1608 feet by 984 feet) marked off
by a wall: the "enclosure of Shamash." An interior wall divides this
area into an ante-courtyard and a courtyard. In the former a temple
was built, with a double colonnade of Hellenistic type surrounding it.
In the latter there is a large edifice, once thought to be a palace and
today considered a sanctuary, consisting of many flanking *iwan*, one of

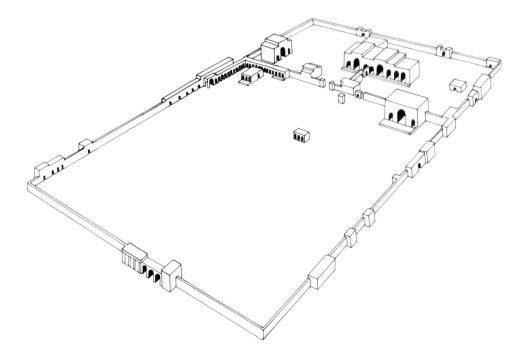

*Hatra: Reconstruction of the so-called Shamash
enclosure. The inner wall divides the enclosure into
an ante-courtyard and a courtyard. In the latter is the
sanctuary consisting of many iwan set next to each
other.*

**Hatra: Detail from the wall decoration of
the sanctuary.**

which leads to the sanctuary proper, a square vaulted room surrounded by a vaulted corridor. The decoration is quite sober — merely some columns and masks.

The temples found in the "enclosure of Shamash" were not the only sacred edifices in Hatra. Others — ten up to the present time — have been discovered outside this zone, no longer isolated but rather set between the houses of the notables and bourgeois of the city. The plan

Hatra: Detail of the outside wall of the sanctuary.

of these sanctuaries follows Mesopotamian tradition: preceding the cella is an oblong room, a sort of ante-cella whose dimensions vary; it may be a simple niche set in front of the entrance or an independent room that juts out. Some temples include additional rooms, probably used by the priests.

All these sanctuaries have yielded a great abundance of sculpture: reliefs, often adorned with paintings; and statues of the gods in the round, reminiscent, in some aspects, of Greek gods; statues of the kings of Hatra, of princesses, priests, generals, all in an attitude of prayer, their right hand raised and opened out. Some statues have been identified by inscriptions; two give the name of the sculptor. All have a rigid frontal attitude and a careful rendering of hair, beards, and clothes — a typically Iranian treatment that is also a characteristic of work of the Sassanian period.

The Sassanians and Their Army

During the entire course of its history, the Parthian dynasty was involved in a struggle with Rome. The fall of this Iranian dynasty was, however, due to a local rebellion which originated in the southwestern region of the country and brought a new Iranian dynasty to power: the Sassanians (A.D. 224–640).

The history of the Sassanian dynasty is marked by conflicts: with the eastern kingdoms of the Kushans and the Ephthalites; and in the west, first with Rome and then with Byzantium. The areas of this last struggle were Armenia and northern Mesopotamia, which fell alternately under the yoke of each western power. During the course of these bitterly fought wars — there were rarely any truces — many Sassanian sovereigns became famous because of their sensational victories. Shapur I was victorious over Valerian near Edessa in 260; the Roman emperor was taken prisoner along with seventy thousand legionnaires. Shapur II was victorious over Julian the Apostate. These successes indicate that the Sassanian army — led first by a commander-in-chief, and then later by four commanders, for the north, south, east and west, respectively — was extremely well organized. The cavalry, which was the army's strong point, included a heavy cavalry made up of the nobles, in which the men, just like the mounts, wore cuirasses; and a light cavalry, where archers were from the lower nobility. Backing up the cavalry was a corps of elephants from the Indies, whose trumpeting, smell, and aspect frightened the horses of the enemy camp. The elephants were led by *cornacs* whose job it was to kill the animals if they ever got upset over the noise of battle and began to stampede through the Iranian ranks. The infantry then followed, made up of farmers drafted into service; they were unreliable troops who did not receive money or recompense of any kind, "disgusting goats, disfigured by filth, who threw away their weapons and turned their backs before entering into battle." This at least was what the emperor Julian told his Roman soldiers in order to instill courage into them. Auxiliary formations, some of which were highly regarded, completed the ranks; these were made up of people from vassal nations who fought on horseback and occupied a privileged position.

Unlike the Parthians, the Sassanians possessed a modern technique of laying siege, utilizing battering rams, catapulted missiles, and mobile towers; they were certainly equal to the Romans in this field. The Sassanian kings took an active part in the wars and personally directed important battles. A monumental throne was set in the middle of the army, protected by the royal escort and by a veritable wall of men consisting of archers and infantrymen. The Iranians had an ingenious system of calculating losses: before the battle the soldiers filed past the king and the general one by one and cast an arrow into one of the large baskets used for this purpose; the baskets were stamped with the royal seal, and after the battle each soldier took back an arrow so that those remaining gave the exact number of men killed or taken prisoner. Al-

Hatra: Statue of a man, with the right hand raised in a gesture of prayer.

Ctesiphon: The ruins of the sixth century A.D. palace. To the right, the vaulted hall in which royal audiences were held.

built 272
abandoned 621

DESCRIPTION OF THE IWAN
OF KISRA BY AL-BUHTURI

The *iwan* is so admirably built that it resembles the shield resting on the side of a strong and valiant man. Its majesty remains, although despoiled of its rich carpets and deprived of its tapestries of white silk.

It is so towering that its raised battlements appear to crown the summits of two mountains, Radhwa and Qudsi; Resplendant in white, they present themselves to the eye as balls of cotton.

One does not know if the *iwan* was made by the hand of man for the genies to live there or whether those spirits have built it for human beings.

Boustani: *Les gens de lettres arabes*

though the Sassanians did not always win, they nonetheless succeeded in blocking the Roman advance in the East for four centuries. And when the peace agreed upon by the successors of the Byzantine emperor Heraclius and the Sassanian king Chosroes II put a definitive end to the wars, the two powers were so weakened that they could not withstand the Arab conquest.

The Structure of Sassanian Society

Sassanian society was composed of a number of classes, but it was distinguished above all by the antagonism between the royal authority and the feudal nobility inherited from the Parthians. The power of these nobles was such that the Iranian sovereigns attempted to counterbalance it with a new class, made up of the important men and the new nobles who furnished the empire with its great dignitaries, administrative heads, and royal functionaries. But the feudal aristocracy fought vigorously to conserve its centuries-old rights and privileges and, by thus weakening the royal power, it was partially responsible for the fall of the Sassanian empire.

The country was administrated — under the king's control — by one man only, the prime minister, who had under his jurisdiction the various "divans" or ministries. The prime minister was responsible for both domestic affairs and foreign policy; he could also take on military command. There were some limitations to his authority: the prime minister could not designate his successor and did not have the right to transfer or dismiss functionaries nominated by the king without special authorization.

The domestic organization was based on the division of the land into provinces, or satrapies, first governed by high dignitaries, and later by military chiefs; a permanent bureaucracy, dependent upon the central power, served as an intermediary. This bureaucracy carried out many jobs; the development and maintenance of the roads, of fundamental importance for the imperial power; the organization and supervision of the postal service, another vital cog in the imperial machine; the establishment of the models and forms for official correspondence, which had to be both detailed and ceremonially proper. The state organization was so good that it was preserved by the Arab conquerors up to the time of the Caliphs of Baghdad, but the feudal organization of society disappeared shortly after the Arab conquest.

The third force of the time, which often aligned itself with the nobility against the king, was the clergy. The priests were organized in a strict hierarchy, like all Sassanian society, and directed by a high priest nominated by the king. The authority of the priests — also known as the Magi — was wide-ranging. It was first of all spiritual, naturally, but it was also legal, even though the supreme judge was the king. The Magi had the authority to "legalize" everyone's life from birth to death, so much so that religion intervened in the smallest matters of everyday life. They were also responsible for teaching, and constituted an economic force as well; they possessed important land-holdings, and various tithes, donations, and compensations left them with considerable assets. There is no exaggeration in the statement that "among the Persians nothing seems legitimate or right if it is not confirmed by a Magus."

A state within a state, the clergy, whose strength lay in its adherence to the official religion, often become fanatical and intolerant. Thus Mazdaism, or Zoroastrianism, the official religion, always succeeded in eliminating the other creeds of the time, whether they were foreign like Christianity or Buddhism, or originated in Iran itself, such as Manichaeism, which claimed to be a universal religion. (Its founder Mani, who lived in the third century A.D., said: "I have come from the land of Babel to make a cry resound in the whole world.") Mazdakism was founded in the fifth century A.D., by the prophet Mazdak, who wanted to establish peace in the world by eliminating the differences between men, which he thought the cause of wars and hate, and by

Page 160:
Naqsh-i-Rustam: Two fire altars. Third to sixth centuries A.D. Height 5 feet, 1 inch and 5 feet, 9 inches, respectively.

Page 161:
Firuzabad: Relief of the victory of Ardashir over Artabanus V. Third century A.D. The relief shows six combatants divided into three groups: the first shows Ardashir knocking Artabanus off his horse with a lance; behind the Sassanian victor, his first-born son Shapur, who succeeded him on the throne, overcomes the grand vizier of the Parthians; then, two attendants, a Sassanian and a Parthian, in combat.

instituting the community of gods and women. Although Manichaeism
was supported by Shapur, for political motives, and Mazdakism by
Kavad in order to check the power of the nobility (in this way he lost
the throne for a certain period), these two religious doctrines were
eliminated from Iran after the martyrdom of their founders. However,
Manichaeism, from the third to the fifteenth century, spread from
Syria and Egypt to central Asia and China. St. Augustine had been a
Manichee for several years in his youth.

Sassanian Art

The last link in the artistic chain of the ancient Middle East, Sassanian art was a direct heir of Parthian art and, for that matter, of *all*
Middle Eastern art of previous times. Its placement on different
registers, the repetition of themes, the symmetry in the composition,
the rock reliefs — all are in fact artistic traditions millennia old. It is
possible to trace some Greco-Roman influences, however, especially in
public works such as bridges and dams; Greco-Roman influence is also
apparent in the plans of certain cities, in the construction of votive
monuments, in the decoration of buildings that have a mosaic covering,
and also in the rendering of certain drapery effects. The vestiges of
cities, of numerous rock reliefs and the decorative arts — jewelry and
textiles — that can be mentioned only in passing here, permit such a
judgment. This art has until recently been neglected by scholars,
probably because it is situated on the threshold between two worlds.
    For the building of their cities, the Sassanians used both the circular

Naqsh-i-Rustam: The investiture of Ardashir I by the god Ahura-Mazda. Third century A.D. Both are on horseback. Ahriman, the spirit of evil, and Artabanus V, the last king of the Parthians, are tread upon by the horses' hooves. An inscription in three languages, Greek, Sassanian, and Parthian, gives the names of the personages. To the right is another rock relief, showing Vahram II surrounded by his family. Third century A.D.

ARDASHIR ADDRESSES THE NOBLES AND PEOPLE AFTER HIS CORONATION

God has made his grace to descend and has established the union and has granted the seal of his favor by delegating to me the power over his servants and his lands in order to restore religion and royalty, which are two twin sisters, and in order to make justice and goodness reign.

Gage: *La montée des Sassanides* (p. 203)

Page 164
Bishapur: The triumph of Shapur. Third century A.D. On the bank of the Bishapur river, two rock reliefs depict Shapur's victory over Gordianus III, Philip the Arabian, and Valerian. This one is divided into four registers (only three are visible in the photograph). The king is depicted on horseback, surrounded by nobles, Persians loaded down with booty, and Roman prisoners.

Page 165
Bishapur: The triumph of Shapur. In the center, the king on horseback rides over the body of Gordianus III. Kneeling in front of him is Philip the Arabian. The Roman emperor Valerian stands behind Shapur, who holds him. The scene is completed by two Persian dignitaries. An angel or genie, bearing a diadem, hovers over the scene. The left part of the relief shows the cavalry; the right, the infantry.

plan of Parthian tradition (as at Firuzabad) and the Hellenistic-Roman plan, in which the two principal east-west and north-south arteries, terminating in gates, intersect at right angles marking the center of the city, while the secondary roads run parallel to the two axes. This is the case with Bishapur, one of the three cities where, according to literary sources, Shapur established colonies of Roman prisoners after his victory over Valerian. Excavations there have uncovered, besides a wall with moats, a fire-temple and some palaces. One of these last is characterized by a large room with a central dome and four *iwan*, giving it a cruciform plan. Surrounded by four corridors, this room, which must have been a sort of audience chamber, was decorated with sixty-four niches, and with sculptured and painted stuccowork whose motifs were typically western: Greek frets, tendrils, and acanthuses.

Bishapur is famous also for its mosaics, which decorate the floor of a courtyard; in these, winged genies, female nudes and geometric designs are set together. Portrait mosaics of men and women, each one different, decorate the floor of an *iwan*. For the most part these are three-quarter portraits with very few profiles; there are also depictions of women fanning themselves or playing instruments. The fire-temple, built to a square plan, still has one of its sides basically intact, which has made it possible to see the remains of the figures of kneeling bulls that supported the roof, attesting to the persistence of the Achaemenian tradition. Finally, in the center of the city, there rose a votive monument erected by Shapur I: two columns with Corinthian capitals set on two pedestals. One of the columns bears an inscription that indicates that a statue of Shapur completed the monument. Of this, only the pedestal remains, flanked by two small fire altars.

In the Sassanian as in the Parthian period the capital was Ctesiphon, on the left bank of the Tigris not far from present-day Baghdad. At Ctesiphon many Sassanian kings were crowned. A palace was built there by Shapur I; according to tradition the Bedouins who came from the desert during the Arab conquest were struck with admiration by

Naqsh-i-Rustam: Triumph of Shapur I, carved below the tomb of Darius. Philip the Arabian is kneeling. Shapur seizes the hand of the emperor Valerian in a sign of domination.

VELENUS, KING OF THE CADUSIANS, ADDRESSES SHAPUR

I thank you for having sent me the auxiliary forces without any losses and in good condition. But I can scarcely congratulate you for having taken as your prisoner of Valerian, prince of princes. I would congratulate you rather if you would set him free: The Romans are never so formidable as when they have been conquered.

ARTABASDE, KING OF THE ARMENIANS, ADDRESSES SHAPUR

I share in your glory but I suspect that you have not so much gained a victory as you have fanned the fires of war.... You have taken only one old man as a prisoner, but you have raised all the people of the earth against you.
Gage: *La montée des Sassanides* (p. 311)

Following pages:
Naqsh-i-Rustam: Vahram II, on horseback, fighting his enemies.

this palace. Unfortunately, the damage wrought by the centuries and by an earthquake has been great, and only a part of a facade and a portico overlooking an *iwan* remain; they once comprised a grandiose architectural complex made of brick and decorated with niches highlighted by columns and arcades set on various levels. The interior of the *iwan* got only a small amount of light, from narrow openings with a diameter ranging from four to six inches. The fragments of marble slabs, stucco panels, the numerous mosaic cubes (a number of which were covered with gold) — all give some idea of the sumptuousness of the decoration of this architecture. Paintings and rugs must have added to this magnificence.

It is within this framework that scenes of court life took place, such as the banquets during which women musicians and dancers — whose graceful figures are rendered in various pieces of goldwork — exhibited themselves. The royal audiences must also be placed in this picture. A curtain closed off the end of the *iwan*, and the crowd had to gather around the opposite end, perhaps even isolated by a balustrade. The most humble as well as the richest subjects came from all over the kingdom and gathered there, and some of them must have waited for days before even hoping to be received by the king. When the curtain opened one might see the great functionaries and dignitaries surrounding a luxurious throne (in a scene similar to the one represented on a rock crystal cup kept at the Bibliotheque Nationale in Paris) with the king the center of attention. St. John Chrysostom, speaking of a fourth century Sassanian king, said that he wore a gilded beard and had the air of a marvelous animal. Thanks to Sassanian sculpture, some idea can be gained of the beauty of the lavishly embroidered royal vestments. For the audiences, the king wore his crown, which was different for each of the Iranian sovereigns, and so heavy that it was suspended over the king's head by means of a thin gold chain fastened to the roof, which only those nearest to him could even see.

The Rock Reliefs

It is the justly celebrated rock reliefs that give the most information about the Sassanian kings' feasts, however. Some are isolated; but most of them are in the province of Fars — at Bishapur, Naqsh-i-Radjab, and Naqsh-i-Rustam. In this last site, they are found in the immediate vicinity of the royal Achaemenian tombs, indicating the preoccupation of the Sassanian kings with establishing themselves as the successors of a great dynasty. The motifs of these reliefs vary little, and they all have a common function: to glorify the person of the king.

Investiture scenes are frequent. The most famous of these is the one representing Ardashir, the founder of the dynasty, receiving the crown, emblem of power, from the god Ahura-Mazda. The two protagonists are on horseback; the horses, whose size is out of proportion with their riders, have their hooves on Artabanus, the last king of the Parthians, and Ahriman, the personification of evil. Ardashir's victory over Artabanus is illustrated by a relief at Firuzabad showing an extraordinary cavalry battle that foreshadows, as has often been pointed out, the tournaments in the Middle Ages.

Another celebrated victory, that of Shapur over Valerian, was the inspiration for many reliefs, the most famous of which — at Naqsh-i-Rustam — shows Shapur on horseback and Valerian kneeling before him. This is a splendid relief, and typical of the Sassanian manner: a static scene that the artist has tried to animate by making the wind play over the clothes of the figures and by paying particular attention to the detailed rendering of the clothes, hair, and the king's beard — details that, from a technical point of view, approach engraving. In the gorges at Bishapur artists have twice depicted this victory. One relief shows the Sassanian king on horseback facing Valerian, who is kneeling and is surrounded by armed soldiers representing various military contingents. The second relief, of majestic proportions, has a similar central theme, but is flanked by four registers. Those on the left are

dedicated to the Iranian cavalry, while on the right we see tributaries, Romans in togas, some standards of the defeated army, and the emperor's chariot.

However, these official scenes are not the only ones depicted in this art of rock relief. Some kings liked to be portrayed surrounded by their families, as is the case with Vahram II, who even on coins is accompanied by the queen and the heir apparent. In this period there were also hunting scenes which perpetuate the ancient tradition. The hunting exploits of the kings were often the decorative theme on Sassanian silver cups. Some sculptors also took it up, as in the famous grotto at Taq-i-Bostan (northeast of Kermanshah). The grotto is really two *iwan* cut out of a ravine in front of a sheet of water. One of them has two particularly animated hunting scenes on its sides; the one a deer-hunting scene, with some musicians present; the other shows boars being chased by the king on a boat, in a marsh with reeds populated by fish and ducks. The king is seen twice in this, first while holding a bow at the beginning of a hunt, and again with the bow lowered, a sign that the killing is over with. These are reliefs that, according to some scholars, give an idea of what Sassanian painting might have been like.

The last phase of ancient Middle Eastern art, Sassanian art, had an unexpected diffusion. Its artists were destined to play a leading role in the iconography of the Middle Ages, thanks to fabrics that reached the Occident during the Crusades, when they were used to wrap sacred relics.

APPENDICES
THE MIDDLE EAST
MONUMENTS THROUGH THE AGES

The Discovery of the Ancient Middle East by the Western World

Any work that professes to describe the civilizations of the ancient Middle East must pay some homage to those historians, travelers, archaeologists, and others who have discovered and maintained these civilizations for our realm of knowledge. There have been too many devoted subjects of this realm to name them all, but we can at least pay tribute to the pioneers who introduced the Middle East to Western civilization.

The most ancient documents that informed Europeans of this region, besides the Bible, are the works of Greek authors, and of these the most accessible is Herodotus. Born in Halicarnassus (in modern Turkey), he was the Greek who deserves his reputation as "the father of history"; sometime around 450 B.C. he seems to have traveled in the Middle East as far as the Tigris and Euphrates Rivers, and although his work was full of errors, it kept that remote world alive for later generations. The other classic of that era is the *Anabasis* by Xenophon, an historian, philosopher, student of Socrates, and general. The *Anabasis* is his account of the retreat of "the ten thousand," those Greek mercenaries who in 401 B.C. had enlisted to help the Persian Cyrus in his dynastic dispute with his brother Artaxerxes. Defeated, they managed to return to their homeland — thanks in part to their commander Xenophon — only after passing through incredibly difficult parts of the Middle East.

In addition to such works — which have an intrinsic interest of which the Middle Eastern elements are but a part — there are various other ancient works from the centuries just before and after the turn of the Christian era. Thus, there was Ctesia, a Greek physician who worked for the Persian court in the fifth century B.C. and who wrote a *History of Syria and Persia*. Most of Ctesia's work has been lost, but some passages were preserved in the work of Diodorus of Sicily, an historian of the first century B.C. Berosus was a Babylonian priest who seems to have flourished around 300 B.C. and wrote a history of Babylon that also passed on information about Babylonian astronomy to the Greek world; quotations from this work are found in the works of Josephus Flavius, the Jewish historian; and Eusebius, a fourth century Christian churchman and writer. Strabo, a geographer who wrote near the beginning of the Christian era, devoted a volume of his works to the countries of the Middle East. All these books, of course, dealt only with the late centuries of Middle Eastern history and all contained many inaccuracies; but again, they kept that region of the world at least on the periphery of Europeans' consciousness.

During the "dark ages" of Europe, however, even these classic works tended to become lost in the shadows; meanwhile, the work of Arabic authors and geographers was all but unknown in the West. Occasional travelers from Europe — such as "the pilgrim of Bordeaux" (A.D. 333) and the nun-pilgrim Heteria (circa 385) — left accounts, but they were restricted to a tiny public. Then there were two rabbis, Benjamin of Tudela, in Spain, and Pethahiah of Ratisbon, in Germany, who visited Jewish communities in the Middle East in the late twelfth century, and while there they visited some of the sites of ancient history. Benjamin, for instance, visited Babylon, but he lacked the courage to venture into the palace of Nebuchadnezzar, "because of the fact that it is a refuge for dragons and poisonous beasts." But the rabbis wrote their accounts in Hebrew and they were not published until 1543; it was about another thirty years before they were translated into Latin.

It was about the same time that two other Europeans made trips to the Middle East. One was John Eldred, an English merchant, and the other was the German physician; Leonhart Rauwolff. Such men went off to the Middle East knowing little more than what Xenophon had described some two thousand years earlier, and their accounts neither added much information nor reached many people. They would look at the great mounds (or *tells*) that covered ancient remains, and they knew the Biblical references to certain sites, but that was about the extent of their "archaeology."

A small step forward was taken with the visit of an Italian aristocrat, Pietro della Valle, in the years 1614 to 1626. He seemed to have an informed interest in antiquities and was capable of writing such descriptions as this of the Tower of Babel: "In the center of a vast and continuous plain, about a quarter of a league from the Euphrates which crosses it at this point going westward, one sees, quite high even today, a confused mass of ruined constructions which form a prodigious heap from the mixture of the various materials; either this was made in this way from the beginning, which is my opinion, or the rubble has mixed up all the ruins and has confusedly reduced them to the form of a huge mountain, from which there appears no sign or point on which one can pass judgment. It is square in shape, in the form of a tower or pyramid with four faces that give on to the four parts of the world."

Even more important than this, Della Valle brought back to Europe from Babylon "some square bricks on which were writing in certain unknown characters"; he also copied some inscriptions at Persepolis. These were not the first such inscriptions that found their way to Europe, but they were among the earliest to inspire interpretation. For a long time, this mysterious writing was seen as anything from "cabalistic figures, talismans" to "mechanical productions or the work of worms or insects." Eventually, a disciplined approach was taken to the decipherment of this writing, beginning with Niebuhr in the eighteenth century, carrying on with the work of Grotefend and Rawlinson in the nineteenth, and eventually involving many other fine scholars. The story of the decipherment of cuneiform is as exciting as that of the excavation of the remains, but it is a full story in itself and we must forego it here. Obviously, though, without the knowledge of cuneiform used to write the Assyrian, Babylonian, Old Persian, and other languages of the ancient Middle East, all the other remains would be lacking a whole dimension.

After Pietro della Valle, increasing numbers of Europeans made trips to the Middle East: some for purely commercial reasons, some for religious motives, some just for the adventures of traveling. Thus, in 1665 and 1677, a French merchant from Lyon, J. Chardin, traveled in Persia and wrote a ten-volume journal. It included detailed drawings of the ruins of Persepolis, and his comment on these ruins is both wise and humorous: "When contemplating this precious monument, it is necessary to do what one does when looking at a lovely person whom age or infirmity have worn out: for the very fact that one sees they still exist, one must imagine how they must have been at one time." Still, none of the visitors during the seventeenth and eighteenth centuries actually added much of significance to Europeans' knowledge of these ancient civilizations. Biblical stories, legends, travelers' tales, wild conjectures — everything received as much weight as any facts arrived at through historical or archaeological analysis.

It was in the early decades of the nineteenth century that began the true investigations of the ancient Middle Eastern world hidden beneath the mounds. Various individuals, groups, factors — and chance — all played their parts. Thus, Britain's East India Company, a privately owned trading organization with offices at Baghdad and Basrah, helped to support some research by assigning agents who had more than a passing interest in the ancient history of the region. The most famous of these was Claudius James Rich, a master of many Eastern languages and resident in Baghdad for many years until his death from cholera while on an expedition to visit the remains at Persepolis. Rich himself did not excavate any major site, but he explored many remains, attracted various scholars and explorers to his home in Baghdad, and brought back to London many objects that formed the first collection of the Department of Oriental Antiquities of the British Museum.

During the next decades, too, came the first official government expeditions to the Middle East. Perhaps the most epic was Britain's Euphrates Expedition, led by Colonel Francis R. Chesney and organized by the government to survey the northern region of Syria and to explore the Tigris and Euphrates Rivers. All the parts for two large paddle steamers were sent and reassembled at the mouth of the Orontes River in 1835; the boats then steamed onto the Euphrates River, where one of the ships capsized (with the loss of twenty men); but the geographic and archaeological surveys of the expedition helped to point the way for those who followed. Meanwhile, another phenomenon was developing. A trip to the Middle East was becoming fashionable among literary figures, especially French Romantic writers like Chateaubriand, Lamartine, and Gerard de Nerval; these men wrote accounts that, if filled with flights of lyricism, also had some solid particles of observation.

By this time, after all the descriptions of surface remains by historians and travelers, merchants and clerics, the ground was prepared for the pioneer archaeologists. The honor of being the first in Mesopotamia is usually accorded to a Frenchman, Paul Emile Botta. Even as a youth, he felt what his vocation would be; while still in his teens, he visited the ruins of a Norman abbey and told a friend that he needed to find "more ancient and more splendid ruins," and that he intended to find them in the East. Eventually he became a physician, but it was his appointment as French consul at Mosul, a city on the upper reaches of the Tigris, that permitted him to satisfy his youthful desire. Botta took up his post in Mosul in 1842 and began at once to seek out the sources of the fragments of pottery and bricks that the natives of the region were always offering for sale. Meanwhile, he began to dig in one of the great mounds across the Tigris from Mosul in hopes of finding ancient Nineveh, but he found nothing that seemed worthy of such a great city.

Then Botta turned his attentions to another great mound about ten miles to the north, a site known as Khorsabad, where local inhabitants told of finding inscribed bricks, walls, and stone carvings. After he sent two men to confirm these reports, Botta himself rode off and set to work excavating; immediately he uncovered some walls with relief carvings: he had discovered the palace and town of the Assyrian king Sargon II, who ruled from 721 to 705 B.C. By April 1843, Botta was writing back to Paris, "I continue to have things cleared away, and I do so with much more interest as I believe I am the first to have discovered sculptures that can apparently be related to the time when Nineveh was flourishing." As reports of Botta's sensational discoveries began to spread, the French extended both official and private support and funds. The first Assyrian monuments reached Paris early in 1847, further confirming the reality of that ancient world.

Meanwhile, an Englishman, Sir Austen Henry Layard, had begun in 1845 to excavate a large mound south of Mosul that turned out to be the site of ancient Nimrud; and in 1849, Layard began to excavate the mound opposite Mosul that Botta had abandoned, and there he found the remains of Nineveh. By this time, too, other men were turning toward the more southern region of Mesopotamia. The first exploratory journeys were made by such Englishmen as William K. Loftus and J. E. Taylor, who made surface investigations at the sites of such cities as Larsa, Uruk, Ur, and Eridu. But the first true excavations in Lower Mesopotamia were accomplished by a Frenchman, Ernest de Sarzec. Between 1877 and 1900, he conducted ten excavation "campaigns," in the course of which he established the reality of a far earlier people than the Assyrians and Babylonians — the Sumerians. In addition to discovering thousands of inscribed tablets, de Sarzec also found such works as the Stele of the Vultures, the silver vase of Entemena, and the statue of Gudea of Lagash.

By this time, France and England were no longer the only European countries interested in Middle Eastern antiquities. Germany had entered the archaeological "competition" in the person of Robert Koldewey, who excavated such sites as Babylon, the Tower of Babel, and the "Hanging Gardens" of Queen Semiramis. Koldewey was an architect by training and he proved especially adept at developing the horizontal method of excavation, by which large complexes are uncovered without neglecting details and objects. By 1889, too, Americans had also begun to excavate in Mesopotamia, at the site of Nippur.

With the opening of the twentieth century, the pioneer era of Middle Eastern archaeology ends, and a new phase begins, marked by more systematic research and more technical means. In addition, archaeological research has taken on a more cooperative and international character. Today, not only are many of the nations of the Western world engaged in excavating but they are doing so alongside archaeologists from the very nations of the sites themselves; and even Japan has archaeological missions working in Iraq, Iran, and Israel. Perhaps something has been lost from those days when solitary, courageous individuals set off across uncharted lands to examine remote ruins, but we may welcome the efforts of all peoples in pushing back the limits of the unknown and filling in the many existing gaps in our knowledge of the ancient Middle East.

Chronological Chart of the Ancient Middle East

Principal Cultures, Dynasties and Rulers of the Ancient Kingdoms of the Middle East.

9000–7000 B.C.

Mesolithic culture of food-gatherers
Iraq: Karim Shahir
Palestine: Natufian & Proto-Neolithic Jericho

7000–5000 B.C.

Pre-Pottery & Pottery
Neolithic
Iraq: Jarmo, Mlefaat
Palestine: Jericho
Anatolia: Mersin, Çatal, Hüyük, Hacilar

5000–4000 B.C.

Chalcolithic
Iraq: Hassuna, Samarra/Eridu
Anatolia: Beycesultan
Iran: Siyalk

4000–3000 B.C.

Mesopotamia: Halaf/Hajji Muhammad
    Ubaid/Uruk

3000–2000 B.C.

Early Bronze Age

Mesopotamia
    Tepe Gawra/Gemdet Nasr
    Early Dynasties: Ur, Lagash, Nippur
    Akkadian Dynasty (2371–2230)
        Sargon (2371–2316)
        Naram-Sin
        Sharkalisharri
    Gutian Dynasty (2250–2120)
    Second Dynasty of Lagash (Gudea)
    Third Dynasty of Ur (2113–2006)
        Ur-Nammu
        Shulgi
        Amar-Sin

2000–1000 B.C.

Middle & Late Bronze Age Mesopotamia
    Elamites
    Isin Dynasty (2017–1797)
    Larsa Dynasty (2010–1761)
    Mari Dynasty (1900–1757)
    Babylonian Dynasty (1894–1595)
        Hammurabi (1792–1750)
    Cassite Dynasty
        Karaindash
    Elamites

Anatolia: Hittites
    Labarnas I (c. 1680)
    Hattusilis I (c. 1650)
    Mursilis I (c. 1620)
    Telipinus (c. 1525)
    Suppululiumas I (1375–1335)

Assyrians
    Tukulti-Ninurta I (1244–1208)
    Tiglath-Pileser I (1115–1077)

1000 B.C. — A.D. 224

Assyrians
    Ashurnasirpal II (883–859)
    Shalmaneser III (858–824)
    Tiglath-Pileser III (745–727)
    Sargon II (721–705)
    Sennacherib (704–681)
    Esarhaddon (680–669)
    Ashurbanipal (668–626)

Neo-Babylonians
    Nabopolassar (626–605)
    Nebuchadnezzar (605–562)
    Nabonidus (555–539)

Achaemenian Dynasty (558–330)
    Cyrus the Great (558–530)
    Cambyses (530–522)
    Darius (522–486)
    Xerxes (486–465)
    Artaxerxes I (465–424)
    Darius II (424–404)
    Artaxerxes II (404–358)
    Artaxerxes III (358–338)
    Darius III Codomannus (338–330)

Alexander the Great (356–323)

Seleucids (301–164)
    Seleucus I (301–280)
    Antiochus III (223–187)
    Antiochus IV (175–164)

Parthians (c. 250 B.C. — A.D. 224)
    Arsaces & Tiridates (c. 250–210 B.C.)
    Mithridates I (174–137 B.C.)
    Mithridates III (c. 123–90 B.C.)
    Vologases III (A.D. 148–192)
    Artabanus V (A.D. 213–224)

A.D. 224–651

Sassanians
    Ardashir (222–241)
    Shapur I (241–272)
    Vahram II (276–293)
    Shapur II (309–379)
    Peroz (459–484)
    Kavad (488–497; 499–531)
    Chosroes I (531–579)
    Chosroes II (590–618)
    Yazdgard III (632–651)

GLOSSARY

Achaemenes: Founder of the Achaemenian dynasty in the seventh century B.C.

Achaemenians: The Persian dynasty that ruled from the reign of Cyrus (558 B.C.) to the death of Darius III Codomannus (330 B.C.)

Adad: Semitic god of storms and the natural elements.

Adapa: The hero of a Mesopotamian poem, who broke the wings of the South Wind.

Ahiram: King of Byblos (thirteenth century B.C.)

Ahriman: Spirit of evil and darkness in the Achaemenian religion.

Ahura-Mazda: Principal divinity of the Achaemenian religion.

Akitu (feast of): New Year's feast in Mesopotamia, during which hierogamy rites (god-marriage) took place.

Akkad: Name of a city (still to be discovered) a region, and a Mesopotamian dynasty whose seat was there (2371–2230 B.C.). It is also called Agade.

Akshak: The seat of the twelfth dynasty after the Flood, not yet discovered; it is thought that this city lies somewhere in the area of Ctesiphon.

Aleppo: A city in northern Syria, mentioned in tablets found at Mari (eighteenth century B.C.).

Alexander the Great: (356–323 B.C.) Son of Philip II of Macedon, conqueror of a vast empire in Asia.

Amanus: A mountain chain north of Antioch.

Amar-Sin: Third king of the third dynasty of Ur (2047–2039 B.C.). Also called Bur-Sin.

Amiti: Daughter of Astyages, King of the Medes, who married Nebuchadnezzar II, king of Babylon.

Ammianus Marcellinus: Latin historian born in Antioch about A.D. 330 who accompanied the emperor Julian the Apostate on his expedition against the Persians.

Amorites: A Semitic population from Amurru.

Amurru: In ancient times, the western region of Mesopotamia, which now corresponds to the mid-Euphrates and Syrian desert area.

Anabasis: *Expedition to the Interior*, an account by Xenophon of the expedition of Cyrus the Younger against Artaxerxes II, and the retreat of the Greek Ten Thousand.

Anahita: Great goddess of the waters in the Iranian religion.

Anatolia: The central part of Asia Minor.

Ante-Cella: In a temple, the room between the courtyard and the cella, or "holy of holies."

Antigonus: One of Alexander's lieutenants. At the division of the empire, he was given Asia Minor.

Anti-Lebanon: A mountain chain that lies to the east of the Lebanon range.

Antiochus III (called the Great): Seleucid emperor, king of Syria (223–187 B.C.)

Anu: Primordial divinity in the Sumerian pantheon, god of the sky.

Apadana: The audience chamber in Achaemenian palaces.

Apamea: Ancient city in Syria, north-north-west of Hims.

Appian: Greek historian of the second century A.D.

Apsu: The underground and fresh water ruled by the god Enki-Ea.

Aqarquf (Dur-Kurigalzu): Capital of the Cassite dynasty, situated west of Baghdad.

Arachosia: Province of the Persian empire.

Aramaeans: Western Semitic population of nomadic origin.

Archivolt: The continuous molding on the curve of an arch.

Ardashir I: Founder of the Sassanian dynasty, king of Iran from A.D. 222 to 241.

Aretas IV: King of the Nabataeans (9 B.C.–A.D. 40).

Arinna: An Anatolian sanctuary, not yet discovered, but known through texts, where a solar god was worshiped.

Armenia: Mountainous region north of Mesopotamia, which corresponds to the Urartu of the ancients.

Arsaces: Founder of the Parthian dynasty in the third century B.C.

Arsacids: Dynasty of the Parthians, or Parthian-Arsacids (c. 250 B.C.–A.D. 224).

Artabanus V: Last king of the Parthian dynasty (c. 213–224).

Ashur (Qalaat Shergat): Ancient city on the right bank of the Tigris, one of the Assyrian capitals.

Ashur: Chief divinity of the Assyrian pantheon.

Ashurbanipal: King of Assyria (668–626 B.C.).

Ashurnasirpal II: King of Assyria (883–859 B.C.).

Assyria: Region in the upper Tigris.

Astyages: King of the Medes (585–550 B.C.) defeated by Cyrus the Great.

Atargatis: A Syrian divinity during the Roman epoch.

Baalbek: Ancient Phoenician city, a Roman colony in the first century A.D.

Baalshamin: "Lord of the skies," a Syrian divinity.

Babylon: Situated south of modern Baghdad, it was the Mesopotamian capital during the first Babylonian dynasty (1894–1595 B.C.), and then again during the Neo-Babylonian period (626–539 B.C.).

Bactria: A region in Asia that corresponds to northern Afghanistan.

Baghdad: Capital of modern Iraq, founded in A.D. 760 by the Caliph el-Mansur.

Basrah: City in southern Iraq, on the Shatt el-Arab River.

Bau: "Mistress of Plenty," female counterpart of the god Ningirsu.

Bavian: A locality thirty-one miles northeast of Nineveh, where there are Assyrian rock reliefs.

Behistun: A site in Kurdistan, eighteen and a half miles east of Kermanshah, where there are rock reliefs of Darius I and of the Parthian period.

Bel: Chief deity of Palmyra.

Belshazar: Son of Nabonidus, king of Babylon (555–539 B.C.).

Beqaa: A plain situated between the Lebanon and the Anti-Lebanon mountains.

Bishapur: Royal Sassanian city in Fars, founded by Shapur I in the third century A.D.

Bit-Hilani: The name given to a type of porticoed edifice of north Syrian or Anatolian origin.

Boghaz Köy: Turkish village near site of ancient Hattusas, the capital of the Hittite empire.

Borsippa (Birs-Nimrud): Ancient site near Babylon.

Brak (Tell): Site in the region of the Khabur, a tributary of the Euphrates.

Byblos: Ancient city on the Mediterranean coast north of Beirut.

Caldarium: The "warm room" in Roman public baths.

Cambyses: Son of Cyrus and Achaemenian king (530–522 B.C.).

Cappadocia: Plateau and steppe region in central Turkey.

Carchemish: Ancient site in Turkey, near the Syrian border.

Carrhae: City in Mesopotamia, now in Turkey, where the Roman army under Crassus was defeated by the Parthians in 53 B.C. (see Harran).

Casio (Jebel Aqra): A mountain in Syria.

Cassites: Invaders from the northeast who put an end to the first dynasty in Babylon and established their own dynasty (c. 1600–1240 B.C.).

Catal Hüyük: Ancient site in Turkey, southeast of Konya.

Cella: The "holy of holies" of a temple, where the god "resides" and where there was usually a statue of the god.

Chardin (J.): Merchant from Lyon, who made several visits to the Middle East in the seventeenth century, an account of which he gave in his *Voyages de M. le Chevalier Chardin, en Perse et autres lieux d'Orient*.

Choga Zanbil (Dur-Untash): An Elamite site about eighteen and a half miles southeast of Susa.

Chosroes II: Sassanian king (A.D. 590–618).

Crassus: Roman banker and politician who, with Caesar and Pompey, formed the first Triumvirate (60 B.C.). He was defeated and killed by the Parthians at Carrhae.

Croesus: King of Lydia (sixth century B.C.).

Ctesiphon: Capital of the Parthian empire and then of the Sassanian empire, on the left bank of the Tigris twenty miles south of Baghdad.

Cuneiform: Name given to the writing—in widespread use throughout the ancient Middle East — whose characters are made up of wedge-shaped marks (*cuneus* is Latin for wedge).

Cyclopic Architecture: A type of architecture that employs large irregular stone blocks; once attributed to mythical Cyclopes.

Cylinder Seal: A small cylindrical object of semiprecious stone, ivory or other durable material, engraved with various representations, often of a religious nature. Rolled across soft clay, it served as a signature or seal.

Cyrus (The Great): Persian king (558–530 B.C.), founder of the Achaemenian dynasty.

Dadusha: King of Eshnunna; some have attributed the "laws of Eshnunna" to him (eighteenth century B.C.).

Darius I: Achaemenian king from (522–486 B.C.)

Darius III Codomannus: The last Achaemenian king (338–330 B.C.), defeated by Alexander the Great.

Decapolis: Ancient confederation of ten Syrian cities.

Diadochi: Name given to Alexander the Great's generals, who divided the empire among themselves after Alexander's death.

Diyala: An affluent of the Tigris.

Dur-Sharrukin (Fortress of Sargon): *See* Khorsabad.

Dura-Europos: An ancient city in Syria, on the right bank of the Euphrates, founded in the Seleucid period.

Dusares: Principal divinity in the Nabataean pantheon.

Ea: Semitic name of the god of the waters, called Enki in Sumerian.

Eanna: The area and sanctuary in Uruk, dedicated to the goddess Ishtar.

Edessa (Urfa): Ancient city in northern Mesopotamia, north-northwest of Harran; now part of Turkey.

Edom: Ancient kingdom south of the Dead Sea.

Elam: Ancient name for the part of Iran east of south central Mesopotamia.

Enki: God of the waters, lord of Eridu.

Enkidu: Gilgamesh's companion.

Enlil: God of the earth, lord of the city of Nippur.

Entemena: King of Lagash at the beginning of the third millennium B.C.

Enuma Elish: "When on high," the first words of the Babylonian poem of the creation.

Ephtalites: A population of Iranian or Turkish-Mongol origin.

Eridu (Abu-Sharain): City in southern Mesopotamia, center of the cult of Enki.

Esagila: "The house that raises its head," the name of the temple of Marduk in Babylon.

Esarhaddon: Assyrian king, son of Sennacherib (680–669 B.C.).

Eshnunna (Tell Asmar): Ancient city in the region of Diyala.

Etana: In Mesopotamian mythology, the shepherd who wished to go into the sky to search for the plant of birth. He failed in his attempt, despite help given him by an eagle.

E-Temen-An-Ki: "House of the foundations of the sky and earth," the name of the *ziggurat* in Babylon in the neo-Babylonian period.

Exedra: In Greek and Roman architecture, a niche or room, most often of semicircular plan; by extension, a meeting hall with benches around the sides.

Fars: A province of southwestern Iran.

Firuzabad: City in the province of Fars, founded by the Sassanian king Ardashir.

Frigidarium: In Roman baths, a room with one or more cold water pools.

Gallienus: Roman emperor from A.D. 259 to 268.

Gaugamela: Site near Arbela in Mesopotamia where Alexander the Great defeated the last Achaemenian king, Darius III Codomannus.

Gemdet-Nasr: Site northeast of Kish, which gave its name to a phase of Mesopotamian protohistory (end of the fourth, beginning of the third millennium B.C.).

Gerwan: A village in northern Iraq, where there are remains of an Assyrian aqueduct.

Gilgamesh: Hero of Sumerian and later Mesopotamian mythology, from Uruk.

Grotefend, Georg: German schoolmaster (1775–1853) whose work was crucial in the deciphering of cuneiform characters.

Gudea: Ruler of Lagash in the Neo-Sumerian period (twenty-first century B.C.).

Gutians: Nomads who invaded Mesopotamia and brought the Akkadian dynasty to an end, reigning in their stead from about 2250 to 2120 B.C.

Hacilar: Turkish site about twelve and a half miles southwest of Burdur, which has important prehistoric architectural remains.

Halaf: A site in the Khabur region which has given its name to a phase of Mesopotamian protohistory.

Hammurabi: Sixth king of the first dynasty of Babylon, (1792–1750 B.C) celebrated for his code of laws.

Hantilis: Great cup-bearer at the Hittite court.

Harmal (Tell): Ancient site on the eastern edge of Baghdad.

Harran: City in upper Mesopotamia, now in Turkey, not far from the Syrian border. *See* Carrhae.

Hassuna: Site south of Mosul, which has given its name to a phase of Mesopotamian protohistory.

Hatra: Capital of a small second century A.D. kingdom, in northern Mesopotamia, southwest of Mosul.

Hatti: A population settled in Anatolia before the arrival of the people who took the name Hittites.

Hattusas: The capital of the Hittite empire, near the Turkish village of Boghaz Köy.

Hattusilis I: Hittite king in the seventeenth century B.C.

Hattusilis III: Hittite king in the thirteenth century B.C.

Hazzi: A god-mountain in the Hittite pantheon.

Hepat: Sun god in the Hittite pantheon.

Hierogamy: The marriage of gods and goddesses; the rites that renew it.

"High Place": The term indicating open-air sanctuaries, set on a height, where the ancients worshiped the gods.

Hines: A village north of Nineveh where there are Assyrian rock reliefs.

Hittites: The Indo-European people who, settling in Anatolia at the beginning of the second millennium B.C., went on to establish the Hittite Empire.

Hrozny (B.): Czech Orientalist (1879–1952), who distinguished himself in the deciphering of Hittite cuneiform characters.

Humbaba: In the Gilgamesh epic, the guard of the cedar forests, killed by Gilgamesh and Enkidu.

Hurrians: A population, relatively unknown, that settled in upper Mesopotamia during the second millennium B.C.

Iasmah-Adad: Son of Shamshi-Adad, king of Ashur, who for a certain period was also king of Mari.

Ideogram: A graphic sign that expresses an idea.

Igigu: Generic name of a group of gods.

Immortals: The name given to the Achaemenian royal guard.

Inshushinak: Chief god in the Elamite religion.

Ionians: Inhabitants of Ionia, a region in Asia Minor between the Gulf of Smyrna and the Gulf of Mendalia.

Iraq: The modern nation whose frontiers correspond roughly to those of ancient Mesopotamia.

Ishkhali: An ancient site in the Diyala region.

Ishtar: The goddess of war and love in the Mesopotamian pantheon.

Ishtar-Kititum: A goddess whose temple was found at Ishkhali.

Isin: A city in lower Mesopotamia which was the seat of two dynasties; it was also the city of Lipit-Ishtar, a king-legislator of the twenty-first century B.C.

Istakhr: An ancient city in Iran, four miles north-northwest of Persepolis.

Iwan: In Parthian and Sassanian architecture, a room with a large opening on one side, often vaulted and often facing a courtyard.

Jarmo: An open-air habitat in northern Iraq, dating from about 6500 to 5500 B.C.

Jerash: Ancient city north of Amman, with notable ruins of the Roman epoch.

Jericho: City in Palestine, settled by Joshua; one of the most ancient of urban sites.

Jerusalem: Royal, holy city, conquered by the Neo-Babylonians in 597 and 586 B.C.

Jupiter Heliopolitanus: Principal god of Baalbek.

Kadesh: City in Syria south of Hims, where a battle was fought between Muwatallis and Ramesses II, in 1299 B.C.

Kanesh: Ancient site in Turkey, north of Kayseri.

Karaindash: Cassite king (fifteenth century B.C.).

Karatepe: Ancient site in Turkey, northeast of Adana.

Kaskans: Barbarians from the north, who made many raids into Asia Minor during the second millennium B.C.

Kavad I: Sassanian king from 488 to 497 and then again from 499 to 531.

Khafage: Ancient site in the Diyala region.

Khani: "Lord of the seal," god of scribes in the Mesopotamian pantheon.

Khazneh Firaun: "The Pharaoh's Treasure," one of the most famous tombs in Petra.

Khorasan: Province in the northeastern part of the Achaemenian empire.

Khorsabad (Dur-Sharrukin): Capital of Sargon II of Assyria (721–705 B.C.), ten miles north-northeast of Mosul.

Kish (el-Oheimir): Sumerian city north-northeast of Babylon, seat of many dynasties.

Kurdistan: A province in southwestern Iran, ancient Susiana.

Kushans: A population of Iranian origin. In the first century, A.D., they had a vast empire corresponding to Afghanistan and part of Russian and Chinese Turkestan.

Labarnas: Hittite king in the seventeenth century B.C.

Lachish: A city in Palestine, west of the Dead Sea.

Lagash (Tello): City in southern Mesopotamia, where Gudea reigned.

Lagides: A dynasty founded by Ptolemy, one of Alexander's generals, in Egypt.

Lamartine (Alphonse de): French poet (1790–1869), author of *Voyage en Orient* and *Nouveau voyage en Orient*.

Lamgi-Mari: King of Mari at the beginning of the third millennium B.C.

Larsa (Senkereh): City in southern Mesopotamia, seat of a dynasty (2010–1761 B.C.).

Layard (Sir Austen Henry): English archaeologist (1817–1894), who carried out excavations at Nineveh and Nimrud.

Lipit-Ishtar: Fifth king of the Isin dynasty (twenty-first century B.C.)

Loftus (Sir William Kenneth): English archaeologist who excavated at Susa in 1851, explored southern Mesopotamia, and worked at Nineveh and Nimrud in 1854.

Lugalzagesi: Sumerian king of the third dynasty of Uruk, defeated by Sargon of Akkad.

Lydia: Region in Asia Minor, on the Aegean Sea.

Magi: Scholars and priests of Median origin.

Malatya: Ancient site in eastern Turkey.

Mallowan (Sir Max Edgar Lucien): British archaeologist, who has carried out excavations at Nineveh, Tell Brak, Nimrud and other sites.

Maltay: Site northwest of Khorsabad, with Assyrian rock reliefs of divine processions.

Mani: Founder of Manichaeism (A.D. 215–277).

Manichaeism: Religious doctrine, which combines Zoroastrian dualism with the Gnostic traditions of lower-Euphrates Christians.

Manishtusu: Son of Sargon and third king of the Akkadian dynasty.

Marduk: Son of the god Ea, and lord of Babylon.

Mari: (Tell Hariri): A city north-northwest of Abu-Kemal, seat of the tenth dynasty after the Universal Flood.

Mazdaism: The Iranian religion, commonly known as Zoroastrianism.

Mazdak: Founder of Mazdakism (sixth century A.D.), a religious doctrine that teaches the community of goods.

Medes: Inhabitants of Media, a region in western Iran.

Megiddo: City in Palestine, southwest of Lake Tiberias.

Mesannepada: King of the first dynasty of Ur (circa 2700 B.C.).

Mitanni: An empire in northern Mesopotamia in the fifteenth and fourteenth centuries B.C.

Mithridates I: Parthian king (174–137 B.C.).

Mlefaat: One of the most ancient Mesopotamian villages, in northeastern Iraq.

Moab: A region east of the Dead Sea.

Mosul: Modern city in northern Iraq, on the right bank of the Tigris opposite ancient Nineveh.

Mursilis I: Hittite king in the late seventeenth century B.C., who led a raid against Babylon.

Muwatallis: Hittite king (1306–1282 B.C.), son and successor of Mursilis II.

Nabonidus: Last king (555–539 B.C.) of the Neo-Babylonian dynasty. (His name was actually Nabuna'id.)

Nabopolassar: Founder of the Neo-Babylonian dynasty (626–605 B.C.).

Nabu: Son of the god Marduk; god of scribes and writing.

Namni: God-mountain in the Hittite pantheon.

Nanna: Sumerian name for the moon god, whose Semitic name is Sin; worshipped especially at Ur.

Naplanum: Founder of the Larsa dynasty (2010–1761 B.C.).

Naqsh-I-Radjab: A cliff three miles north of Persepolis, with Sassanian bas-reliefs.

Naqsh-I-Rustam: A site with Sassanian bas-reliefs and Persian tombs, three and a half miles north of Persepolis.

Naram-Sin: Grandson of Sargon and king of Addad (circa 2300 B.C.).

Nebi-Yunus: One of the two *tell* (the other is Quyungik) that covered the ancient city of Nineveh.

Nebuchadnezzar I: King of the second dynasty of Isin (twelfth century B.C.).

Nebuchadnezzar II: King (605–562) of the Neo-Babylonian dynasty.

Neo-Babylonian: The era in Mesopotamia between the reigns of Nabopolassar and Nabonidus (626–539 B.C.).

Nergal: God of the underworld in the Mesopotamian pantheon.

Niebuhr, Karsten: Eighteenth-century German who visited Persepolis and made valuable contributions to decipherment of cuneiform.

Nimrud: One of the Assyrian capitals, south of Nineveh.

Nineveh: One of the Assyrian capitals, on the right bank of the Tigris.

Ningal: Goddess, female counterpart of the moon god Nanna.

Ningirsu: God of fertility, worshiped in Lagash.

Ninlil: Goddess, female counterpart of the god Enlil, lord of Nippur.

Ninmah: Goddess in the Mesopotamian pantheon.

Ninni-Zaza: A goddess whose temple was discovered at Mari.

Ninurta: God of war in the Mesopotamian pantheon.

Nippur: Sumerian city where the god Enlil reigned.

Nisaba: Mesopotamian god of vegetation and writing.

Nusku: Mesopotamian god of fire, symbolized by a lamp.

Odenathus I: Arab prince of Palmyra (third century A.D.).

Odenathus II: Arab prince of Palmyra, married to Zenobia (third century A.D.).

Orontes: A river in central Syria, now called Nahr el-Asi.

Paleolithic: A phase of pre-history characterized by chipped stone tools.

Palmyra: Caravan track city in the heart of the Syrian desert, with notable remains from the Roman period.

Parrot (André): French archaeologist, who has excavated at Lagash, Larsa, and Mari. Director of the Louvre Museum.

Parthians: A tribe of Iranian origin who founded the Parthian-Arsacid dynasty (250 B.C.–A.D. 224).

Pasargadae: The first Achaemenian capital, sixty-two miles north-northeast of Shiraz.

People of the Sea: A mixed group of people that came from the north and west and invaded the Middle East about 1200 B.C.; they probably included the Biblical Philistines.

Peristyle: A range of columns surrounding a building or open court.

Phoenicia: Region along the Mediterranean coast, from Syria on the north to about Carmel, Israel, on the south.

Phrygia: A region of central Asia Minor.

Propylaeum: Monumental entranceway.

Puduhepa: Hittite queen, wife of Hattusilis III (thirteenth century B.C.).

Pulu: Another name for the Assyrian King Tiglath-Pileser III. He is mentioned in the Bible under this name.

Python: One of Alexander the Great's generals.

Qarqar: Ancient site on the Orontes River, northwest of Hims.

Quyungik: One of the *tell* that cover the ancient city of Nineveh.

Ramad: Prehistoric site near Damascus.

Ramesses II: Egyptian pharaoh of the nineteenth dynasty; married a daughter of the Hittite king Hattusilis III.

Rawlinson (Sir Henry Creswicke): English Orientalist (1810–1895), considered the "father of Assyriology."

Rich (C. J.): English Consul-General at Baghdad and representative of the East India Company (1787–1822), who explored many Mesopotamian sites.

Rimush: Son of Sargon, king of the Akkadian dynasty.

Roxana: Daughter of an Iranian noble, and wife of Alexander the Great.

Samaria: City in Palestine, capital of the kingdom of Israel.

Samarra: City on the left bank of the Tigris, north of Baghdad. It has given its name to a phase of Mesopotamian protohistory.

Samsu-Iluna: Son and successor of Hammurabi, king of Babylon.

Sardis: Ancient city in Asia Minor.

Sargon of Akkad: Founder of the Akkadian dynasty (2371–2316 B.C.).

Sargon II of Assyria: King of Assyria from 721 to 705 B.C.

Sarzec (Ernest de): French Vice-Consul at Basrah, instigator of excavations at Lagash.

Sassan: An Iranian priest, eponymous ancestor of the Sassanian dynasty founded by his grandson Ardashir.

Sassanians: Iranian dynasty (A.D. 224–651).

Satrapy: The name of a province of the Achaemenian empire, administered by a Satrap.

Sawwan (Tell es-): Ancient site about six miles south of Samarra.

Scythians: Population of Iranian origin, which from the eighth century B.C. on invaded Urartu and Assyria many times.

Seleucids: Dynasty that reigned (301–164 B.C.) over a part of the Middle East after Alexander's death.

Seleucus: One of Alexander's generals, founder of the Seleucid dynasty.

Semites: An ethnic group originating in Arabia that settled in ancient western Asia.

Sennacherib: King of Assyria (704–681 B.C.).

Shalmaneser I: Assyrian king in the thirteenth century B.C.

Shalmaneser III: Assyrian king (858–824 B.C.), son of Ashurnasirpal II.

Shamash: God-sun, worshiped especially at Sippar and Larsa.

Shamash-Shum-Ukin: Son of Esarhaddon, brother of Ashurbanipal, king of Babylon (seventh century B.C.).

Shamshi-Adad I: King of Assyria (eighteenth century B.C.).

Shapur I: Sassanian king, son of Ardashir I (A.D. 241–272).

Shapur II: Sassanian king (A.D. 309–379).

Sharkalisharri: King of the Akkadian dynasty.

Sharruma: Hittite god, son of Teshub and Hepat.

Shilak-Inshushinak: Elamite king in the twelfth century B.C., son of Shutruk-Nahhunte.

Shulgi: Second king of the third dynasty of Ur (2113–2006 B.C.). Also called Dungi.

Shutruk-Nahhunte: Elamite king who carried out raids into Babylonia in the twelfth century B.C.

Sibitti: The seven sky gods, or those stars identical to the Pleiades.

Sidon: Phoenician port south of Beirut.

Sin: Semitic name of the moon god in the Mesopotamian pantheon.

Sinahutsur: Brother of Sargon II or Assyria.

Sind: Province in Pakistan.

Sippar (Abu Habba): City in Akkad, north-northwest of Babylon.

Smerdes: Son of Cyrus, who for a certain period usurped the Achaemenian throne.

Smith (George): Celebrated English Assyriologist (1840–1876).

Sultan Tepe: Turkish site about ten miles southeast of Urfa (Edessa).

Sumerians: Population of non-Semitic ethnic origin, which came to Mesopotamia and settled before the fourth millennium B.C.

Sumu-Abum: Founder of the first dynasty of Babylon (1894–1595 B.C.).

Suppiluliumas: Hittite king (1375–1335 B.C.).

Susa: City in southwestern Iran, capital of Elam.

Susiana: The center of the Elamite kingdom in southwestern Iran.

Taq-I-Bostan: Site seven miles northeast of Kermanshah, in Iran.

Taylor (J. E.): English Consul at Basra, who explored Ur and its surroundings.

Telipinu: Hittite god, son of the storm-god.

Telipinus: Hittite king in the late sixteenth century B.C.

Tell: The Arab name for an artificial hill, formed by the accumulation of ancient ruins.

Temenos: The sacred enclosure, where sanctuaries were located in ancient cities.

Tepe Gawra: Ancient site northwest of Nineveh.

Tepidarium: The resting room, of mild temperature, in Roman public baths.

Teshub: Hittite god of the natural elements.

Thebes: Ancient capital of upper Egypt.

Thermae: Roman public baths.

Tiamat: Personification of the salt waters, adversary of Marduk in the Mesopotamian poem of the creation.

Tiglath-Pileser I: Assyrian king from 1115 to 1077 B.C.

Tiglath-Pileser III: Assyrian king from 745–727 B.C.

Triton: A sea deity.

Tudhaliyas IV: Hittite king (circa 1250 B.C.).

Tukulti-Ninurta I: Assyrian king from 1244 to 1208 B.C.

Tyre: Ancient Phoenician city south of Sidon.

Ubaid: A site near Ur, which has given its name to a phase of Mesopotamian proto-history (fourth millennium B.C.).

Ugarit (Ras Shamra): Ancient site on the Mediterranean coast south; it was one of the most important Phoenician cities in the second millennium B.C.

Umma: Ancient site in Lower Mesopotamia, thirty-one miles northwest of Lagash.

Untash-Gal: Elamite king in the thirteenth century B.C.

Uqair: Ancient site northwest of Babylon.

Ur: Ancient city, the seat of three dynasties; mentioned in the Bible as "Ur of the Chaldeans" (Genesis XI, 31).

Urartu: The ancient kingdom that corresponded roughly to present-day Armenia.

Ur-Nammu: Founder of the third dynasty of Ur, legislator (twenty-first century B.C.).

Uruk: Sumerian city, the seat of many dynasties; city of Gilgamesh.

Urukagina: King of Lagash (twenty-fourth century B.C.).

Ut-Napishtim: Mesopotamian hero who survived the Flood.

Utu: Sumerian name for the god-sun (Semitic name: Shamash).

Utu-Hegal: King of Uruk (twenty-second century B.C.).

Valerian: Roman emperor from A.D. 253 to 260, taken prisoner by the Sassanians. He died in captivity.

Van (Lake): A lake in eastern Turkey.

Wadi Musa: "The Torrent of Moses," a stream at Petra.

Wahballat: Son of Zenobia, the queen of Palmyra.

Winckler (Hugo): German archaeologist and Orientalist (1863–1913); the first to conduct excavations at Boghaz Köy (1906–1912).

Wood (Robert): English traveler who was the first to visit Palmyra, in 1751.

Woolley (Sir Leonard): English archaeologist, who carried out excavations at Ur (1880–1960).

Xerxes: Achaemenian king from 486 to 465 B.C.

Yazilikaya: Hittite rock sanctuary, about one mile from Boghaz Köy.

Zagros: Mountainous region northeast of Mesopotamia.

Zarife: Cane huts still seen in the villages of southern Iraq.

Zenobia: Queen of Palmyra from A.D. 267 to 272.

Zidantas: Participant in the plot that caused the death of the Hittite king Mursilis.

Ziggurat: In Mesopotamian sacred architecture, the name given to step-towers on which temples were built.

Zimrilim: Last king of Mari (eighteenth century B.C.), defeated by Hammurabi of Babylon.

Zoroaster: Prophet and reformer of the Mazdaic religion (sixth century B.C.).

RECOMMENDED READING

From the many books available on all the various aspects of these ancient Middle Eastern peoples and civilizations, we offer here merely a selection of the most accessible ones — in terms of price, current editions, and level of approach.

Badawy, Alexander: *Architecture in Ancient Egypt and the Near East* (MIT Press, 1965)
Chiera, Edward: *They Wrote on Clay* (Chicago Univ., 1938)
Contenau, Georges: *Everyday Life in Babylon and Assyria* (Norton, 1966)
Cottrell, Leonard, *The Quest for Sumer* (Putnam, 1965).
DuRy, C.: *Art of the Ancient Near and Middle East* (Abrams, 1969)
Fiore, Silvestro: *Voices from the Clay: The Development of Assyro-Babylonian Literature* (Oklahoma Univ., 1965)
Frankfort, Henri: *The Birth of Civilization in the Near East* (Doubleday, 1959)
    Kingship and the Gods (Chicago Univ., 1948)
Gaster, Theodor: *The Oldest Stories in the World* (Beacon Press, 1958)
Ghirshman, Roman: *Iran* (Penguin)
    Art of Ancient Iran (Braziller)
Glueck, Nelson: *Deities and Dolphins: The Story of the Nabataeans* (Farrar, Straus & Giroux, 1965)
Gurney, Oliver: *The Hittites* (Penguin, 1961)
Kramer, Samuel: *History Begins at Sumer* (Doubleday, 1959)
Lloyd, Seton: *The Art of the Ancient Near East* (Praeger, 1961) *Foundations in the Dust* (Penguin, 1955)
Mellaart, James: *The Earliest Civilizations of the Near East* (McGraw-Hill, 1966)
Michalowski, Kazimierz: *Palmyra* (Praeger, 1970)
Piggott, Stuart, ed.: *The Dawn of Civilization* (McGraw-Hill, 1961)
Pritchard, James B.: *The Ancient Near East in Pictures* (Princeton Univ. Press)
    Ancient Near Eastern Texts Relating to the Old Testament (Princeton Univ. Press)
Roux, Georges: *Ancient Iraq:* (Penguin, 1966)
Saggs, H. W.: *The Greatness That Was Babylon* (NAL, 1968)

RECOMMENDED VIEWING

Obviously there is nothing that can compare with a visit to the actual sites described in this book, and the modern age of jet travel and organized tourism has made even these remote places accessible. As it happens, though, almost all the works of art have been removed, most of them to major European museums and to museums in the homelands of the sites. North Americans, however, are fortunate in having several fine collections of works from these ancient peoples and civilizations; the most comprehensive are:

> The Metropolitan Museum of Art, New York, New York
> The Museum of Fine Arts, Boston, Massachusetts
> Oriental Institute Museum, Chicago Illinois
> University Museum, Philadelphia, Pennsylvania

Listed below are the other collections — most of them open, within certain restrictions, to the general public — that offer people everywhere a chance to make the acquaintance of some of the productions of this ancient world.

California: Los Angeles County Museum
Colorado: Denver Art Museum
Connecticut: New Haven: *Yale University Art Gallery
Illinois: Chicago: Field Museum of Natural History
Maine: Brunswick: Bowdoin College Museum of Art
Maryland: Baltimore: *Walters Art Gallery
Massachusetts: Amherst: Amherst College Museum
     Cambridge: *Fogg Art Museum, Harvard University
Michigan: Ann Arbor: *Kelsey Museum of Ancient & Medieval Archaeology
    *Detroit Institute of Art
Missouri: Kansas City: *Nelson Gallery & Atkins Museum of Fine Arts
    St. Louis: *City Art Museum
New Hampshire: Hanover: Dartmouth College Museum
New York: New York City: *Brooklyn Museum
Ohio: *Cincinnati Art Museum
    *Cleveland Museum of Art
    *Toledo Museum of Art
Washington: *Seattle Art Museum
Washington, D.C.: *Freer Gallery of Art
    The Dumbarton Oaks Research Library & Collection
CANADA: Toronto: *Royal Ontario Museum

* better than others on this list

INDEX

188

SOURCES AND ACKNOWLEDGMENTS

The original ancient texts that appear in translation throughout the margins of this book (on the pages indicated here, at left) are quoted through the courtesy of the following authors and publishers:

16 20, 59, 60
Ancient Near Eastern Texts Relating to the Old Testament, ed. by James B. Pritchard, 3rd edn., with Supplement (copyright © 1969 by Princeton University Press): pp. 265 and 267, transl. Leo Oppenheim; pp. 356 and 393, transl. Albrecht Goetze. Reprinted by permission of Princeton University Press.

18, 34
History Begins at Sumer, by Samuel Noah Kramer. Doubleday-Anchor edition published in 1959 by Doubleday & Co., Inc.

18, 24, 71
R. Labat, A. Caquot, M. Sznycer, M. Vieyra, Les Religions du Proche-Orient asiatique. Textes sacrés babyloniens, ougaritiques, hittites, Paris, Fayard-Denoël, 1970.

29
M. Lambert, Textes commerciaux de Lagash, in Revue d'Assyriologie et d'Archéologie orientale, XLVII, Paris, Presses Universitaires de France, 1953.

31
Fr. Thureau-Dangin, Les inscriptions de Sumer et d'Akkad, Paris, E. Leroux, 1905.

32
La Lune. Mythes et rites, Collection "Sources Orientales," V, Paris, Editions du Seuil, 1962.

40
Les Hommes d'Etat célèbres, under the direction of J. Pirenne, Vol. I: Le monde antique jusqu'à la chute de l'empire romain, Paris, Editions Lucien Mazenod, 1969.

44
M. J. Steve, Tchoga Zanbil (Dur Untash) III. Textes élamites et accadiens de Tchoga Zanbil, Paris, Geuthner, 1967.

48
J.-R. Kupper, Correspondence de Kibri-Dagan. Archives royales de Mari, III, Paris, Imprimerie Nationale, 1950.

52
A. Finet, Annuaire de l'Institut de Philologie et d'Histoire orientales et slaves, XIV, Bruxelles, 1957.

52
Ch. F. Jean, Lettres diverses. Archives royales de Mari, II, Paris, Imprimerie Nationale, 1950.

60
Le Monde du Sorcier, Collection "Sources Orientales," VII, Paris Editions du Seuil, 1966.

60
Le Jugement des morts, Collection "Sources Orientales," IV, Paris, Editions du Seuil, 1961.

66
Th. Dombert, Der Sakralturm. I Teil: Ziggurat, 1920.

66, 71
Henri Frankfort, Kingship and the Gods, Copyright © 1948 by The University of Chicago Press.

66, 71
M. Vieyra, Les Assyriens, Collection "Le temps qui court," Paris, Editions du Seuil, 1961.

80
D. J. Wiseman, Chronicles of Chaldaean Kings (626–556 B.C.) In The British Museum, Copyright © 1956 by the Trustees of the British Museum.

80
M. Rutten, Babylone, Collection "Que sais-je," Paris, Presses Universitaire de France, 1948.

98
A. T. Olmstead, History of the Persian Empire, Copyright © 1948 by the University of Chicago Press.

105, 110
Erich F. Schmidt, Persepolis, I (Vol. LXVIII of the University of Chicago Oriental Institute Publications), Copyright © 1953 by The University of Chicago Press.

115
George G. Cameron, "The Monument of King Darius at Bisitun," in Archaeology, Autumn 1960, Vol. 13, No. 3. The Archaeological Institute of America.

118
Corpus Inscriptionum Semiticarum. Pars Secunda, n. 350, Paris, Klincksieck, 1889.

134, 150, 162, 167
J. Gage, La montée des Sassanides et l'heure de Palmyre, Collection "Le Memorial des Siècles," Paris, Albin Michel, 1964.

156
B. Boustani, Les gens de lettres arabes (translated from the Arabic by Henri Marchal), Beyrouth.

The drawings of buildings, reconstructions of structures, and site plans are the work of Giuliano and Giovanni Battista Minelli, who made use of materials in the following volumes through the courtesy of their publishers: E. Akurgal, *Ancient Civilisation and Ruins of Turkey* (Istanbul, Mobil Oil Türk A.S. Public Affairs, 1969). R. Ghirshman, *Tchoga-Zanbil*, Vol. II (Paris, Geuthner, 1968). R. Ghirshman, *Iran, Parthes et Sassanides* (Paris, Gallimard, 1962). Oliver Gurney, *The Hittites* (London, Penguin, 1954). Max E. L. Mallowan, *Nimrud and its Remains* (London, Collins, 1966). André Parrot, *Mission Archéologique de Mari, I: Le temple d'Ishtar* (Paris, Geuthner, 1956). André Parrot *Mission Archéologique de Mari, III: Les temples d'Ishtarat et de Ninni-Zaza* (Paris, Geuthner, 1967). André Parrot, *Archéologie Mésopotamienne, I* (Paris, Albin Michel, 1946). André Parrot, *Sumer* (Paris, Gallimard, 1960). André Parrot, *Assur*, 2nd edition (Paris, Gallimard, 1969). *Quarterly of the Department of Antiquities in Palestine* VII (Paris, Letanzey et Ané, 1938). E. Strommenger, *Fünfjahrtausende Mesopotamien* (München, Hirmer Verlag, 1962). *Syria*, 3-4 (Paris, Geuthner, 1969). E. Unger, *Babylon*. A. Varagnac, *L'homme avant l'écriture* (Paris, A.R. Colin, 1959). Sir Leonard Woolley, *Excavations at Ur* (London, E. Benn Ltd. ,1954). *Zeitschrift für Assyriologie*, Walter de Gruyter, AF Band 49, S.I. ff. (Berlin, 1950). *Ziggourat et Temples de Tchoga-Zanbil in Iranica Antiqua* (Leiden, E.J. Brill).

Grateful acknowledgment also to: The Oriental Institute, University of Chicago, for the reconstruction made by H.D. Hill of the temple of Ishtar-Kititum; The Republic of Iraq, Ministry of Information, Directorate General of Antiquities, for the plan of Hatra and of Tell Harmal; the General Director of Antiquities and Museums of Damascus, Syria, for the plan of Palmyra.